JOHN FERGUSON

JOHN FERGUSON
1836–1906
Irish Issues in Scottish Politics

E. W. McFARLAND

TUCKWELL PRESS

First published in Great Britain in 2003 by
Tuckwell Press Ltd
The Mill House
Phantassie
East Linton
East Lothian, Scotland

ISBN 1 86232 164 7

A catalogue record of this book
is available on request from
the British Library

Printed & bound by Antony Rowe Ltd, Eastbourne

Contents

Illustrations

Acknowledgements

Thanks to Marianna Birkeland and (as always) Jim Whiston for assistance. Thanks also to Ewen Cameron, Catriona Macdonald, Andrew Newby and Pam Rogers.

I am grateful to the following for permission to use archival and illustrative material: The Board of Trinity College Dublin; East Dunbarton District Libraries; Glasgow City Archives; Adam McNaughton; Enda Ryan, History and Glasgow Room, Mitchell Library, Glasgow; National Archives of Scotland; National Library of Ireland; National Library of Scotland; New York Public Library; National Archives of Scotland; Scottish Liberal Democrats; Strathclyde Passenger Authority. I apologise for any omissions in this respect.

I am happy to acknowledge a grant from the Arts and Humanities Research Board which helped towards the fieldwork for this book. Support was also provided by the School of Social Sciences, Glasgow Caledonian University.

Abbreviations

GCA	Glasgow City Archives
HGA	Home Government Association
HGB	Home Government Branch
HRCGB	Home Rule Confederation of Great Britain
HRL	Home Rule League
ILP	Independent Labour Party
INL	Irish National League
INLGB	Irish National League of Great Britain
INLL	Irish National Land League
IPHRA	Irish Protestant Home Rule Association
IRB	Irish Republican Brotherhood
NAI	National Archives of Ireland
NAS	National Archives of Scotland
NLI	National Library of Ireland
NLLGB	National Land League of Great Britian
NLS	National Library of Scotland
NYPL	New York Public Library
PRONI	Public Record Office of Northern Ireland
SDF	Social Democratic Federation
SLRL	Scottish Land Restoration League
SLRU	Scottish Land Restoration Union
SRO	Scottish Record Office
TCD	Trinity College Dublin
UIL	United Irish League
UILGB	United Irish League of Great Britain
WMEC	Workers' Municipal Electoral Committee

Preface

I suspect that John Ferguson would forgive me for not making this book a personal biography. When approached once for his own reminiscences, he confessed that self-examination was not in his line of thought and work. Instead he was proud that his life had been one of 'public action, defending or propounding the advanced doctrines of human happiness'.[1]

He was the epitome of the Victorian public man. Upright, hirsute, and clad in his velvet frock coat and large-brimmed black felt hat, he pursued a myriad of causes with intense energy. Whether holding forth at St Patrick's Day demonstrations on the necessity for Home Rule, or buttonholing fellow commuters to win their support for the taxation of land values, he remained convinced of the ultimate triumph of his mission. Fiercely proud, there were definite elements of theatricality in the face he showed to the world. The dangerous Irish firebrand whom the authorities believed was capable of 'thrusting himself' upon Queen Victoria when she visited Glasgow in 1888 was found on closer acquaintance to be 'a true gentleman'.[2]

Ferguson was distinguished both by the length and breadth of his political activism. A compulsive joiner, he was drawn wholeheartedly into the Victorian web of progressive endeavour. The Reform League, the Liberal Party, the Irish Land League, the Scottish Labour Party were a only few of the organisations in which he served. In four decades, he met – and outlived – many of the luminaries in Irish nationalism and British democratic politics: Charles Bradlaugh, John Martin, Isaac Butt, Michael Davitt, Charles Stuart Parnell and John Redmond, all found hospitality at his villa, Benburb. He also became one of the leading publishers of Irish music and literature, helping shape the collective memory and common culture of the Irish at home and abroad. In his campaigning work the friction of distance meant little to him. Leaving Glasgow, he would speed across the North Channel, address meetings throughout the country, returning by way of Dublin or London to attend to his business affairs.

Here is the attraction of Ferguson for the biographer. While he may not have been able to dictate history on the scale of a Gladstone or Parnell, he stands out as a vital *mediating* figure, possessing the uncanny gift of being present at the right historical moment. In a period when political change was becoming increasingly fragmented, his life has a unifying sweep, embodying many of the themes which preoccupied late nineteenth-century society: the impact of empire and the challenge of nationalism; the emergence of class as political rallying point; the tension between individualist and collectivist impulses in national and civic government.

In Ferguson, the rationalist coexisted with the romantic visionary. He discovered in the teachings of Christ, 'the highest evolution of political economy, as the divine blessing upon the human intellect . . .'[3] Equally, he drew strength from his identification with two of the great imagined collectivities of his day: 'the nation' and 'the democracy'. While it was his life's mission to reconcile these in a single crusade for human progress, this task was not helped by hesitancy in specifying exactly how he visualised their membership. What if the Protestant minority did not want to be part of his 'Irish nation'? What if 'the democracy' were no longer willing to be represented by his 'great Liberal Party'? Despite his proclaimed adherence to 'eternal verities of God', his attempt to address these questions necessitated repeated tactical shifts and reversals of policy which revealed a consummate political operator.

My interest in John Ferguson began almost ten years ago while researching the history of the Orange Institution in nineteenth-century Scotland. There was something endearing about this figure defiantly marching to a different beat from his fellow Ulster Protestants. There are two immediate motivations in tracing his biography. In the first place, his influential role in Irish politics seems neglected, perhaps because his career was conducted outside the charmed circle of Irish parliamentarians.

Secondly, although he has claimed a place in the historiography of late-Victorian Scotland, this is usually as a player in a much larger drama in which Irish migrants come to terms with Scottish society, or battle is joined for independent labour representation.[4]

Fortunately, despite the lack of substantial personal papers, there is a rich cache of material available on Ferguson's intriguing career. As befits the story of a life lived in the public realm, we may not be able capture his interior monologue, but we can at least observe Ferguson through the eyes of his contemporaries, notably in the correspondence and memoirs of major nationalist figures, such as Butt, Davitt and Dillon. Since rhetoric was the life blood of his career, we can also 'hear' his own distinctive voice, not only through his countless articles and newspaper letters, but above all through his printed speeches.

Writing the obituary of his friend Hugh Murphy in 1903, Ferguson hoped for a biographer to do justice to 'a true and brilliant life'.[5] The man himself deserves no less.

Notes

1 *Irish Packet,* 14 Nov. 1903.

2 Glasgow City Archives (GCA), TD 602/15, J. Blackburn to the Lord Provost of Glasgow, 18 Aug. 1888.

3 *Glasgow Herald,* 6 Jan. 1892.

4 For example, Ian Wood's, 'Irish Immigrants and Scottish Radicalism' in I. Macdougall, *Essays in Scottish Labour History,* Edinburgh, 1978, pp. 65–89 is a seminal study. Much useful material is also contained in unpublished theses such as P.W. Morris, 'The Irish in Glasgow and the Labour Movement 1891–22', (University of Oxford B.Phil. Thesis, 1989), and Jim Smyth's excellent and encyclopaedic, 'Labour and Socialism in Glasgow 1880–1914: the Electoral Challenge Prior to Democracy', (University of Edinburgh Ph.D. Thesis, 1987). Note also Smyth's, *Labour in Glasgow 1896–1936* (E.Linton, 2000).

5 *Glasgow Star,* 29 Aug. 1903.

CHAPTER ONE

A Young Protestant Conservative

When John Ferguson turned from his favourite subjects of Home Rule and the Single Tax and 'dropped into poetry', he loved to boast a lineage of 'genuine Irish descent' which stretched from Fergus Mac Erc, Prince of the north Antrim kingdom of Dalriada and descendent of Conn of the Hundred Battles.[1] In characteristic style, the suspicion that Ferguson himself might be a scion of more recent settler stock was expansively swept aside. His ambitious genealogical claims perhaps reflected some sensitivity to the increasing confluence of Irishness, Catholicism and nationalism during the later nineteenth century, but they were also part of a lifelong process in which he actively sought to weave a new 'public self' from the material of his Irish Protestant background and personal democratic mission.

In reality, his origins owed more to the strong farmers of Antrim and the Belfast shopocracy than to the heroes of *Uladh*. He was born in Belfast on 18 April 1836.[2] While Glasgow contemporaries freely applied an Ulster Presbyterian label to him, his family background illustrated in microcosm the mobile and intricate nature of developing confessional and political identities in the province.[3] His parents, Leonard J. Ferguson and Charlotte Ferris had been married on 31 November 1831 at Glenavy Parish Church, County Antrim by the Church of Ireland incumbent, Mr Bell.[4] This was an inter-denominational marriage between a Presbyterian and an Episcopalian at a time when such arrangements were still controversial. The whole issue regarding the recognition of Presbyterian marriages had been a highly emotive one in Ulster. Indeed, it was not until 1844 that an act was passed to allow Presbyterians and members of the Church of Ireland to be married by a Presbyterian minister.[5]

Leonard Ferguson came from an Antrim family of Presbyterian

tenant farmers, who in the previous generation had 'turned out' in the 1798 United Irishmen's Rebellion.[6] His own father had taken his Presbyterian pike to Antrim Bridge on 7 June 1798, a fateful battle at which rebel troops under Henry Joy McCracken were defeated by Crown forces.[7] For good measure, another kinsman was the radical martyr, William Orr, a young Antrim farmer, hung in October 1797 for offences under the Insurrection Act.[8]

While 'Remember Orr' became a watchword for United Irishmen, Presbyterians in succeeding decades were to regard their radical past with a mixture of covert pride, denial and ambivalence.[9] In the case of Ferguson's family, outright rejection seems to have prevailed, for it was not until his early manhood that John was made aware of his family's United Irish connections. On the contrary, his father was a staunch upholder of conservatism. This was already a tenacious and vigorous tradition in Ireland at the time of Ferguson's birth, but suspicious of resurgent Catholicism, many more Presbyterians were set to follow Leonard's example and align themselves with the 'natural' party of Protestantism in the coming decades.[10]

The Tory credentials of Ferguson's Anglican mother, Charlotte, were more straightforward. She was the third daughter of John Ferris, formerly a substantial tenant farmer of Glenavy in the barony of Upper Masserene, County Antrim.[11] Forming a portion of the vast estates confiscated from the ancient O'Neil family, the parish had originally been settled by colonists in the Elizabethan period and was subsequently inhabited by the descendents of soldiers who had been quartered there during the Williamite campaigns. 'Ferris' was one of the commonest names among a local population who were described in 1832 as having, 'a peculiar cast of countenance . . . very fine high and broad foreheads and general light hair, and the freedom from the Scottish accent or Irish brogue . . . a manly race both in their persons and in their manners.'[12] Although the Ferris family for generations had been ardent adherents of 'the Orange and Protestant Ascendancy party . . .', Ferguson's ancestral speculations might have led him to conclude that they shared the same 'Mac Fhearghuis' bloodlines as himself.[13]

Belfast and Glenavy

John Ferguson's earliest years were spent in Belfast – that 'violent-talking but feeble-thinking city', as he later remembered it.[14] Around the time of his son's birth, Leonard had established himself a provision merchant, obtaining premises in Gamble Street, near Donegal Quay.[15] The 1830s and 40s were decades of transition and optimism for 'the first town in Ireland for trade'. Its strategic location at the head of the Lagan valley well equipped it to handle the commercial traffic, which boomed as the interior of the province was opened up.[16] Between 1831 and 1841, the population had risen from 50,000 to over 75,000. Meanwhile, the civic design of the Georgian town, so gratifying to the eye of Wolfe Tone, was rapidly overtaken by sprawling, unplanned extensions.[17]

Leonard's business was ideally positioned at Belfast's new commercial heart. Gamble Street, which had only appeared on the map in 1831, was a thoroughfare of taverns, pawnbrokers, lodgings and caravanserai, only yards away from Belfast's bustling harbour.[18] Reflecting the city's rising prosperity, the Lagan of Ferguson's boyhood was a scene of constant movement. Lighters scuttled across the river, while larger vessels eased their way down from Garmoyle to discharge their cargoes of timber and luxury goods on the quays and receive home-produced linen and provisions in return. By 1843, the family's residence was a few streets away in the rather more salubrious Stanley Place, a mixed commercial and residential district.[19] John, it seemed, would eventually enter his inheritance as a member of an industrious, independent merchant community.

Belfast's expansion had a bleaker aspect. The 1830s had also witnessed a sharp decline in community relations, partly under the strain of largely Roman Catholic rural migration, but also reflecting the promptings of fundamentalist Protestant preachers.[20] The sectarian riots which were to haunt the city had first appeared during the 1832 elections, followed by a further outburst in 1845. Another disturbing feature of the city's growing pains was to have an even more direct bearing on the Ferguson family fortunes. Despite being hailed by contemporaries as 'a clean Manchester', Belfast had the worst mortality rate in Ireland. The city was particularly susceptible to epidemic diseases. Even as late as 1852, life expectancy was calculated at nine years and half the living population was under twenty.[21] In these unhealthy conditions, growing business opportunities were no defence and Leonard Ferguson died around 1844. John, who was left without any memory of his father, now escaped the city. In the company of his sister Margaret, his mother took him to her father's home in Glenavy, County Antrim.

There is a real sense in which the Irish nationalists of Ferguson's generation were raised under the shadow of the Great Famine and 'the Black Year of 47'. The family of Michael Davitt suffered directly and, while surviving, were left destitute and facing eviction from their Mayo homestead.[22] Tim Healy's family had among their treasured possessions a crucifix made out of wood from the death-carts of Bantry.[23] In contrast, Ferguson's upbringing in Antrim was to mark him out from many of his later colleagues as much as his religion. In the wake of the personal tragedy of his father's death, the recollections of his rural boyhood were to be those of comfort and security, rather than distress and dispossession.

Glenavy was hardly the obvious cradle for a radical land reformer. The situation of the parish, beside the Glenavy River, was cheerfully and prettily wooded and watered, resembling 'a rich English district'.[24] Although the village itself appeared rather dirty and straggling, the surrounding countryside was well-cultivated and diversified. The soil along Lough Neagh, which the Ferris family farmed, was reckoned particularly fertile.[25] Observers had noted the inhabitants' taste for gardens and orchards, which they attributed to their English extraction, but cereal-growing predominated, the chief crops being wheat, oats, barely and rye. Potatoes were traditionally considered a preparation crop, rather than a means of subsistence, and the farmers' method of cultivating them was 'anything but Irish'.[26] When this crop failed in Antrim, the local landlord the Marquis of Hertford offered assistance to the most needy in a manner that saw him favourably compared to other absentees, such as Lord Londonderry.[27] This response followed on a pattern of benevolent estate management. Rents had been moderate and although the 'three lives' leases which prevailed in the parish were usually considered an uncertain tenure, tenants had confidence in renewal and could expect a 'fining down' of their rent one quarter with each new lease.[28] While, as elsewhere in Ireland, the rural crisis bore down heaviest on cotters and labourers, the substantial tenant farmers of Glenavy could be confident of maintaining their status as 'an independent, respectable and enlightened class'.[29] Admittedly, their watches, beaver hats and other signs of rising consumption were threatened by the increased poor law rates and low grain prices of the late 1840s, but these irritants were counterbalanced by an improved transport infrastructure and the inducement of an expanding Belfast market for farm produce.

It was not only material circumstances that insulated the young Ferguson from bitter famine memories. The rural society in which he was growing up was one of widening ethnic and class divisions. As a boy, he had little contact with Catholics, who were very few in Glenavy and 'humbler in their stations than the others'.[30] The few he did meet were labourers, whom, he recalled, 'must have lost all idea of Irish Nationality, as nothing ever occurred amongst them to excite my though of it'.[31] The one exception, Teresa McManus, was a *Seanbhean Bhocht* figure, straight from romantic Irish literature. As he recollected:

> Twice every week an old woman, bent-down, with a long blue coat covering her rags, lifted the latch of the farmhouse kitchen and entered . . . She was nearly blind and said to

be ninety years old. A greyhound that lay in a corner of a huge fireplace as soon as he heard [her] voice, muttering her blessing upon the house, rose lazily and went elsewhere . . . This in an Orange Yeoman's house, with the cavalry sabre and dress sword of the owner crossed above her head, told tales of a country and its people, to me in everything but the name, unknown . . . [of] the 'thrublesome times', 'and augh, darlin,' said she, 'sure the bloody Yeomanry were murdherin' and burnin' the whole country"[32]

Yet these fleeting images of another Ireland had to compete with the more insistent collective memory among Ulster Protestants of the 1641 Rebellion. Ferguson's boyhood was haunted by bloody images of Portadown Bridge, where men walked across the Bann upon the unburied bodies of murdered Protestants.[33] His informal socialisation was reinforced by a conventional education. Ferguson attended school in nearby Crumlin, possibly at the town's small academy, run by a Presbyterian clergyman, Rev. Nathaniel Alexander. This respectable school was well-supported and offered classics, mathematics, algebra and 'all the subjects necessary for 'an English and mercantile education'.[34] Ferguson gave particular attention to ancient and modern History: 'Irish History was, of course, left out as being, in the estimation of his teachers, dangerous for a loyal Protestant and Unionist'.[35]

The romance of improvement

Ferguson, aged fourteen, returned to Belfast to begin his working life. It seemed highly unlikely that his earlier upbringing as a young Protestant Conservative would be challenged in this new setting. The 1850s had witnessed rapid industrialisation and a massive building boom, with the bulk of the city's 119,000 population now settled in religiously-segregated quarters. The area behind York Street, running into Waring Street and Corporation Street, near where the Ferguson family had lived, was, for example, now almost exclusively Catholic.[36] Periodic sectarian disturbances had persisted, culminating in ten days of rioting in July 1857, in the wake of an inflammatory sermon delivered by Rev. Henry Drew from his pulpit at Christ Church.[37] The city was also an uncompromising Tory redoubt, under the iron rule of John Bates, a solicitor whose gerrymandering tactics were successful in limiting the impact of the Liberal vote – already mainly Catholic. Nowhere was the cumulative social and political exclusion of the minority community better illustrated than in the city's Chamber of Commerce, where 186 out of 194 members were Protestant.[38] As the Fenian activist Frank Roney remembered:

> In Ulster, at that time, every phase of life, public and private, was tinctured with a sectarian bias. Before engaging in any enterprise however insignificant, or forming any acquaintance however necessary, the question of religious belief always took precedence. Doubt of the honesty of the person with whom you were obliged to do business almost always existed until association and experience proved your misgivings unfounded.[39]

His own Protestantism unquestioned, Ferguson was apprenticed to a stationery company. By the early 1850s there were some half dozen of these firms in the city, servicing an expanding business community.[40] Although his mature talents may have been better suited to a career in journalism or the law, favoured by many distinguished nationalist contemporaries, he did not seem to resent the trade to which he was sent.[41] Yet, while he worked hard to master his new calling – rising from apprentice to journeyman, and later, traveller in the firm – routine business life was clearly insufficient to satisfy his growing sense of intellectual enquiry.

Patrick Joyce has written of the Victorian 'inner-directed self' which drove a culture of self-improvement and self-help. Thus the individual was liberated from dependence and secured the conditions by which responsibility could be exercised in a new 'social' realm.[42] John Ferguson's voracious pursuit of knowledge in his Belfast years was indeed to play an important role in his eventual moulding as a public figure. He devoted his spare time to study, employing his own carefully devised system, which gave each night in the week a separate subject. Saturday was set aside for newspapers and politics, while Sunday was left as a day of religious contemplation.[43] His choice of subjects reflected in part the rampant Utilitarian ethics of a business city. He began with religious manuals, but quickly expanded into logic and political economy. History remained a favourite subject, his programme including Gibbon, Alison, Thiers and Hume. But, on languages he held definite views. He studied English literature, French and German – of the latter he became a fluent speaker – but classics he held to be of no practical utility in commercial life.[44]

Books were not the only source of his education. He also obtained training in free public discussion from his membership of the clubs and societies with which mid-Victorian Belfast was well supplied.[45] Again, he initially confined himself to religious organisations. He had become a communicant of St John's, May's Fields, a new Church of Ireland congregation which had been formed in 1853.[46] He also joined the Church of Ireland Young Men's Society, established in 1850, 'for the spiritual, moral and intellectual improvement of its members . . .'[47] Here the independent and disputative streak which was to be a hallmark of his later political life was soon to flourish. Evangelical fervour, allied with fears of Catholic encroachment, was developing to reinforce common Protestantism in 1850s Belfast.[48] Given his family background, it is hardly surprising that Ferguson was more enthusiastic in embracing this ecumenical spirit than some of his Church of Ireland colleagues. On one occasion he received the severe censure of the Society's Committee for speaking on the platforms of the Presbyterian and Methodist Young Men's Societies.[49]

In his next act of religious resistance, his opponent was more formidable. The Rev. Charles Seaver, the first Rector of St John's, was a charismatic and powerful pastor whose theology was evangelical, low church and conservative.[50] Casting himself as the Thomas Chalmers of Belfast, he had set out to inspire his congregation of merchants and manufacturers to undertake home missionary work which 'under Divine Blessing, would . . . bind the higher and lower ranks of society in bonds which no factious demagogue would be able to sever'.[51] Undeterred by Seaver's fearsome reputation, Ferguson, aged only twenty-one, was quick to respond when he disagreed with his views on predestination. After an hour's discussion in a church class, he publicly cornered the rector, maintaining that as God was without sin, he could not Himself fix or compel man to sin.[52] For this impertinence he was ostracised from his religious connections, two years before the great evangelical revival swept Ulster.[53]

There were compensations in his developing secular studies. Here he benefited from Belfast's expanding and enlightened provision of adult education. From the 1840s, the demand had grown for higher educational standards in business and industry.[54] By the end of the next decade, the city's Queen's College was offering evening lectures in science and literature, aimed at members of the commercial classes, 'for whom ordinary academic courses were inappropriate or out of reach'.[55] It was at this point Ferguson encountered T. E. Cliffe Leslie, Professor of Jurisprudence and Political Economy at Queen's College.[56] Leslie was primarily an economist with a particular interest in land reform, a topical issue when set against the agricultural depression in Ireland from 1859 to 1863. He lectured and wrote against the deductive approach of classical economy, tacking economic questions from a comparative and historical perspective. The progress of a society, he argued, relied not in restricting the rise in population, but on the ratio of the progress of population and the increase of productive power, together with the improved economy of the producer.[57] While his poor health and residence in London ensured that his impact on the

College was slight, Cliffe Leslie's influence on Ferguson and his developing interest in land economics, was to be great and lasting.[58]

Typified in his response to Leslie's teachings, Ferguson's Belfast years had given him the intellectual materials which were calculated to undermine the sectarian commonplaces of his boyhood. Nevertheless, while he had gained the rudiments of a broad liberal education, his learning retained an abstract and unfocused quality. For all the attractions of inductive method, the principles he had painfully acquired through evening lectures and private study had still to be applied to the economic and social questions that surrounded him in his native province. Ferguson now seized upon the letters of Dennis Holland, published in the *Ulsterman*, in which the author attempted to call public attention to 'landlord oppression and rural misery' in Donegal.[59] Holland had travelled among the peasantry during the winter of 1857, and presented an emotional testimony of 'the cry from help form that bleak north-west coast'. His vivid sketches began to bring home to Ferguson the human dimension of the land question in a way Leslie's logical exegesis could not:

> ... a grim, black marsh district, where human creatures ... crouch and shiver by the little steaming turf-heap which gives no blaze (so wet it is), but fills with smoke the wretched hut where the ragged cow and the little sheep are huddled together with father, mother and children.[60]

It was to be the beginning of a lifetime's passion. He was not alone in beginning to chaff at the security of the Protestant fold, but few faced a more challenging personal struggle. Prominent Presbyterian ministers like Isaac Nelson and, in a later generation, J. B. Armour, could at least lay claim to the Ulster radical tradition from which Ferguson's upbringing had estranged him.[61] Even Charles Stewart Parnell was able to rebel against the Protestant landlord class without rebelling against his family, who were proud of their distinguished role in eighteenth-century Patriot politics.[62] In Ferguson's case, however, Toryism and rigorous evangelical Protestantism and were the rallying points of both his class and his family circle. The result was a defensive overlap of political, religious and personal identities, which produced a dread of 'turncoats'. Already, his Belfast friends were offended at his broad range of reading material and attempted to confine him to the orthodox *Belfast Newsletter*.[63] It was clear that the next phase of Ferguson's intellectual and political development could proceed only once he had left his accustomed surroundings. He never lost touch with political events in Ulster, returning frequently on business and campaigning trips, but this early departure from his native province, had one important implication. In physically separating himself from the evolving *mentalité* of its Protestant population, he also risked failing to grasp their deep and abiding hostility to nationalist aspirations.

Notes

1 J. Denvir, *The Life Story of an Old Rebel* (Dublin, 1910), p. 176.

2 *Glasgow Observer* , 28 Apr. 1906.

3 *Daily Record* 24 Apr. 1906. The *Record* admitted that, 'his temperament differed . . . from that of the modern Ulster Presbyterian'. Later commentators have often understandably made the same assumption: T. W. Moody, *Michael Davitt and the Irish Revolution* (Oxford, 1982), p. 125.

4 Public Records Office Northern Ireland (PRONI), Glenavy Parich Register, Mic 1/44. National Archives, Ireland (NAI), WW36, Marriage Licence Bonds, Down Connor and Dromore 1721–1845.

5 A. R. Scott, *The Ulster Revival of 1859* (Ballymena, 1994), p. 28.

6 In the mid-nineteenth century the Ferguson name was mainly concentrated in the barony of Upper Antrim and in

the parish of Newtownards, Co. Down: R. Bell, *The Book of Ulster Surnames* (St Paul, Min., 1988) p. 65.

7 *Irish Packet*, 14 Nov. 1903.

8 *The Press*, 17 Oct. 1797. He is remembered in one of William Drennan's best poems, 'The Wake of William Orr'.

9 See I. McBride, 'Memory and Forgetting: Ulster Presbyterianism after 1798', in T. Bartlett *et al.* eds., *The Irish Rebellion of 1798. A Bicentennial Perspective* (Dublin, 2001).

10 K. T. Hoppen, *Elections, Politics and Society in Ireland, 1832–1885* (Oxford, 1984), p. 278.

11 *Belfast Newsletter*, 2 Dec. 1836.

12 A. Day and P. McWilliams,*Ordnance Survey Memoirs of Ireland. Parishes of Antrim,Volume VII, 1832–8,* (Belfast, 1993), pp. 86, 89.

13 *Glasgow Star,* 28 Apr. 1906; Bell, *Ulster Surnames,* pp. 65–6.

14 *Glasgow Observer,* 12 Sept. 1893.

15 *Matier's Belfast Directory 1836.*

16 R. Sweetman, 'The development of the port', in J. C. Beckett *et al., Belfast: The Making of the City* (Belfast, 1983), pp. 57–70; E. Jones, *A Social Geography of Belfast* (Oxford, 1960), p. 40.

17 *Ibid.*, p. 50.

18 *Martin's Belfast Directory 1842–3.*

19 *Henderson's New Belfast Directory 1843–4.*

20 F. Heatley, 'Community relations and religious geography 1800–86', in Beckett (ed.), *Making, p. 135*

21 J. McCracken, 'Early Victorian Belfast', in J. C. Beckett and R. E. Glasscock (eds.), *Belfast, Origin and Growth of an Industrial City* (London, 1967), p. 88; J. Bardon, *Belfast, An Illustrated History* (Belfast, 1982), p. 104.

22 Moody, *Davitt*, p. 9.

23 T. M. Healy *Letters and Leaders of My Day* (London, 1928), vol. I, pp. 16–7. For the rest of his life A. J. Kettle was to look on pre-famine Ireland as an idyll of 'honey bees in almost every garden': L. J. Kettle (ed.), *The Material for Victory. Being the Memoirs of Andrew J. Kettle* (Dublin, 1958), p. 5.

24 *Ordnance Survey Memoirs*, p. 84.

25 PRONI, Tithe Applotment Book, 1834, Parish of Glenavy, FIN/5A/147. John Ferris had already given up his farm by the time his daughter returned, but continued to hold a property in Glenavy townland. Other members of the Ferris family were large proprietors. William Ferris, for example, cultivated over 123 acres in the townland of Deerpark, and Thomas Ferris, over 98 acres. The average Glenavy farm was between 30–40 acres.

26 *Ibid.*, p. 77.

27 C. Dallat, 'The famine in Antrim', in L. Kinealy and T. Parkhall (eds.), *The Famine in Ulster*, (Belfast, 1997), p. 15. However, for a contrary view of Hertford see, *Belfast Vindicator* 22 Apr. 1846, quoted in J. Killen (ed.), *The Famine Decade. Contemporary Accounts 1841–1851* (Belfast, 1995), p. 61.

28 *Ordnance Survey Memoirs*, p. 87.

29 L. Kennedy, 'The rural economy, 1820–1914', in L. Kennedy and P. Ollerenshaw, *An Economic History of Ulster 1820–1939* (Manchester, 1985), p. 38.

30 *Ordnance Survey Memoirs*, p. 86.

31 *Irish Packet*, 14 Nov. 1903.

32 *Ibid.*

33 John Ferguson, *Three Centuries of Irish History. From the Reign of Mary the Catholic to that of Victoria the Protestant. An Unbroken Record of Confiscation and Persecution, Mixed with*

Massacre, and Terminating in Extermination by Unjust and Ruinous Taxation, (Glasgow [c.1897]), pp. 1–2.

34 *Ordnance Survey Memoirs,* p. 74.

35 *Glasgow Star,* 28 Apr. 1906.

36 F. Heatley, 'Community relations and religious geography 1800–86', in Becket (ed.), *Making,* p. 135.

37 *Report of the Commissioners of Enquiry into the Origin and Character of the Riots in Belfast in July and September 1857* (Dublin, 1858).

38 Hoppen, *Elections,* p. 271.

39 I. B. Cross (ed.), *Frank Roney. Irish Rebel and California Labor Leader* (Berkely, 1931), p. 11.

40 *Belfast and Ulster Directory 1852.*

41 He reacted angrily when one admirer suggested that he would have made a distinguished lawyer: *Kirkintilloch Herald,* 2 May 1906.

42 P. Joyce, *Democratic Subjects* (Cambridge, 1994), pp. 16, 161–76.

43 *Glasgow Observer,* 28 Apr. 1906.

44 *Ibid.* An echo perhaps of Bentham's view in *Rationale of Reward* that Potemkin would have been better occupied playing solitaire than reading the *Iliad.*

45 By the 1850's, the city could boast, for example: The Belfast Social Enquiry Society; The Young Men's Intellectual Improvement Association; The Belfast Natural History and Philosophy Society; The Belfast Society for the Promotion of Knowledge; an Essayist Club and several minor literary societies.

46 *Belfast and Ulster Directory 1852.* It was situated on the corner of Oxford Street, not far from Ferguson's boyhood home.

47 *Belfast and Ulster Directory 1856.*

48 F. Holmes, *Henry Cooke* (Belfast, 1981), pp. 115–6.

49 *Glasgow Star*, 28 Apr. 1906.

50 Scott, *Ulster Revival*, pp. 104–5.

51 Rev. Charles Seaver, *The Sunday School. A Nursery for the Church. A Lecture Delivered before the Belfast Sabbath School Union* (Belfast 1856), p. 5.

52 *Glasgow Star*, 28 Apr. 1906.

53 Seaver was to be its leading Episcopalian figure: Rev. Charles Seaver, *The Ulster Revival. A paper read before the Evangelical Alliance, 22 September 1859*, (Belfast, 1859).

54 J. Jameson, *History of the Royal Belfast Academical Institute* (Belfast, 1959), p. 97.

55 T. W. Moody and J. C. Beckett, *Queen's Belfast 1845–1949. The History of a University* (London, 1959) p. 159.

56 Moody and Beckett, *Queen's Belfast*, p. 596.

57 For his early work see, *On the Self Dependency of the Working Classes under the Law of Competition* (Dublin 1851); see also *An Inquiry into the Progress and Conditions of Mechanics and Literary Institutions* (Dublin, 1852) and *Military Systems of Europe Economically Considered* (London, 1856).

58 See for example *Glasgow Observer*, 27 Jun. 1891; *Glasgow Echo* 1 Sept. 1894.

59 Holland's notes were reprinted as, *The Landlord in Donegal. Pictures from the Wilds* (Belfast, nd.).

60 Holland, *Landlord*, p. 1. Ferguson's fascination with Holland was to continue. In 1879, Cameron & Ferguson published his novel, *Donal Dun O'Byrne: a Tale of the Rising in Wexford in 1798*.

61 *Northern Whig*, 9 Mar. 1888; J. R. B. McMinn, *Against the Tide. A Calendar of the Papers of the Rev. J. B. Armour, Irish Presbyterian Minister and Home Ruler 1869–1914* (Belfast, 1985).

62 P. Bew, *Parnell* (Dublin, 1991), p. 6.

63 *Glasgow Star,* 28 Apr. 1906.

CHAPTER TWO

The Patriotic Soul and the Democratic Intellect

Emigration was a fact of nineteenth-century Ulster life, with the passage to Scotland both speedy and cheap. For 3/– the young Ferguson could book a steerage berth in Belfast and arrive in Glasgow in eight hours.[1] He came in 1859 or 1860 – he could never quite recall the date – in search of a new beginning.[2]

The scale of his adoptive city, with a population more than three times that of Belfast, must have been daunting to a new arrival in his early twenties, but much would also have been familiar.[3] Glasgow's townscape had suffered from a brash building mania earlier in the century, but its public spaces and expanding residential suburbs also reflected the progress and confidence of the city's bourgeoisie. From the 1840s, an industrial base had developed, more flexible and diversified than Belfast's, yet equally adapted to the needs of imperial trade. Glasgow too shared the social costs of rapid expansion. Levels of deprivation, evident in overcrowded housing and unregulated, low-wage working conditions, were probably worse than most comparable British cities.[4]

In time, these issues were to form Ferguson's battleground, but in the early 1860s his first task was to establish himself in his new surroundings. He had moved from being a junior member of the religious and commercial ascendancy in Belfast to a more complex, marginal status in Glasgow. Here, while his Protestantism was not a hindrance, neither was it a passport to social acceptance and business success. A young provincial in the second city of Empire, Ferguson responded by seizing the expanding opportunities for material and personal advance, which his situation offered.

Shortly after his arrival, he became a traveller in the wholesale stationery and printers' firm, Cameron & Co. The business had only been established in 1860, but during the next decade it proceeded to thrive. In 1864, it moved into the export business, relocating in larger and more prestigious premises in West Nile Street in the centre of the city's business district.[5] By 1867, Ferguson had become a full partner.[6] His domestic life had also prospered. In 1862 he had married Mary Ochiltree, 'a lady of high culture who had been given a splendid education'.[7] She was some three years older than Ferguson, the daughter of Matthew Ochiltree, a prosperous linen draper of Markethill, County Armagh.[8] Although her native parish of Mullaghback was predominately Presbyterian and Methodist, she shared Ferguson's Anglican, Tory upbringing.[9] The couple settled in West Cumberland Street on border of Gorbals and Tradeston, one of the older, better class streets in a bustling, densely populated area, which had long been a magnet for Irish settlement.[10] In true Victorian fashion, three children, John, William Bertram Ochiltree, and Anna Bertram Ochiltree, were born in quick succession between 1865 and 1869. A fourth daughter, Elizabeth, was born in 1875, when Mary Ferguson was in her forties, but died in childhood.[11]

Glasgow held a greater significance for John Ferguson than the building of family and business networks. Migration also marked his intellectual coming of age and the beginning of his public life. He was set to commit himself to the causes of Home Rule, radical democracy and social reform, but, just as there was little agreement over which took priority in his political career, there were competing accounts of how this 'conversion' had come about.

Becoming an Irishman

At the end of the eighteenth century, Ulster radicals, proud of their own enlightenment, were apt to patronise the efforts of their Scottish counterparts. It was a mark of how far the political trajectories of the two societies had diverged in the next century that the Scottish press could adopt a similar tone when explaining the blossoming of Ferguson's career in progressive politics, which, they believed, was due to 'the more liberal atmosphere of Scotland'.[12] There can be little doubt that the move from Tory Belfast to Liberal Glasgow did provide an enabling environment for Ferguson. Political reform was the rallying call which united a varied coalition of social groups, with Glasgow voters returning a Conservative MP only once between 1832 and 1886. The city also expressed its liberal credentials in support for the values of Free Trade, individual rights, manhood suffrage and 'a collective creed of intellectual and religious freedom'.[13] Indeed, Ferguson's own business partner Duncan Cameron, a free-thinking republican and land reformer, was part of this very milieu.

For the *Glasgow Observer*, the voice of the Catholic Irish, it was Ferguson's entry into nationalist politics that held the most fascination. His case offered an example of a Protestant Irishman finding secular salvation in the national cause. At first, all his friends in Glasgow were, like himself, Irish Protestants who formed around 25 per cent of the Irish-born population.[14] Indistinguishable to the host population from their Catholic countrymen, many struggled to safeguard their social position by using familiar networks of influence, such as Orangeism, and being 'more British than the British'.[15] Here Ferguson's response was presented as a melodrama of conflict and redemption:

> It was only after coming to Scotland that Mr Ferguson seemed to discover his inborn patriotism. He was not long here before his discovered that it would be necessary for him to take one side or the other – either for or against the land of his birth. A struggle ensued of which only he could tell the heart-searching nature ... His social and business leanings were towards the old life, but his patriotic soul yearned above that, and the promptings of patriotism and duty overcame the other feeling.[16]

His personal account of his struggle, offered in 1894, when

he was already a well-established public figure, also takes
the form of a quasi-religious conversion.[17] He was drawn one
evening by the loud and animated discussion coming from the
old Eclectic Hall, in Dunlop Street. The subject was 'Ireland
and Popery'. 'The Pope was been discussed in all the moods
and tenses, and two or three Irish Catholics were fighting their
political battles against great odds'. Having little knowledge of
the Roman Catholic Church, Ferguson initially stayed silent, but
was drawn in when the debate turned to Ireland. Now, he found
his humanitarian principles on the land issue, nurtured by Cliffe
Leslie, brushed aside by Scots who were traducing the country
and its people, seeming to think that Irish tenant-right was a
robbing of landlords and a principle that, 'only Papists . . . could
think of admitting'.

Clearly his first public appearance in Glasgow had revealed
a darker side to a city which prided itself on progress, touching
on a current of feeling which regarded Ireland and Irish issues
with undisguised hostility, ignorance and condescension. As the
Glasgow Herald explained in 1865, a considerable portion of the
Irish people persisted in tampering with rebellion because, 'it . . .
must be kept moving on in some shape, or the brave rollicking
boys, who knock each other down for sheer love would, "get blue
moulded for the want of a bating"'.[18] Yet, Ferguson's education
had ensured that his own awareness of Irish issues was limited.
He had been 'completely beaten' in the Eclectic Hall debate, not
because he lacked energy in putting his case, but because his
information was deficient. Indeed, he was fond of saying it was
not until he found himself in Glasgow that, *'I discovered not only
Ireland, but that I was an Irishman*[19]

It was through the medium of this newly acquired Irish identity
that he now came to make sense of his migrant experience. His
'education in Nationality' was to be active and rapid one, pursued
with the omnivorous energy he had previously devoted to works
of political economy. For the next few years, his leisure time was
spent on 'national literature'. This included the shilling volumes

of the 'Library of Ireland', a venture originally established through the inspiration of the Young Irelander, Thomas Davis in 1845. Its purpose was to foster national self-awareness, by making works such as Thomas McNevin's, *History of the Irish Volunteers* and John Mitchel's, *Life of Aohd O'Neill* available to the widest possible public.[20] Ferguson also tackled the seventeenth-century poet and historian Geoffrey Keating's, *History of Ireland*, while for lighter reading, he selected another Davis creation, the *Nation*, and other nationally-minded periodicals. These he read mainly on Sundays, having relaxed his earlier Sabbatarian principles.

The industry of these years was to have a lasting impression. History was to remain of prime importance to him, believing that, 'a Nation's life . . . depends for its health and progress on the study of the past'. The British ignorance of Irish history, he argued, sprang from an unwillingness to acknowledge the 'stain on the character of the English nation' in its dealings with Ireland.[21] Young Ireland authors, such as Mitchel and Thomas D'Arcy McGee, were influential, with Ferguson eagerly absorbing their latest productions: *The Last Conquest of Ireland (Perhaps)* (1861); and *A Popular History of Ireland to the Emancipation of the Catholics* (1864). The vision which emerged was one of Irish history's heroic sweep – a continuous process of English conquest and despoliation, through which the nationhood of Ireland, 'the Poland of the West', had remained inviolable:

> Vernal-like from death and mourning,
> Sprang our coffined Fatherland –
> Phoenix-like from out the burning,
> Sepulchre and Spies o'erturning.
> Courage, Brothers – hand to hand –
> God's with Ireland, hand to hand.[22]

In this romantic narrative of struggle and endurance, Ferguson was no mere onlooker, but a living participant: a new nationalist perhaps, but one 'of the very oldest tribe of [the] Irish race . . .'[23]

His mother presented him with an added bonus. One evening, when Ferguson was declaiming the virtues of one of the most extreme Young Irelanders – the Ulsterman, John Mitchel – and attacking Protestants for their failure to rally likewise to the Irish cause, Mrs Ferguson interjected: 'Your father's family held these views . . . so there's rebel blood in your veins'. 'By Saint Patrick', cried her son, 'I felt it, and was never more pleased to hear anything in my life'.[24]

Becoming a Radical

In finding Ireland, he may have lost the support of his friends and relations, but his personal and intellectual martyrdom was far from complete. Mary Ferguson followed her husband in her devotion to the new cause and continued to support him throughout his career. It was also significant that some of the philosophical mentors he had studied since his Belfast days had already presented critical views on the Irish question, reflecting their abiding hostility to establishment interests in church and state, and their admiration for European nationalism.[25] This consideration may place Ferguson's Damascus-like conversion in a less dramatic light. A more gradual process is likely through which his self-education exposed him to the social and political discourses of his day – of which nationalism was one of the most prominent. Indeed, his presence in the Eclectic Hall on that fateful night could scarcely have been accidental. This was the headquarters of the Eclectic Society, a group which had grown out of Owenite Socialism, but had also fallen under the spell of Charles Bradlaugh's radical and individualistic approach to social reform.[26] It had become a meeting place for the city's freethinkers and provided a forum for the discussion of a varied range of subjects: political, scientific, social and religious.

Critically, Ferguson's own brand of eclecticism and his reading into the broader canon of radical philosophy was to continue. This meant that, despite being absorbed for the moment in the fate of the Irish 'national spirit', he was also able to place himself in the even greater historical drama of unfolding reason and the progress of humanity. It was a sentiment which he later used poetry to capture:

> Through the ages an unceasing purpose runs,
> And the thoughts of men are broadened
> With the process of the suns.[27]

Perhaps as a result of his lack of formal education, he was apt to parade his learning, a trait which gave his opponents ample opportunity for ridicule.[28] In times when his constitutional principles were called into question he also was inclined to recite his intellectual authorities as a defensive mantra, yet for his admirers, his natural scholarship conferred an honoured niche among nationalist contemporaries. His learning did more than lend polish to his political activities. He approached the acquisition of useful knowledge in the spirit of one preparing for battle. He was determined to have his information 'bright and keen, for the next encounter with the enemy'.[29] The weapons lay close to hand, for, as with nationalist history, the publication of some of the seminal texts of radicalism was intertwined with his own emergence as a public figure. His knowledge of French and German opened up the world of continental philosophy, but it was Herbert Spencer and John Stuart Mill that he initially adopted as his intellectual guides.

If today, Spencer seems a half-forgotten figure, a rather desiccated synthetic philosopher and apologist for unfettered capitalism, his contemporary readers certainly did not regard him in this unflattering light. One of the most influential of Victorian thinkers, he intrigued radical intellectuals from Beatrice Webb to Havelock Ellis, who was 'fascinated by that all-seeing gaze . . . It was not so much his clearness and positiveness, but rather the sum of the vastness and complexity of all things, of a great mystery which surrounds us and which we cannot penetrate'.[30] For Ferguson, the attraction offers a revealing insight into his intellectual and personal development during the 1860s.

Spencer's *Social Statistics*, which first appeared in 1851, had already challenged the validity of aristocratic titles to land, a position immediately attractive to a young radical. It was, however, his *First Principles* (1862) and *Principles of Biology* (1864–7), which began to set out an altogether more ambitious and enveloping world view. 'The philosopher of Darwinism', Spencer was a system-builder and one of the earliest exponents of sociology and evolutionary theory.[31] He offered an apparently verifiable theory of social change which was heavily organicist, arguing that social evolution was the evolution of function meeting needs. His application of the scientific method to human nature also taught a generation of reformers the relevance of 'facts', relating to social organisation. Henceforth, social science investigation, with its intellectual synthesis of observation and measurement and its systematic ordering of data for comparative purposes could be used to 'solve' social problems, replete with the confidence of nineteenth century biology. Above all, despite his own innate pessimism, Spencer's 'revelation' of fundamental laws of nature and society held out the hope that truth and progress were attainable objects.

Even the philosopher's fierce defence of individualistic polity had a radical component which struck a chord for those who like Ferguson had turned their backs on traditional allegiances. His wider popularity in the Victorian age may even capture elements of a generational revolt. For the new army of lower middle class workers, clerks or elementary school teachers, who had left the functional dependence of parents and home town and had migrated to the city, Spencer's individualism offered the possibility of a new identity and the search for new models of behaviour. His own biography also offered compelling parallels with Ferguson's recent experiences. Already provincial outsider, Spencer commitment to 'science' cast him also as an iconoclast, one who was determined to ignore pressure to confirm to traditional authorities: Webb recalled him not merely refusing to go to church on a Sunday morning, but walking in the opposite direction against the tide of believers.[32] Most importantly, Spencer symbolised the triumph of the democratic intellect. He was, like Ferguson, almost entirely self-educated and proud of it. The message he held out was that access to knowledge and an adequate understanding of the world did not depend on being part of a favoured class, or on attendance at the ancient universities, but could be undertaken on one's own account – even if the end result was sometimes awkward and even misbegotten.

As Ferguson set out to build his own philosophical and political system, Mill's attraction is perhaps easier to grasp. His writings on Irish landholding were to be a major influence on many in the nationalist movement.[33] In these he made a decisive break with earlier radical thought on the economic dimensions of the Irish Question. John Bright's diagnosis in the 1840s had cited the monopoly of land ownership, absence of capital, lack of demand for labour and a surplus population as the key problems. For the next twenty years his prescription of free trade in land and the introduction of English capitalist farming remained the radical orthodoxy.[34] In contrast, Mill's *Principles of Political Economy* (1848–65), and his pamphlet *England and Ireland* (1868) firmly set out the historicist case for reform, advocating the conversion of tenants into peasant proprietors and cooperative production as the solution.[35] This attempt to settle the Irish land question on Irish terms was an impressive novelty, yet there was much more in Mill's developing body of work to stimulate Ferguson's wider quest for knowledge. *On Liberty* (1859) had, for example, further advanced the case of individualism, establishing the criteria for distinguishing between individual responsibility and cases where 'society' should intervene. The book also argued for the widest possible scope for freedom of speech and attacked religious intolerance, arguing that true beliefs gain strength when they have to be upheld publically in the face of opposition.

Absorbing these high-minded precepts, Ferguson, continued to develop a cast of mind which was analytical, concrete and historical. He developed a particular fascination for social statistics, amazing contemporaries by his capacity for 'absorbing facts and rendering them subservient to an argumentative purpose that overbore all contentions of opponents . . .'[36] The practical conviction was also growing that, as he later expressed it: 'It is within human power to make conditions in which all men can have opportunities of lives worth living'.[37] This was a principle which was calculated to propel him from philosophical speculation into the active politics of British radicalism.

With customary good timing, one of his first major political outings was to take part in the inaugural meeting of the Reform League in London.[38] This body had more tortuous origins than he liked to admit, representing an alliance between metropolitan middle class radicals and industrial artisans of the type that he was later to advocate for Glasgow.[39] It had grown out earlier progressive movements, such as the Universal League, but its development also coincided with inspiring international agitation in Poland and Italy. A series of conferences, held to draw up policy and settle organisational details, culminated in its formal inauguration at St Martin's Hall on 23 March 1865.[40]

Ferguson was still too junior a figure to be included in any of the Reform League's committees, but the episode did offer useful political experience. Looking to Mill, Bright and Gladstone for inspiration, the objects of the League were to advance universal manhood suffrage and the secret ballot, thus breaking the aristocratic stranglehold on government. It conveyed its message through the medium of pamphlets, songs and poems, but also offered lectures, not only on the themes of suffrage and the ballot, but also on British constitutional theory.[41] A further vital element in its strategy was the use of large public demonstrations, intended to force a dialogue between Parliament and the people. The most famous of these in July 1866 – the so-called 'Hyde Park Riot' – saw Ferguson as a member of the 5000–strong crowd who forced entrance and tore down the park railings in an attempt to establish the right of public meeting in Royal Parks.[42]

Extra-parliamentary activity of this type gave rise to controversy within the League, antagonising those who were concerned to respect the limits of legality, but Ferguson struck up a lasting friendship with the leading exponent of the more advanced strategy, Charles Bradlaugh, the champion of scientific materialism.[43] Back in Glasgow, his political energy found further outlets in the city's loosely organised 'Democratic party' which operated from Democratic Hall, in Nelson Street, Trongate.[44] Many of its leading lights were former Chartist activists and advanced radicals, such as James Adams, who had been secretary of the last Glasgow Chartist society. The veteran town councillors, James Martin and James Moir were also drawn in, but its membership represented the future as much as the past, including Gavin B. Clark, who was to become the Crofters' MP for Caithness and President of the Highland Land League.

The Glasgow democrats campaigned on a range of social and political questions, which also anticipated Ferguson's later concerns. Their first campaign to dismantle the credit or tally system, a notable source of working men's indebtedness, met with some success in promoting legislation to allow freedom of contract. Agitation on the land question was more disappointing. Despite a meeting by Ernest Jones in the City Hall, they discovered great difficulty in convincing the urban population that the issue concerned them.[45] By the autumn of 1866, these issues were becoming increasingly eclipsed by the question of franchise, with the establishment of the National Scottish Reform League for the purpose of organising a mass Reform demonstration.[46] Again progress was uneven. The rally, addressed by John Bright in October, marked an impressive and orderly show of strength, representing all shades of opinion within the national reform movement.[47] Despite this apparent unity, the Scottish leadership rapidly became dominated by a middle class group who wanted the League to become a wing of the Liberal Party. Over the next two years leading up to the 1868 General Election, splits among the reformers, particularly over the issue of independent labour representation, became increasingly debilitating as the movement began to overreach itself.[48]

Radicalism was the beginning of a complex political apprenticeship for Ferguson. Yet, even in the thick of action at Hyde Park, he had not forgotten Ireland: 'as we forced the rails . . . and stood before the soldiers, the thought passed through my head how different if we had been Irishmen at Phoenix Park . . .'[49] In this he was not alone. Irish issues also had an insistent presence on the British reform agenda. The Reform League's sister organisation, the Dublin-based, Irish National Reform League demanded sweeping agricultural, industrial and political change, with a delegate meeting called in London in March 1867 to support justice for Ireland.[50] Yet, it was the Irish Question which was also to illustrate with particular clarity, the constraints and divisions of British radicalism. Some of these limitations would have been apparent from Ferguson's reading of Mill's, *England and Ireland*. For, while escaping from English preconceptions in his analysis of Ireland's economic position, Mill continued to support political union as a beneficial and permanent arrangement.[51] Even Ferguson's new associate, Bradlaugh, who had direct experience of Ireland through his early military service, shared Mill's reservations, arguing in his *Irish Question* (1868) for radical change in landholding to sweep away traditional landlordism, while still accepting the principle of British dominion.

By the time these reflections appeared, the moral legitimacy of Britain's right to rule in Ireland had already been challenged from a new source. The rise of the Fenian movement not only tested the parameters of radical thought, but also compromised the unity of radical organisations, including the Reform League. For Ferguson, the fluid political situation of 1860s, one to which the British radicals had themselves contributed, proved that a single organisation was unlikely to encapsulate the breadth of his developing political vision. It was now that his attention was forced from the indissoluble nation of the Young Ireland Library to the less rarefied politics of the Glasgow Irish community.

Fenian Fever

For its determined band of adherents in Scotland, loyalty to
Fenianism created the same mentality of 'independence' and
'advancement' which Ferguson had gained through the medium
of self-education.[52] The Irish Republican Brotherhood (IRB) had
been established in Dublin in 1858, originally as an oath-bound
military society – the 'Fenian' title was borrowed during the
1860s from its American counterpart. Influenced by European
conspiratorial societies, its central doctrine was the right of the
Irish people to obtain a separate republic, if necessary by physical
force. To this end, it attempted to recruit from all classes and
creeds, albeit meeting with most success among young, urban
Catholics in lower-ranking occupational groups.

While traditional nationalist historians have viewed the
Fenians as a link in the chain of republican succession, the thrust
of revisionist interpretations has been to place the movement in
its full social, economic and intellectual setting.[53] Typically, in this
re-appraisal, it appears as embedded in the crisis-ridden decades
between 1850 and 1870, a reaction against the new social order that
was emerging, yet at the same time an attempt by those alienated
to find a place in it.[54] For all their warlike aspect, the Fenians by
no means stood outside the social norms of the Victorian age.

Fenianism reached the Irish in Scotland in the early 1860s.
Here, it found a large and far from homogenous community,
increasingly frustrated at its powerlessness and isolation from
the mainstream of Scottish society. The heavy post-Famine
migration waves had now subsided, and on average only 8000
new immigrants from Ireland were arriving each year during the
1860s.[55] Although the number of Irish-born residents in Scotland
was consequently stabilising at around 207,000 between 1851 and
1871, this was still a very significant population, the majority of
which was Roman Catholic. In 1871, 40 per cent of the largest Irish

communities and 70 per cent of communities with the largest Irish in percentage terms were in Scotland, most notably Glasgow, Greenock, Dundee, Edinburgh, Paisley, Ayr and Airdrie.[56] Even in this company, Glasgow stood out. According to the 1861 census, Irish-born citizens totalled 63,574, but the Irish themselves consistently reckoned their numbers at a quarter of the city's estimated population of 500,000, with contemporary claiming that, 'Dublin excepted, Glasgow has the largest Catholic population in any city in the three kingdoms'.[57] Despite a developing commercial and professional middle class, concentration of the majority in the poorest housing and in low-paid casual employment in heavy industry seemed bound to persist.

These handicaps apart, the rising ambitions of the community could not be concealed. The *Glasgow Free Press* had been established in 1851 to work for Ireland and expose the grievances of the Catholic Irish in Scotland. A decade later, it was still bemoaning the lack of Irish-born priests, while condemning the internal divisions which, it believed, prevented the Irish becoming 'a solid phalanx of power' in their city of adoption.[58] The remedy, it argued, was for the Glasgow Irish to 'bestir themselves' by joining improving organisations such as Irish National Association of Scotland.[59]

While the secret IRB network equally sought to boost its members ethnic identity and self-worth, it was determined to operate outside the narrow clerical and constitutionalist channels through which the struggle for national and community advancement had previously been confined. It is difficult to quantify the organisation's impact. It was claimed that 25,000 Fenians were active in Scotland, but less dramatic estimates of 18,000 Fenians on the whole British mainland and of around 2500 in the Glasgow area may be more realistic.[60]

Was John Ferguson drawn into their ranks?[61] Historians of Home Rule, from McDonagh onwards have generally assumed that he was a member of the IRB, but, given that this was a conspiratorial movement, the truth is very difficult to determine.[62]

From the vantage point of the early twentieth century, it the issue still caused some of his obituarists confusion and embarrassment. For some, the Fenian episode was far enough distant to assume the mantle of heroic failure. The *Observer* stated that although Ferguson was by nature a constitutionalist, he had nevertheless 'the courage of a soldier', and until later times when he saw the possibility of persuading England to a peaceable settlement of the Irish difficulty, 'he would have no hesitation whatever in allying himself with those who sough the short way out of Ireland's misery and who felt that she should strike for her own flag.'[63] Similarly the *Record* noted that while often lamenting the need for secret societies, he expressed himself 'as feeling that the logic of "the blow" was useful, however it might be dealt'.[64] These speculations brought an angry riposte from a close colleague, Arthur Murphy, that while held in respect by advanced nationalists, he had no association with the physical force movement.[65]

Ferguson himself insisted, while testifying in front of the *Times-Parnell Commission* in 1888, that he had never actually joined the IRB.[66] Instead, he proudly proclaimed his adherence to British republicanism, claiming that he had 'probably' only taken part publicly in Irish political affairs in 1869 or 1870. Prior to this he informed the Commission – with some sarcasm –that had confined his interest to 'writing and speaking at literary and other societies and in every way which a modest youth of the time was able to adopt'. Established to consider serious accusations against the motives of Land League agitation in Ireland, the Commission was hardly a forum which encouraged openness, and in less guarded occasions he was happy justify the Fenians as 'the cream of the Irish race.[67] However, another Home Rule contemporary, such as William O'Brien, who had himself joined the IRB in his teens, also believed that, while undoubtedly one of 'the extreme men', Ferguson was never 'a sworn revolutionist'.[68]

While Fenianism did present a great emotional appeal, there were also sound reasons to hesitate over adherence in the

1860s. The single-mindedness of its military oath to uphold the virtually-established republic offered one potential stumbling block to an activist of Ferguson's eclectic philosophical outlook and expanding political contacts. Michael Davitt, who himself had been an IRB activist, later condemned it as the 'silly oath of secrecy' and even the leading Fenian, John O'Leary found it 'repugnant'.[69] The organisation's rather nebulous social reform policy was also unlikely to displace his rigorous self-education in political economy and statistical methods. Fenianism did develop a radical reputation on the land issue, dear to Ferguson's heart. As the *Press* suggested, 'whatever was political and national in its objects was subordinate to the social one, that is of destroying landlordism'.[70] Yet, there was little practical indication of how this might be achieved.

It did not, however, require an actual oath to engage with tide of Fenian-inspired nationalism. The term 'Fenian' itself acquired a remarkable elasticity. For the *Free Press* 'Fenianism' meant 'the desire of Irishmen to have their country free from the bondage which unites her to England . . .'[71] In this sense, he was indeed a Fenian – or at least, like John Dillon, a 'cool Fenian', who knew 'the extreme party' and was known by them.[72] Certainly, in the midst of the Fenian crisis, he was able to seize on the business opportunities which it presented. Despite O'Leary's strictures on the right of patriots to perpetrate bad verses, Fenianism had revived the tradition of Irish street ballads, with activists such as Charles Kickham and John O'Kegan Casey eagerly composing songs.[73] When in Dublin in 1866, Ferguson discovered from H. J. Gill, the Irish publisher, that there was no song book available in Ireland containing the older patriotic ballads, including Michael Joseph McCann's 'O Domhnaill Abu', he pressed Cameron & Co to produce a new edition. Unfortunately, the Irish authorities were now on the offensive, suppressing songs which had circulated with impunity for twenty years. Ferguson's first project, *The Green Flag of Erin* was seized, as was a later cheap edition of songs by Thomas Moore and Thomas Davis.[74] This incident did not deter him from producing *Songs of A Rising Nation*, another collection of 'Battle Ballads' by Ellen Forrester and her son Arthur, the IRB organiser, which emerged in 1869.[75]

The element of ambiguity in Ferguson's political allegiance was later to prove useful in his role as a broker between the physical force and constitutionalist wings of nationalism. His experience during these years was a formative influence in a more indirect sense. The Fenian crisis set out in stark relief the materials with which he would have to labour during his active career in politics. On a positive note, they revealed the numerical muscle and collective aspirations of the Irish community in the West of Scotland. More negatively, they exposed both the antagonism and incomprehension of many of the host population and the ideological and social fissures present among the Irish themselves.

Like the rest of Britain, Scotland experienced 'Fenian Fever' which peaked at the end of 1867.[76] This followed the failed Fenian military operations on the British mainland at Chester Castle, Manchester and Clerkenwell Gaol, but also fed on the shadowy nature of the local movement. The main contribution to the resulting moral panic was made by the press and authorities. The Irish population in Scotland were soon regarded as part of 'the enemy within', with their public and private meetings branded 'quasi-Fenian' and subject to close surveillance.[77]

While the mainstream press was the most outspoken on the Fenian menace, there was little comfort from Ferguson's local allies in the reform movement. Serious discussions did take place between the Fenians and English republicans, including Bradlaugh, but there was no such rapprochement in Scotland. Admitting that dissent was justified over issues such as the Established Church and the land question, the radical *Glasgow Sentinel* believed that this could only be removed by a reformed British parliament and not by the panecea of 'independence'.[78] Moreover, it rejected the calls of John Bright and 'those demanding leniency for Fenian prisoners that anyone disaffected with government has the right to overthrow it'.[79]

In this atmosphere of isolation and suspicion, the response of the Irish themselves was far from unified. As in Ireland, the Catholic clergy were implacably opposed to Fenianism and sought to blunt native hostility by dissuading their parishioners from involvement.[80] The position of *Free Press* was more complex. Initially hostile to what it believed was an insult to the nation's intelligence, it became convinced that Fenianism was a formidable vehicle for Irish grievances. Yet, its understanding of the movement was it was similarly tempered by an awareness of the vulnerability of the Irish community in Glasgow, for many of whom economic survival remained the primary objective.

Fenianism has been credited with the 're-nationalisation' of Irish politics.[81] Whether from prudence or necessity, it was soon evident that in Scotland this impulse would be largely directed through constitutional channels. The agitation during 1869 to win amnesty for Fenian prisoners caught the imagination of the local Irish population, but so had the Reform agitation of three years previously. For the *Free Press,* this had marked 'the TIDE OF DEMOCRACY setting in', and it waited expectantly to see how any large reform measure would benefit Ireland.[82] The 1868 Reform Act raised expectations further and in the general election of that year, new voters from the Glasgow Irish were among those who assisted the cause of the progressive candidates.[83] Even when Glastonian Liberalism was judged by some to have lost its momentum after the disestablishment of the Church of Ireland in 1869, it was to not to '. . . scaffolds, chains and exiles' tears' that the majority turned, but to open agitation for home government.

In John Ferguson's retrospective analysis, the Fenians conspired unwisely for themselves, but wisely for the nation. He believed that they had made constitutional struggle possible: 'As a military movement', he admitted, 'its results were little better than a fiasco, but out of it sprang the intelligent, well-directed movement called Home Rule, of which the world has heard much, and will hear more.'[84] This new movement was set to engage his own political energies and charisma more effectively than any underground organisation.

Notes

1   Royal Mail Packets made daily trips between the cities
    (Sunday excepted): *Belfast Newsletter* 8 Jul. 1860. The demand
    for fast day sailings was evident in the introduction of
    purpose-built steamers, such as G. & J. Burn's *Giraffe*:
    C. Duckworth and G. Langmuir, *Clyde and Other Coastal
    Steamers* (Prescot 1977), p. 13.

2   The emigration rate (per 1000) for Ulster in 1851–61 was
    17.3, this dropped to 10.7 in the next decade: W. E. Vaughan
    and A. J. Fitzpatrick, *Irish Population Statistics: Population*
    (Dublin, 1978), pp. 311–21.

3   C. Withers, 'The demographic history of the city 1831–1912',
    in W. H. Fraser and I. Maver (eds.), *Glasgow 1830–1912*
    (Manchester, 1996), pp. 142–3.

4   W. H. Fraser, *ibid.*, p. 4; Maver, *Glasgow* (Edinburgh, 2000),
    pp. 133–142.

5   *Glasgow Directory 1859–64*. The business had developed out
    of the firm of Cameron, Clark and Co. of St Enoch Square
    and Argyle Street. Duncan Cameron split from his parter
    Joseph Clark in 1860 and relocated the firm's office in
    Queen Street the following year.

6   *Glasgow Directory 1867*. This is the first listing of the business
    under the title 'Cameron & Ferguson'.

7   *Glasgow Observer*, 28 Apr. 1906.

8   *Slater's Directory of Ireland 1856; Griffith's Valuation 1864*, Town
    of Markethill: Matthew's premises in the Main Street had a
    rateable value of £ 15, one of the highest in the town.

9   A. Day and P. McWilliams, *Ordnance Survey Memoirs of
    Ireland. Parishes of Armagh,Volume I, 1835–8,* (Belfast, 1993),
    pp. 94–7.

10 *Glasgow Directory 1865*. The Ferguson's neighbours were a

watchmaker, a builder and a deputy-clerk. For a profile of the area see, W. Watson, *Report on the Vital Social and Economic Statistics of Glasgow for 1868* (Glasgow 1869), p. 46. The population density was reckoned at 92 per acre.

11 Edinburgh, National Archives of Scotland (NAS), Census 1871.

12 *Glasgow Echo*, 1 Sept. 1894.

13 J. F. McCaffrey, 'Political issues and developments', in Fraser and Maver, *Glasgow*, p. 199.

14 G. Walker, 'The Protestant Irish in Scotland', in T. Devine (ed.), *Irish Immigrants in Scottish Society* (Edinburgh, 1990), p. 49.

15 *Glasgow Star*, 28 Apr. 1906.

16 *Glasgow Observer*, 28 Apr. 1906.

17 *Glasgow Echo*, 1 Sept. 1894.

18 *Glasgow Herald*, 6 Sept. 1865.

19 *Irish Packet*, 14 Nov. 1903.

20 Thomas Davis, *Prose Writings, Essays on Ireland* (London, 1890), pp. 224–6. His original aim was 'to give to the country a National Library, exact enough for the wisest, high enough for the purest, and cheap enough for all readers . . .'

21 *Three Centuries*, pp. 1–2.

22 *Ibid.*, p. 134.

23 *Glasgow Star*, 28 Apr. 1906.

24 *Ibid.*

25 F. D'Arcy, 'Charles Bradlaugh and the Irish Question: A Study in the Nature and Limits of British radicalism, 1853–91', in C. McCartney (ed.), *Studies in Irish History* (Dublin, 1979), p. 228–9. The commitment to Ireland dating from

the 1840s in John Bright's speeches attracted the approval of Michael Davitt: *The Fall of Feudalism in Ireland, or the Story of the Land League Revolution* (Shannon, 1970), pp. 101–2.

26 *Glasgow Sentinel*, 25 Nov. 1865, *Forward*, 11 Jun. 1910.

27 *The Land for the People. An Appeal to All who Work by Brain or Hand*, (Glasgow [c.1881]), p. 30.

28 *The Bailie*, 6 Aug. 1879.

29 *Glasgow Star*, 28 Apr. 1906.

30 Quoted in C. J. Nottingham, *The Pursuit of Serenity: Havelock Ellis and the New Politics* (Amsterdam, 1999), p. 27. For Webb's reaction, see *Diary of Beatrice Webb*, vol. 1 ed. N. J. Mackenzie (London 1982), p. 8.

31 D. Macrae, *The Man versus the State*, (Harmondsworth, 1962).

32 Beatrice Webb, *My Apprenticeship* (London, 1926).

33 E. D. Steele, 'J. S. Mill and the Irish Question: the principles of political economy, 1848–65', *Historical Journal*, xii (1970), pp. 216–36. For Michael Davitt, *Principles of Political Economy* 'seemed like the articles of a new social chapter': *Leaves from a Prison Diary* (London, 1885) p. 247. See also, *Fall of Feudalism*, pp. 101–2.

34 See R. D. Collison Black, *Economic Thought and the Irish Question, 1817–1870* (Cambridge, 1960); D'Arcy, 'Charles Bradlaugh' p. 229.

35 *England and Ireland*, p. 13.

36 *Daily Record*, 24 Apr. 1906.

37 John Ferguson, *Glasgow, the City of Progress*, (Glasgow 1900), p. 7.

38 *Glasgow Echo*, 1 Sept. 1894.

39 D. D. Bell, 'The Reform League and its Origins to 1867', (University of Oxford D. Phil. Thesis, 1961).

40 Not the Guild Hall, as Ferguson recalled.

41 See *Glasgow Sentinel*, 9 May 1865 for its 'Address to the Working Classes'.

42 *Glasgow Sentinel*, 28 Jul. 1866.

43 Kettle, *Material for Victory*. p. 42.

44 *Forward*, 11 June 1910.

45 *Ibid*.18 June 1910.

46 W.H. Fraser, *Scottish Popular Politics* (2000), pp.79–85; 'Trade unions, reform and the election of 1868 in Scotland', *Scottish Historical Review*, xiv, (1967), p. 144.

47 *Scottish National Reform League: Great Reform Demonstration in Glasgow, Tuesday 16 October 1866* (Glasgow, 1866).

48 *Glasgow Sentinel*, 27 Jun. 1868 reported that little had been heard of the League for twelve months. See also W. H. Fraser, *Alexander Campbell and the Search for Socialism* (Manchester, 1996), pp. 163–6.

49 *Three Centuries*, p. 68.

50 Bell, 'Reform League', p. 376.

51 D'Arcy, 'Charles Bradlaugh', p. 230; H Bradlaugh Bonner, *Charles Bradlaugh* (London, 1895), vol. I.

52 For a full discussion of the issues below, see E. W. McFarland '"A reality and yet impalpable": The Fenian panic in Mid-Victorian Scotland, in *Scottish Historical Review*, LXXVI, 6, No.206, pp. 199–223.

53 J. Hutchinson, 'Irish nationalism' in D. G. Boyce and A. O'Day, *The Revisionist Controversy in Irish History* (London, 1996), pp. 100–16.

54 R V. Comerford, *The Fenians in Context* (Dublin, 1985), p. 8.

55 B. Collins, 'The origins of Irish immigration into Scotland', in T.Devine (ed.), *Irish Immigrants and Scottish Society in the Nineteenth and Twentieth Centuries* (Edinburgh 1990), p. 11.

56 Collins, 'Origins', p. 8; C. Pooley, 'Segregation or integration? The residential experience of the Irish in Mid-Victorian Britain', in R. Swift and S. Gilley (eds.), *The Irish in Britain, 1815–1939,* (London, 1989), p. 63.

57 *Glasgow Free Press,* 11 May 1861; 23 Jun. 1865; *Irish Catholic Banner* 20, 27 Jun. 1868.

58 *Ibid.,* 11 May 1861; J. E. Handley, *The Irish in Modern Scotland* (Cork, 1947), pp. 47–92.

59 *Ibid.,* 7 Jan., 22 Jul., 23 Sept 1865 for activities.

60 *North British Daily Mail,* 16 Oct. 1867; 23 Sept. 1865; A. O'Day, 'The political organisation of the Irish in Britain 1867–1890', in Swift and Gilley, *Irish in Britain,* p. 111. *North British Daily Mail,* 21 Oct. 1867.

61 *Three Centuries,* p. 65.

62 M. McDonagh, *The Home Rule Movement* (Dublin, 1920), p. 20.

63 *Glasgow Observer,* 28 Apr. 1906.

64 *Daily Record,* 24 Apr. 1906.

65 *Glasgow Star,* 28 Apr. 1906

66 *Special Commission Act 1888. Report of Proceedings before the Commissioners appointed by the Act. Reprinted from The Times* (London, 1890), vol.iii, p. 285.

67 *Glasgow Observer,* 5 Mar. 1892.

68 W. O'Brien, *Recollections* (London 1905), 140.

69 Davitt, *Fall of Feudalism,* p. 111; G. Moran, *Father Patrick Lavelle. A Radical Priest in County Mayo* (Dublin, 1994),p. 86.

70 *Glasgow Free Press,* 27 Oct. 1866.

71 *Glasgow Free Press,* 19 Jan. 1867.

72 F. S. L. Lyons, *John Dillon: A Biography* (London, 1968), p. 22.

73 J. O'Leary *Recollections of Fenians and Fenianism,* vol. II, (London, 1896), p. 78; G. Zimmerman, *Songs of the Irish Rebellion,* (Dublin, 1967), pp. 48, 259–60.

74 NAI, Chief Secretary's Office Registered Papers, CR 126, Nov. 7 1866, case of John Hughes, bookseller.

75 *Irishman,* 27 Mar. 1869: for Forrester see, Moody, *Davitt,* pp. 48–65. A 'people's edition' priced 1/– was produced alongside the more expensive version.

76 McFarland, 'Fenian Panic', pp. 210–17.

77 *North British Daily Mail,* 2 Oct. 1867. Even the Protestant Irish could not escape the net. The prospect of the Orangemen of Glasgow using Fenianism to demarcate themselves from their Catholic countrymen merely prompted the *Mail* to warn of 'the likely repetition of those scenes of bloodshed which disgraced Belfast . . .'

78 *Glasgow Sentinel,* 16 Feb. 1867.

79 *Ibid.,* 11 May 1867. See also, 28 Dec. 1867.

80 J. Lynch to P. Cullen 7 Feb. 1867, Cullen Papers, quoted in Moran, *Father Patrick Lavelle,* p. 77.

81 D. G. Boyce, *Nationalism in Ireland* (London, 1982), p. 183.

82 *Glasgow Free Press,* 13, 20 Oct., 1867.

83 NAI, Fenian Papers, 5084R: report of amnesty meeting in Glasgow; McCaffrey, 'Political Issues and Developments', p. 201.

84 *Three Centuries,* p. 134.

CHAPTER THREE

A Dark and Terrible Time

The first Home Rule movement was born of an unlikely and unstable coalition and led by that 'compendium of honest compromise', Isaac Butt.[1] It was the contradictions and opportunities implicit in this new wave of Irish politics which galvanised John Ferguson as he began his political career in earnest.

Forty-nine of the leading merchants and professional men of Dublin attended a private meeting in Bilton's Hotel on the evening of 19 May 1870. The pluralism of this distinguished gathering was astonishing, with Protestant landowners, nationalist repealers and Fenians all in attendance.[2] The common factor binding the participants was dissatisfaction with the current arrangements for governing Ireland. The landowners were drawn in through their resentment against Gladstone's disestablishment of the Church of Ireland. Middle-class Catholics were attracted by their disappointment at his Land Act and education policy. The Fenians remained watchful, but largely benevolent, believing that, 'by taking part in every political or semi-political movement, [they] could exercise much influence, and mould these movements to [their] own end'.[3] Nor was there any dissent when Butt proposed that the solution to their concerns was the establishment of an Irish parliament with full control of domestic affairs. The discussion had only lasted upwards of an hour, but out of it emerged a committee which by July was able to present to the public the 'Home Government Association of Ireland'.

The new association initially appeared to realise the Young Ireland dream of a truly comprehensive Irish nationalism, but unity began to dissipate almost at once. Any nationalist wishing to combine his countrymen in a single movement had to realise that the new national aim could not hope to mobilise popular support without attacking historic grievances.[4] Land reform, for example, might appear as *the* national issue, but only if the 'nation' was defined as Catholic Ireland. Instead, to many Protestants the land question appeared as a 'sectional interest' which threatened the very basis of their identity and security. If the movement pressed its case too energetically and on a broad front it would alienate its right wing, yet the very existence of this 'Orange' element in its ranks distanced Liberals and the Catholic Clergy.

Reflecting this dilemma and recoiling from the widespread suspicion directed against it, the Home Government Association (HGA) was reluctant to move beyond the role of a metropolitan pressure group. What they intended to do, explained Butt, was merely to bring the Home Rule question before the public mind. In practice, as Thornley suggests, the movement was thus immediately 'divorced from the main sources of Irish political energy'.[5] Its initial refusal to affiliate local branches and coordinate organisation at this level and its lack of enthusiasm for electoral struggles meant that the burden of fighting the cause of Home Rule was left to local enthusiasts who, like Ferguson, were often relatively new to politics. Indeed, it was the more 'advanced' men on the British mainland who most eagerly eagerly seized the initiative and who were to attempt to shape Home Rule to suit their own purposes. In these circumstances, the dichotomy between 'national' and 'local' politics becomes difficult to sustain. The HGA was a movement for overtly national aims, yet its momentum in the 1870s came from local migrant communities for whom, 'the rising cause of the Fatherland,' meant gaining recognition in their cities of adoption.

The Grand Old Master

It was one of the ironies in John Ferguson's career that both he and his arch-conservative father shared a political hero in the shape of Isaac Butt.[6] Indeed, there was much to admire in this most endearing and exasperating of Irish politicians.

Born the son of a Donegal rector in 1815, Butt had once been even more firmly embedded in the Ascendancy than Ferguson. He had no need for the discipline of self-improvement, having been elected Professor of Political Economy at Trinity College, Dublin while still in his early twenties. By the 1840s, Butt was 'the rising hope of the Irish Protestant Conservative Party', championing them against Daniel O'Connell in the great debate on Repeal in the Dublin Corporation. It was his legal career, however, which led him to desert the Tory standard. Early doubts had arisen when he had defended the Young Ireland leaders in 1848, but his advocacy in the case of Fenian prisoners in the mid-1860s finally convinced him that self-government was the only pathway for Ireland.[7]

Butt was essentially an old-fashioned Whig. He had a warm and winning personality, coupled with an appearance which immediately inspired affection in his friends and opponents:

> Looking at the clean-shaven, round mobile, face, decidedly Irish in cast, with its large sensitive mouth and thick lips, one thought of an old comedian ... Butt was in fact, about equal parts lion and lamb – bold and daring in mind, with a temperament placid and easy-going[8]

Unfortunately, this amiable and relaxed quality – allied to an accumulating burden of debt and drink – left him poorly equipped to weather the storms of nationalist politics. As Ferguson commented, 'he expected to exercise the devils of bigotry and cupidity by generous sentiment'.[9]

They had first met in the late 1860s, when he gained the benefit of Butt's legal advice on the seizure of his firm's song books by Dublin Castle.[10] However, it was in his guise as a land reformer that the younger man was really drawn to him. Butt's reputation as a moderate home ruler has often obscured his role in promoting the tenant right movement and assisting its recovery from the collapse of the early 1850s. By the time of Ferguson's approach, he had become the movement's most radical spokesman and most successful propagandist. In *Land Tenure and Ireland: a Plea for the Celtic Race* (1866) and *The Irish People and the Irish Land* (1867) he set out a powerful case for the security of tenure and argued for a campaign of serious agitation.

With his virtues ascendant in these years, Butt was an invigorating acquaintance. His relationship with Ferguson flourished both personally and professionally. As one of 'Butt's young men', Ferguson was invited into private discussions in the 'Conspiracy chamber' as Butt called the round room in his house in Eccles St., Dublin. By 1870, Cameron & Ferguson were entrusted with the publication his *Ireland's Appeal for Amnesty*.[11] Nor was he above using the young radical into frighten the landed interest into supporting Home Rule. Although he generally preferred Ferguson to suppress his advanced views when speaking in public in Ireland, he unleashed him on a private meeting of 'Tory and Whig Protestants and Union Jack Catholics' where his listeners were reminded that they were not by the law of England the owners of the land, but only 'enstated' in it, and that the state could 'resume possession of its inalienable property', if it was clear they no longer served society usefully.

> Now gentlemen, said Isaac Butt, mark my words the doctrine Ferguson has stated the true economic doctrine of this question – the law of nature –which will ultimately prevail. It will win in England before long. Let it be done like '82 of all classes, and the people will be so grateful to you that for fifty years these questions will be kept out of Ireland. Hold back now and you last chance is gone. Radical reform will sweep Ireland of feudalism long before wealthy Britain feels its force.[12]

In later years, Ferguson held the memory of his 'Grand Old Master' in deep reverence, invoking his, 'glorious wit, humour and legal lore'.[13] In practice, as their working relationship developed during the 1870s, he became Butt's candid friend and critic, flattering, cajoling and threatening as the situation demanded. The land question which had brought them together would eventually become one of many bones of contention between them, but there one issue on which they remained in harmony. This was Butt's grand scheme of 'federal home rule'. For both men, this offered the best settlement of relations between Britain and Ireland, combining legislative independence with partnership in a great imperial destiny. While other young followers of Butt may have found his imperial nationalism a shade idiosyncratic, for Ferguson it became was to prove an abiding preoccupation.

Unlike subsequent versions of Home Rule' which envisaged a devolutionary system of government, Butt's scheme was truly federal. His plan was to combine home rule for Ireland with a central governing body for the whole United Kingdom in which England and Scotland would also be represented. An Irish House of Lords would be retained to soothe the aristocracy, but the Irish House of Commons would have supreme domestic control, 'except in those matters which the Federal Constitution might specifically reserve to the Imperial Assembly'.[14]

This in itself was a sweeping and imaginative design. However, there was much more to Home Rule than a precise formula for government. For conservatives it meant a more palatable alternative to 'Repeal of the Union'. For moderate nationalists, it meant a subordinate Irish parliament. For Fenians, it meant the first step to a separate republic.[15] In fact, the term was loaded with deeper symbols and meanings and acted as a code for a range of expectations which were often ill-defined, but deeply felt.[16] It is against this background that Ferguson's attraction to the Home Rule cause can best be understood. At a massive open air demonstration in Glasgow in 1874, he imparted his own radical version of the grandeur of the federal scheme to a massive audience:

He pleaded for Federalism in order that social reforms might receive the attention of a national parliament . . . that the moors, the swamps and the waste land might wave with golden harvests and food for men, instead of being rejected as they are now. He pleaded for Federalism that pauperism might be dealt with; that freedom instead of flowing into a festering channel, might be driven into a channel of honest toil. He pleaded for Federalism that education – that child of heaven – might touch the hearts and intellects of the people, and say to the surging, boiling ocean of liberalism that existed in every town – 'Peace be still'. He pleaded for Federalism that the sewers of the city might no longer vomit forth miasma and death; that men might have penny trains, and be driven into the country that peace might be found and where flower plots before their doors might refine their hearts and occupy their hands.

That was a picture of the glorious future which might be accomplished under a scheme of national independence . . .[17]

A gentleman leader

The first step in creating the New Jerusalem of Home Rule was to establish a local outpost in Glasgow. By October 1871, Butt's Dublin-based association had only 850 members, but the decision was taken to set up district associations, with funds set aside to pay lecturers to tour the British mainland. Ferguson had already anticipated the move. On St Patrick's night 1871, a small gathering of local Irishmen had been held at the Old Tontine Hotel, Trongate. A 'very young and boyish' Ferguson informed them of Butt's movement in Dublin. He followed this up by chairing an organising committee, which arranged for Butt to visit the city during November. [18]

The response to his initiative displayed the hunger of many of his fellow Irishmen for political involvement. On the evening of Butt's lecture on Tuesday 14 November, the City Hall was dangerously packed with an audience of 'largely composed of working men'. Butt spoke eloquently and at considerable length, but his customary fastidiousness prevented the formation of a local Home Rule Association which had been the object of the exercise. On his advice, no Home Rule motion was put to the meeting as this had not been publicly intimated in advance, and 'it was unfair to bear down by the weigh of their majority the opinion of the minority'.[19] Instead, the Glasgow Home Rule Association was formally inaugurated on 19 December at the Choral Hall in West Nile Street. Ferguson became its president, with a governing council drawn from the leading business and professional men among the city's Irish population.[20]

This mobilisation of the Glasgow Irish represented an attempt to reshape their activities in line with the political realities of the early 1870s. As such, Ferguson's project faced a number of external and internal pressures. With the Fenian panic still uppermost in their minds, one immediate constraint was the antipathy of many of the host population to this latest burst of assertiveness. The Butt meeting had been for the most part an exercise in studied moderation. Butt himself had publicly expressed his pleasure that the audience included 'Irish and Scotch', informing his Dublin associates on his return that he had 'great faith in the efforts of the Scotch people'.[21] In fact, the response of the local press was swift and scathing, with the *Glasgow Herald* cheerfully highlighting one of Ferguson's more intemperate asides to the effect that Home Rule might have to be won by illegitimate means if legitimate pathways failed. This was the beginning of a vendetta which saw an infuriated Ferguson set aside his liberal principles of free speech to suggest that dueling be reinstated to bridle 'the mouths and pens of ruffians' who perpetrated 'national insult'.[22] More constructively, it also led him in 1875 to be one of the leading promoters of the Irish in Britain's own newspaper, the *United Irishman*.[23]

As the political temperature rose during the 1870s, local hostility also found expression in threats directed at visiting Irish speakers.[24] Violence was also directed personally at Ferguson, as the most visible exponent of Irish demands. He remembered this as a decade of struggle and isolation – 'a dark and terrible time' – when his children were taunted as they went to school and bullets were put through the window of his home. Looking back in later years, he rather revelled in this role as a prophet in the wilderness, carried through his travails by the poetic sentiments that:

> . . . truth must prevail! Meanwhile endure.
> Of wordly peace, let worldlings boast,
> Amidst the storms of life, be sure,
> The loftiest spirit suffers most.[25]

More difficult to romanticise were the technical problems which surrounded the political organisation of the Catholic Irish community. By 1871, 14.32 per cent of the city's 447,732 population were of Irish birth, including both Catholics and Protestants.[26] Yet despite this numerical presence, the Irish were not residentially segregated in a pattern which would allow them to dominate any single parliamentary constituency. Throughout the 1870s, they were to remain concentrated in the east of the city, in the areas of Bellgrove, Calton and Barrowfield, or on a line running from the Gorbals through St Rollox and Port Dundas and on to Cowcaddens. Further sizable groupings lay south of the river in Lauriston and Kingston, and in Kelvinhaugh, Sandyford and Maryhill in the North. The social and economic characteristics of the population were also unfavourable. Although the 1868 Reform Act had broadly been an empowering measure, many of the Glasgow Irish did not conform to its ideal type of the 'respectable' skilled working man. The new franchise was tightly bound to the operation of the poor law, excluding those who had been in receipt of parochial relief in the year prior to the revision of the register. To be registered onto the parliamentary electoral role, voters had also to pass the barriers of an occupiers' franchise which demanded the prompt payment of rates, a twelve months residential qualification, or a complex lodgers' franchise. These were difficult to surmount for a shifting population, with many in irregular employment and in the cheaper end of the housing market.[27]

Even if a majority of the Glasgow Irish could be moulded towards the cause, there remained serious ideological and tactical divisions within the Glasgow Home Rule camp. These meant that Ferguson performed a different balancing act from Butt's in Dublin, but one which was no less demanding. Although he was later to sum up the key division as being between 'a Republican party and a strictly Conservative party', local realities were more complex.[28] One difficulty was the clergy's suspicion to any uncontrollable secular movement which might threaten their traditional role as the leaders of the Irish community. An even more active goad were the Fenians, who for an underground movement were remarkably vociferous and visible in the area. They were led by John Torley, the manager of a Dumbarton chemical works, who represented Scotland on the IRB Supreme Council.[29] This group had already shown their impatience with constitutional agitation in 1869, when they had rushed the stage at a Glasgow meeting seeking amnesty for Fenian prisoners by constitutional means, with cries of 'Gammon!' and 'Where were the spouters when they were wanted!'[30]

Against this background, Ferguson's plan was to educate, organise, persuade and placate. First, the Irish themselves must be shepherded out of their apathy and into an awareness of their rights and duties as citizens. The host population, their press and political parties must also be made aware of the community's legitimate demands – not least their claim to be taken seriously as a major interest group in the developing politics of West of Scotland. For this purpose, the Irish vote had to be solid and unified and deployed to the maximum effect. The Home Rule campaign must therefore win support from the main shapers of opinion within their own community – or at least possess sufficient credibility to marginalise those who could not be won over.

This was a strategy which, Ferguson determined, would be largely played out in the public domain. Central to his tactics were the deployment of mass meetings and elaborate demonstrations.

These 'public rituals' were designed originally as a defensive mechanism against calls to drive all the Irishmen out of Scotland, but increasingly during the 1870s they became opportunities for the Irish to display their numerical strength, responsibility and seriousness of purpose. Featuring visits from front rank figures in the Home Rule movement, they were also public testimony to Ferguson's influence in the inner counsels of the national organisation. His own appearance on the platform was inspirational. Forsaking John Butt's nostrum that 'orators should be shaved', he sported a flowing beard which complemented 'his mane of jet-black hair, the flash of his fanatical eye, the erect courage of the Northern Protestant'.[31] The experience of his oratory impressed itself deeply upon contemporaries, not least for his ability to pluck telling statistics from his voluminous reading and flatten hecklers by reciting large quantities of blank verse.[32] Indeed, as Davitt once commented, finding something to say after a speech of John Ferguson was as difficult as picking up a crumb of bread in a Dartmoor cell.[33]

His underlying educative mission also found an expression in the correspondence columns of a variety of newspapers from Patrick Ford's *Irish World* to the mainstream Scottish press. By 1894, he estimated that he had seen over 1400 articles and letters published, his literary style growing more purple and prolix as the years passed by.[34] Informed by copious research, his interventions stimulated his readership to enlarge their own knowledge on political and economic questions. His endorsement of Newman's *Apologia* was reckoned enough to send more than one Irishman rushing to his local library.[35]

Ferguson's personal magnetism was matched by the uniqueness of his social, confessional and political profile. It was eloquent testimony on the Irish community's political development by the early 1870s, that they should have felt the need for such an unorthodox champion. He was now one of the community's small group of business leaders. His personal prosperity had continued to grow, with the family moving from Tradeston to a

large house in Cobden Place, Prospecthill by 1870. By 1873, they
had acquired an impressive villa in the new railway suburb of
Lenzie, ten miles outside Glasgow.[36] Ferguson named it 'Benburb',
after his favourite battle in which Owen Roe O'Neill defeated the
Covenanter army in 1580. The house was to become his campaign
base for the next thirty years. His daughter, Anna likened it to
'a small foreign settlement in the midst of a hostile population',
for it was here that her father played host distinguished visitors
after they had fulfilled their speaking obligations in Glasgow.
The Ferguson children were to be fortunate in a rich fund of
memories, from Isaac Butt's solemn benediction to O'Connor
Power's lusty singing voice.[37]

His social advance was underpinned by the success of his
publishing enterprise. In retrospect, he was anxious to present
Cameron & Ferguson as a political project originally inspired
by Isaac Butt.[38] On a visit to Lenzie, he claimed, they had been
chatting nostalgically about the cheap Irish literature sold by
hawkers at fairs and markets, when Butt had raised the serious
issue of the government's attempts to suppress the patriotic
songbooks of their day. 'Fletcher of Saltoun was right', proclaimed
Butt, '"Give me the making of a people's ballads and I care not
who makes their laws."'

In reality, Butt's vision was coupled with his own acute
business sense. His entry into Irish politics caused his publishing
business to suffer initially, as some local clients closed their
accounts, but the firm's main market was increasingly in Ireland
and the Irish communities of Great Britain and America.[39]
Here, the song books, popular histories, patriotic novels and
'monster' joke books which formed the staple of their output
were a lucrative business. Sold cheaply in a range of outlets,
their popularity reflected a increasingly literate and anglicised
public.[40] Ferguson's catalogue was particularly prodigious,
including popular arrangements of both nationalist *and* Orange
melodies. His nationalist colleagues initially regarded his role
as 'the purveyor of Orange Ballads' with bemused tolerance,
trusting that he approached them with 'eye of a folklorist,

rather than a politician'.[41] The financial security which resulted was, however, vital in underpinning his political activities. The contrast was clear with the careers of the Belfast labour pioneer, Alexander Bowman, or the land activist, Andrew Kettle, both of whom were edged out of public life due to economic pressures.[42] Ferguson's successful business background was also at a premium in a commercial city where politics were run on business lines, offering him at least one element of common ground with the political managers of the Liberal Party, already viewed as a potential ally for the Irish.[43]

Although he had forsaken the conservative evangelism of his youth, he remained a firm Protestant. He was influenced by aesthetic considerations in his choice of worship, finding Anglican services 'more beautiful than any of the Scottish churches'.[44] In 1873, he became a communicant of St Cyprian's, the new Scottish Episcopalian church in Lenzie, but his taste for disputation had not deserted him. Within three years he had left the church in protest, after the Vestry committee had deposed two incumbents in succession – one for 'his ritualistic mode of conducting services, such as reading the communion with his back turned to the congregation'.[45] His strongly individualistic streak, coupled with the mixed denominational background of his own family, encouraged a generous pluralism in matters of religion. Displaying the continuing legacy of Spencer, he regarded Protestantism as 'more adapted to the law of evolution than Catholicism', but the Reformation principle of private judgement in matters of religion, he had taught him 'to treat Catholicism with the respect due to an ancient and noble force for God and human progress, which still holds within its folds the largest portion of the Christian world'.[46]

Ferguson's Protestantism, shared by other leaders of the national Home Rule movement, such as Butt and John Martin, was of major significance to the Glasgow Irish. On one hand, it located their struggle firmly within the Young Ireland tradition of a non-sectarian nationalism and thus helped counter the 'Home Rule – Rome Rule' claims which were already becoming vocal in

the early 1870s.[47] He nevertheless remained acutely conscious of
the anomaly of a Protestant leading an overwhelmingly Catholic
organisation. He was ever anxious to acknowledge the role his
own religion had played in Irish history, condemning conduct
which, 'made Protestantism stink in the nostrils of any Catholic
country'.[48] On a number of occasions in the early 1870s he even
attempted to resign his presidency in favour of a Catholic, but
the community's willingness to retain him may also have owed
much to the symbolic value of having a Protestant nationalist as
leader.[49] The 'old Orange blood of the North' and his subsequent
'conversion' which he referred to frequently in his speeches helped
convince them of the justice of their own cause.[50] Here was a man
whose unswerving principles had exiled him from his 'own sort',
but was now doing battle for the righteous people in whose arms
he had found refuge. This selflessness was a further important
component in the public image of 'Honest John Ferguson' which
was now being rapidly drawn.

In this sense, despite his commercial background, there was
something of the 'gentleman leader' in Ferguson's relationship
with the Glasgow Irish. In terms of his political radicalism,
however, he stood out as clearly a man of his times. Required by
Butt to curb his views while in Ireland, he was unrestrained on
his home ground. Coterminous with his efforts in the Home Rule
cause were attempts to establish a Republican society in Glasgow,
assisted by Sir Charles Dilke, the parliamentary radical and warm
supporter of Irish issues.[51]

Republicanism was enjoying a brief vogue in Britain, as the
Queen's isolation from official duties and the economic burden
of the civil list were set against the example of the new French
Republic established in September 1870. Although the local
radical press had balked at the cost of the wedding of Princess
Louise condemning 'those with royalty on the brain', Ferguson's
republican project found it difficult to establish a foothold in
Glasgow.[52] His first attempts to hire a hall in December 1871 for
a lecture by a member of the London Republican Union on 'The

Principles of Republicanism and the Superiority of a Republic over a Monarchy', were thwarted by local Council's Bazaar Committee.[53] Drawing on his old Democratic Hall associates, a Republican Club was subsequently founded in 1872, with Ferguson as president and G. B. Clark as secretary. Its manifesto, advocating the abolition of the monarchy, disestablishment and full adult male suffrage, testified to advanced Liberal principles rather than any revolutionary designs.[54] Despite visits from Dilke and Bradlaugh during the course of the year, success was elusive.[55] Opposition sprang from both extremes of the political spectrum. Bradlaugh's meeting in October was disrupted by protesting Orangemen, while the official IRB line on such gatherings was to welcome the general spread of republican principles, while restraining rank and file participation for fear that their organisation's own integrity might be compromised.[56] These setbacks did little to blunt Ferguson's enthusiasm for British republicanism. The cause was apparently forging ahead nationally and a conference was called in Birmingham in May 1873 to establish a National Republican League.[57] Anxious that the Irish should not be excluded, 'fiery Ferguson' became instrumental in ensuring that federal Home Rule became one of the new League's policy planks, alongside the abolition of heriditary privilege and the introduction of universal suffrage. Even so, he had to tread delicately. The 'Glasgow Home Rule Association', he explained, could not easily fall in with a republican association, as its very principle was 'the King, Lords and Commons of Ireland', and although its work was 'not to separate from but to share the future fate of England . . . a large portion of the Irish nation was determined to have nothing to do with English parties'.[58]

Personal politics of this stamp helped set much of the combative and independent spirit which Home Rule acquired in the city. Although compromise was necessary to prevent outright splits in the community, the result was not be a bland constitutionalist middle ground. For Ferguson, who retained a particularly strong attachment to the concept of popular sovereignty, 'justice for

Ireland' required to be set in the context of the larger British radical agenda of 'equality and opportunity for all citizens in a well-ordered state'. While his 'advanced' profile reflected this intellectual republicanism, rather than any purist attachment to a virtually established 'Irish republic', the iconoclasm this stance entailed was comprehensible to those local and national figures more conventionally committed to the Fenian project.[59]

Building a movement

For the next three years, Ferguson's political energies had a double focus. While undertaking patient organisational and propaganda work in Glasgow, he also campaigned to inject an assertive policy nationally into the Home Rule movement. These two imperatives were closely linked, for a powerful local base would offer Ferguson a mandate to influence the evolution of national policy. There was also an awkward dilemma here. Like other British-based activists in the 1870s, he encountered disdain from the old guard in the Dublin leadership who were contemptuous of the lowly social origins of the expatriate 'raiders' and suspicious of any attempt to 'dictate to Irish Home Rulers'.[60] Failure to make Home Rule a credible nationalist vehicle, however, might tempt some of his most energetic and advanced of his local supporters to turn from constitutional protest and re-embrace the Fenian 'private system' to realise their aims.

The immediate task was to maintain local momentum. The first openly political celebration of St Patrick's Day in Glasgow was organised in the City Hall in March 1872. Under Ferguson's chairmanship, these became regular gala events. On this occasion, amnesty for Fenian political prisoners was a dominant theme, and patriotic entertainment in song and verse, mingled with keynote speeches from the veteran nationalist, John Martin MP and A. M. Sullivan, editor of the *Nation*, who would shortly join Cameron & Ferguson's growing band of nationalist authors.[61] Ferguson established the judicious tone of evening by setting out his own credentials as a constitutionalist Home Ruler.

> He was not for separation between, England, Ireland and Scotland . . . He would not condescend to press men very long by dwelling on that point – they could just infer whatever they chose. He could honour the British flag highly, it was a glorious flag, and had memorable associations clustering around it, which no man would honour more highly than the Irishman, if it were possible for the Irishmen to do so without treason to their own Green flag.[62]

Soon afterwards, the rapid expansion of the Home Government Branch let to a move to new rented premises in the Campbell Arcade, Trongate.[63] The establishment of 'Home Rule Hall' now gave the branch its first permanent base and provided vital social and cultural facilities. The premises, which were retained till a move to East Nile Street in the late 1870s, contained a newsroom, meeting space and a library – with 200 volumes donated by Ferguson – so that 'work of an amusing and agreeable nature' could balance the sterner duties of 'obtaining that position in political and municipal affairs which our numbers and intelligence entitle us.'[64] Further growth over the next two years led to the inauguration of seven new branches in the city and the establishment of a coordinating Central Council.

Ferguson's pioneering work was not confined to Glasgow. A vacuum was already being created by the HGA's unwillingness to harness the great wave of optimism which had encouraged launch of local associations like his own. Ferguson commented caustically that, 'The Home Rule Association in Dublin are doing nothing, and people are beginning to see it'.[65] The travel required by his business interests placed him in an ideal position for carrying out alternative missionising work in England. Here he acted in conjunction with the Manchester-based Fenian, John Barry, a highly capable and intelligent activist whose role has often been allowed to overshadow Ferguson's own.[66] Ferguson also saw his native Ulster as a legitimate sphere of influence. Boasting that he had 'a longer arm than some think', he used the St Patrick's day demonstration of 1872 to persuade J. G. Biggar to form a Belfast Home Rule Association on the Glasgow model. Circumstances in his native city, however, were less favourable than Glasgow, and he was soon forced to plead for Butt's support to prevent the Belfast Home Rulers from being 'laughed into a corner'.[67]

This was only one of many appeals to get Butt – 'our great leader' – to take a more active personal role in putting life into the local branches. By the summer of 1872, a note of desperation was beginning to creep into his correspondence with the older man. 'John Ferguson', he insisted, 'has no other motive in this or any other political action than a sincere desire to do my part in the work which will be done for Ireland . . . Yes, even if the terrible misfortune happened to us that Isaac Butt fell away from the national cause!'[68]

These frustrations were now brought to a head by the HGA's electoral strategy. Problems stemmed from its very success. By 1872, Home Rule candidates had contested eight by-elections, winning six of them. The lesson to be learned was that while conservative Home Rulers were defeated, candidates with stronger nationalist credentials, like John Martin, could rally the electorate behind Home Rule and thus persuade ambitious Liberals and the Catholic clergy to adopt a more conciliatory attitude in order to safeguard their local influence.[69] Whereas Butt was squeamish over such 'dictation', fearing popular excesses would alienate his conservative supporters, Ferguson, who had become a member of the HGA Council in August, eagerly accepted the challenge. Taking a longer term view, he argued that 'more active agency is required to find out the popular opinion where it has defined itself [or] the first general election will find an enthusiastic and willing people, talking about what should be done, but for want of direction . . . at the mercy of the two English parties once more'.[70]

An ideal opportunity to test this more robust approach appeared when a vacancy arose for the representation of Londonderry City. Ferguson had been closely watching the position from the end of 1870. He had worked up a body of 'new men' in the city, with a local Home Rule Association formed in September 1872.[71] Hopes were particularly high as the by-election would be the first contest in Ireland since the introduction of the secret ballot. Ferguson again prevailed his associate, Biggar to stand and shuttled between Glasgow and Londonderry during November to act as his campaign manager.

Joe Biggar was certainly a colourful candidate. A Belfast provision merchant, he was to turn from Presbyterianism and the curing of pigs to embrace Home Rule, Catholicism and the IRB. His ugly and misshapen appearance and rasping voice did not prevent several amorous adventures and at least two illegitimate offspring, and while many contemporaries believed that his abrasive exterior hid the kindest of hearts, his relationship with the high-minded Ferguson was to remain a rather tense one.[72] The whole Londonderry episode was in fact to prove one of Ferguson's more impetuous undertakings. Essentially, Home Rule activists were fighting against the prevalent localism of Irish politics. Quickly, he realised that to stand any chance of success he would need public intervention by the HGA and preferably by Butt himself. The result was a series of frantic imprecations to Butt, with his demands being gradually scaled down from a personal appearance, to an address – 'worth another fifty votes' – or even to a letter of support to assist the flagging campaign.[73] Any lingering hopes were dispelled when the Catholic clergy threw their weight behind the Liberal candidate and Catholic, Christopher Palles. Indirectly, their intervention gave victory to the Conservative, while Biggar gained only 89 votes and lost £1000 in expenses. Ferguson was 'dull, beaten and humiliated', and 'wild with rage', commenting that in all his life he had never felt so bitterly.[74] However, in his fury at pusillanimous Catholic electors, he overlooked the more disturbing evidence of political and sectarian polarisation in Ulster which was clear from the refusal of Presbyterian voters to support either a Catholic Liberal or the Home Rule cause.[75]

Shunned by the HGA leadership, Londonderry had been a blow to the advanced Home Rulers and to Ferguson's personal prestige. His relationship with Butt, recovered for the time being, but a stronger determination set in that Home Rule must be taken in hand to prevent further drift and fragmentation. This was a view which which had been anticipated by John Barry and the advanced wing on the mainland. Ferguson had previously resisted participation in a convention in Liverpool during 1872 to urge the HGA to action as 'divisive', but now he saw no alternative, but to make common cause.[76]

In his own chronology, 1873 was the point from which he dated the creation of a real Home Rule movement.[77] Two key developments influenced this perception. In early January, Ferguson chaired the Manchester conference of delegates from the British-based Home Rule associations, out of which the Home Rule Confederation of Great Britain (HRCGB) was founded. The distinctive social profile of the British movement was at once evident from the proceedings. The audience was largely working class, with a leadership drawn, like Ferguson and Barry, from the business and commercial classes. As Ferguson expressed it with relish: 'Home Rule has arisen out of the necessities created by honest poor men'.[78] Butt, who was elected the body's President, addressed the meeting only reluctantly because of the 'Fenian' character of its chief organisers.[79] He insisted on maintaining a focused approach for the HRCGB's work, refusing to endorse other issues beside Home Rule. Ferguson, who became Vice-President, for the moment concurred. This was a surprising position given his own activities in Glasgow, but may suggest the return of his buoyant belief that the goals of the Home Rule were capable of rapid fulfilment.[80] At least the Manchester conference, and its successor in Birmingham, did make some practical headway in establishing an infrastructure which could direct the vote in

British constituencies. Six District Councils were established, with Ferguson chairing the Scottish body which met in Glasgow.[81]

The next step in building a unified national organisation was the conference held at the Rotunda, Dublin in November 1873, a gathering in which again Ferguson played a key role. His standing with the advanced nationalist wing was clear from his participation in a critical meeting on the eve of the conference. This event marked what has been termed the first 'new departure' in Irish politics.[82] Here, in company which included the Cork MP, Joseph Ronayne and the leading Fenians, Pat Egan, John Nolan, John O'Connor Power and Charles Doran, he helped win approval for a plan of 'cordial cooperation' in which Butt's movement received an IRB pledge of support for a trial period of three years. The public discussions which followed over the next four days were equally stormy, but confirmed the endorsement of Butt's initiative.[83] As usual, Ferguson was repeatedly on his feet, animated by the parliamentary duties of Home Rule representatives. When some speakers quibbled over being bound by a strict pledge to support the Federalist scheme, he drew on his broader political radicalism to reply:

> He could not master his indignation at the notion that on account of gentlemen of wealth and respectability, their movement should be turned out of doors. The day of the people had come, and they would use it. At the hustings there would be a determined fight against the men who hung back or came forward merely from the force of Home Rule voters outside and not from honest convictions (loud applause).[84]

Even after exhaustive debate, the issue surrounding the conduct of Irish members was still not fully resolved. As Butt defended the individual rights of MPs, a potent source of conflict was laid down for the future. A new organisation, the Home Rule League (HRL), did at least emerge from the Dublin sessions, but this fell short of the HRCGB as a party machine, functioning instead as a loose body of subscribers. Nevertheless, Ferguson was expansive on the prospects for Home Rule and on the role which the migrant communities could play on the day of battle :

> ... he might say he represented two to three millions of Irishmen across the water, who were about to shake, in the interest of old Ireland, many a Whig seat and many a Conservative seat in England and Scotland, where they could not extract the Home Rule pledge. Liverpool, Manchester and Glasgow were in their hands (cheers).[85]

This confidence reflected the growing political edge which the activities of the Glasgow Irish had acquired in the interim between the Manchester and Dublin conferences. Behind the usual patriotic platform bluster of these months had been the serious aim of setting out the community's political agenda. The main tasks remained organising the Irish vote and deploying it to maximum effect. Time was of the essence, as Gladstone's government had just been defeated over the Irish Education Bill. The Irish looked to autumn 1874 as the ideal date for a general election, as by this point their registration work would be well advanced.[86] The favourable showing of Catholic candidates in the School Board Elections in 1873 also gave grounds for hope. The Irishmen of Glasgow, Ferguson declared, numbered some 150,000, of whom 15,000 were voters or would be able to register in time for the election.[87] Personal ambition may also have been at work in these calculations – as he reminded his audience at the Dublin conference that these were votes which 'could propel him into the British Parliament'.[88] He was certainly willing to set aside his admiration for Gladstone to argue that the block should be deployed tactically.

> As regards the election, it was better to have open enemies than secret friends, better for them to have a weak Conservative party from which they could extort anything, that have a strong Liberal government which would allow

the Prime Minister to ignore the Irish vote. Let Isaac Butt have sixty Home Rule MPs at his back and he would hold the British Parliament in his power . . . They should equalise the Conservative and Liberal parties in the country – to get a nice balance so that the Irish sixty could go in and turn the scale.[89]

Expectations again rose in August with the first great open air political demonstration held by the Glasgow Irish. Ostensibly organised to commemorate the birthday of Daniel O'Connell, this exercise also represented a major expression of community power. Just as their public meetings 'claimed' the City Hall, O'Connell processions – of which this was the prototype – took over the neutral civic space. Glasgow, with its grid of spacious public streets, was to prove an ideal marching city. On this occasion some 6,000 to 7,000 people from a range of community organisations took part, closing off the city for an hour and a half. For Ferguson, it was the proudest day of his life'. Their conduct had shown that, 'they were peaceable citizens; but while walking within the lines of the law, they were determined to obtain by legal and constitutional means the salvation of their country'.[90] Yet, these mass public demonstrations also had an unwelcome mirror image which he could not ignore. The Catholic Irish were not the only migrant group seeking recognition in Scottish society and politics. The Orange Institution, with its large Ulster Protestant membership, had also began to use parading in the early 1870s to display their growing strength and 'orderliness'.[91] Indeed, the Orangemen, for whom Ferguson reserved special venom as 'the henchmen of England', were destined to haunt his political career like a discordant chorus.

Even the crowning attraction of his programme for the Home Rule year brought its own difficulties. He had proposed that Butt undertake a Scottish tour in December. This posed countless logistical headaches, but was essential to keep the Scottish branches within the HRCGB, as some were unwilling to pay into a fund from which they could see no benefit.[92] While the venture succeeded in this respect, it also opened up the sporadic rivalry between the main centres of Irish settlement in Scotland, resulting in an undignified tug-of-war over Butt's speaking dates.[93]

These sensitivities were swept aside when the general election was suddenly called in mid-January 1874. For the Home Rule League the *coup* was staggering and brought dismay at the incompleteness of their preparations.[94] Ferguson was also wrong-footed and hastily called on Irish voters not to make promises until the Executive of the Confederation's Scottish Council had reached a decision. With the Liberals in similar disarray, an independent 'Irish interests' candidate for Glasgow was endorsed in the shape of the Hon. Francis Kerr. Crucially, this Catholic gentleman – late of the Papal Zouaves – could attract the widespread clerical support which Ferguson could not.[95] The outcome of the strategy was disappointing, but far from the debacle of Londonderry. Kerr received over 4000 first preferences, evidence of a small, but disciplined electoral core. This was sufficient to split the Liberal vote and allow in the first Tory MP for Glasgow since the Great Reform Act. A sheepish Ferguson was forced to scale down his next forecast of the Irish vote to 10,000, declaring that stronger exertions were needed to get names onto the voters' roll.[96]

There was compensation in the national picture, as his prediction of an 'Irish sixty' had proved accurate. Isaac Butt was returned along with fifty-nine other Irish members professing sympathy for Home Rule. Ferguson had repeatedly prepared his audiences for this new dawn for the Irish cause. His own fate and that of the wider Home Rule movement now depended on Butt's parliamentary performance.

Notes

1 Davitt, *Fall of Feudalism*, p. 85.

2 A. M. Sullivan, *New Ireland* (Glasgow, 1877), p. 339; see also, Trinity College Dublin (TCD) Galbraith Papers, 3839, Diary, 19 May 1870.

3 A Fenian 'Centre' quoted in, R. B. O'Brien, *Charles Stewart Parnell* (London, 1898), vol. i, p. 65.

4 Boyce, *Nationalism*, p. 195.

5 D. A. Thornley, *Isaac Butt and Home Rule* (London, 1964), p. 96.

6 *Glasgow Observer,* 28 Apr. 1906.

7 Sullivan, *New Ireland,* pp. 342–3; Davitt, *Fall of Feudalism,* pp. 79–99.

8 McDonagh, *Home Rule Movement*, p. 8.

9 *Glasgow Observer,* 9 Jan. 1892.

10 *Glasgow Examiner,* 28 Apr. 1906.

11 *Glasgow Observer,* 9 Jan. 1892; National Library of Ireland (NLI), Cameron & Ferguson Memo to I. Butt, 8 Mar. 1870, Butt Ms. 86992 (4). Typically, Butt quibbled with the green cover of his pamphlet. Ferguson's exasperated response was that green was the colour 'so universally associated with Ireland that we automatically apply it to all books of an Irish character'.

12 *Glasgow Observer,* 21 Jun. 1891. He was referring to Volunteer agitation of 1782 which resulted in an enhanced degree of 'self-legislation' for the Irish parliament.

13 *Irish Packet,* 14 Nov. 1903.

14 Thornley, *Butt,* pp. 97–102.

15 McDonagh, *Home Rule Movement*, p. 13.

16 A. O'Day, 'Home Rule and the Historians', in *Revisionist Controversy,* p. 155.

17 *Glasgow Herald,* 17 Aug. 1874.

18 For the recollections of Thomas Boyd who had been present, see: *Glasgow Star,* 13 Mar. 1914. Ferguson was convinced the need for an 'educational and improving' organisation among the Glasgow Irish: *Glasgow Herald.,* 28 Oct. 1871; *Nation,* 3 Jun. 1871.

19 *Ibid.,* 15 Nov. 1871.

20 *Freeman's Journal*, 5 Dec. 1871.

21 *Glasgow Herald*, 22 Nov. 1871.

22 *Ibid.*, 15 Nov. 1871; 18 Mar. 1873.

23 John Denvir, *Life Story of an Old Rebel* (Dublin, 1910), p. 130.

24 *Glasgow Herald*, 18 Sept. 1872. Rev Issac Nelson was informed that he would be 'sent back as luggage' if he came to speak in Glasgow.

25 *North British Daily Mail*, 20 Apr. 1900.

26 M. Flinn (ed.), *Scottish Population History*, Cambridge, 1977.

27 M. Dyer, *Men of Property and Intelligence. The Scottish Electoral System prior to 1884* (Aberdeen, 1996), p. 110; I. G. C. Hutchison, 'Politics and Society in Mid Victorian Glasgow 1846–86', University of Edinburgh Ph.D. Thesis, 1975, pp. 270–8; Handley, *Irish in Modern Scotland*, pp. 122–63. Denvir suggested that the mining communities of Lanarkshire had a greater degree of stability and thus were more conducive to enfranchisement: *The Irish in Britain from the Earliest Times to the Fall of Parnell* (London, 1892), p. 446.

28 *Special Commission*, vol. iii, p. 295.

29 T. W. Moody, 'The IRB Supreme Council 1868–78', *Irish Historical Studies*, xix (1975), p. 286–322. *Glasgow Observer*, 21 Sept 1887 for portrait.

30 *Glasgow Herald*, 28 Nov. 1869.

31 O'Brien, *Recollections*, p. 140.

32 *Glasgow Herald*, 28 Apr. 1906; *North British Daily Mail*, 3 Apr. 1888.

33 *Glasgow Herald*, 26 Oct. 1882.

34 *Glasgow Echo*, 1 September 1894.

35 *Scottish Leader*, 8 Jan. 1889.

36 *Glasgow Directory 1871–1873*. Benburb was one of the largest

houses in Lenzie with a rateable value of £100: *Valuation Role 1876–7.*

37 *Glasgow Observer,* 15 Mar. 1913.

38 *Irish Packet,* 14 Nov. 1903.

39 *Glasgow Echo,* 1 Sept. 1894. .

40 Hoppen, *Elections, Politics and Society,* p. 456–7. The firm were also agents for some of the major music publishers, such as Chappell and Co

41 TCD, Davitt MSS 9420/2732, R. McGhee to M. Davitt 15 Sept. 1900: it was especially amusing to think of him sitting on a public platform on the Lord's Day 'side by side with that saintly Catholic' – Tim Healy. See also *Glasgow Observer,* 25 Aug. 1900.

42 T. Bowman, *Peoples' Champion. The Life of Alexander Bowman, Pioneer of Labour Politics in Ireland.* (Belfast, 1997); Kettle, *Material for Victory.*

43 J. F. McCaffrey, 'Political Reactions in Glasgow Constituences in the General Elections of 1885 and 1886' (University of Glasgow Ph.D. Thesis, 1970), p. 308.

44 *Glasgow Echo* , 1 Sept. 1894.

45 St Cyprian's Church, Minute Book, Lenzie Episcopal Church, 8 Sept. 1873; 2 Feb. 1876.

46 *Three Centuries,* p. 77.

47 See, *Glasgow Herald,* 18 Sept. 1872; 18 Mar. 1874. Note Denvir's qualified regret on J. G. Biggar's conversion to Catholicism – 'he was more service to our cause as a Protestant, there being to few of them in our ranks': *Life Story,* p. 182.

48 *Ibid.,* pp. 5–6.

49 *North British Daily Mail,* 2 Aug. 1875.

50 *Freeman's Journal,* 22 Nov. 1873.

51 *Special Commission,* vol. iii, p. 285. Dilke supported

disestablishment, land reform and deliberative assembly for Ireland. He was also a fellow disciple of Mill: S. Gwynn and G. M. Tuckwell, *Life of Rt. Hon. Sir Charles Dilke* (London, 1917).

52 *Glasgow Sentinel,* 19 Sept. 1870; 23 Mar 1871.

53 *Glasgow Herald,* 9 Dec. 1871.

54 Ferguson's partner Duncan Cameron was also involved: *North British Daily Mail,* 10 Jan.   1872.

55 *Freeman's Journal* 2 Apr. 1872; *North British Daily Mail,* 1 Oct. 1872.

56 L. O'Broin, *Revolutionary Underground. The Story of the IRB 1858–1924* (Dublin, 1976), p. 7.

57 Hypatica Bradlaugh Bonner, *Charles Bradlaugh. His Life and Work* (London, 1895), vol. 2, pp. 106–7.

58 *Scotsman,* 13 May 1873.

59 Significantly, he found it easy to work with pragmatic men like the 'constitutionalist Fenian' and prosperous Dublin businessman, Patrick Egan who also had thrown in their lot with Butt, while holding ideologues such as the New York or Paris-based IRB leaders, Thomas Luby and John O'Leary in distaste: NLI, J. Ferguson to I. Butt 21 Dec. 1875, Butt MSS 8697.

60 *The Nation* 28 Sept; 26 Oct. 1878.

61 Sullivan's, *New Ireland* became on of the firm's most popular productions.

62 *Glasgow Herald,* 19 Mar. 1872. His early attempts to combine the dictates of imperial unity and national freedom can be compared with those of his fellow Protestant Home Ruler, Alfred Webb. See, *Why I Desire Home Rule* (Dublin, 1874).

63 *Glasgow Observer,* 8 Oct. 1887.

64 *Ibid.,* 18 Sept. 1872; *Nation* 15 Dec. 1872.

65 NLI, Butt MSS 8694, J. Ferguson to I. Butt, 14 Aug. 1875.

66 Particularly evident in the case of Healy who was Barry's kinsman and who described his as 'the ablest man of Irish blood in Britain', *Letters and Leaders*, vol. 1. p. 30. For a more balanced account see, John Denvir, *Life Story*, pp. 171–3.

67 NLI, Butt MSS 8694, J. Ferguson to I. Butt, 15 Oct., 21 Dec. 1872.

68 Ibid., J. Ferguson to I. Butt, 14 Aug. 1872.

69 Thornley, *Butt*, p. 131.

70 NLI, Butt MSS 8694, J. Ferguson to I. Butt, 15 Oct. 1872.

71 Ibid., J. Ferguson to I. Butt, 14 Aug. 1872.

72 *The Bailie*, Aug. 22 1877; Sullivan, *New Ireland*, pp. 414–5; Healy, *Letters and Leaders*, vol. 1, pp. 39–44; O'Brien, *Recollections*, pp. 259–65. For his later displeasure with Biggar: NLI, Butt MSS 8697, J. Ferguson to I. Butt, 21 Dec. 1875.

73 NLI, Butt MSS 8694, J. Ferguson to I. Butt, 3 Nov., 12 Nov. 1872.

74 Even the 'very leaders had to give up J.B.': ibid., J. Ferguson to I. Butt, 3, 20, 25 Nov. 1872.

75 Hoppen, *Elections*, p. 269.

76 NLI, Butt MSS 8694, J. Ferguson to I. Butt, 2 Oct. 1872: he believed any such meeting should   be in Dublin.

77 *Special Commission*, vol. iii, p. 295.

78 *Freeman's Journal*, 21 Nov. 1873.

79 Denvir, *Life Story*, pp. 173–5.

80 *Nation*, 11 January 1873. Ferguson's position may also reflect his personal irritation at the Amnesty Campaign. The non-appearance of John 'Amnesty' Nolan at a Glasgow Amnesty meeting the previous November had forced him to speak, even though his father-in-law had just died. He promised

to 'take care we have no more "amnesty meetings"': NLI, Butt MSS 8694, J. Ferguson to I. Butt, 14 Nov. 1872:

81 A. O'Day, 'The Political Organisation of the Irish in Britain 1867–1890', in R. Swift and S. Gilley (eds.),*The Irish in Britain 1815–1939* (London, 1989), p. 193. A system of branch subscriptions was also organised

82 O'Brien, *Recollections*, pp. 139–40; Moody, *Davitt*, p. 123. It is not impossible that Ferguson had taken the formal IRB oath by this point – *pace* his evidence to the Special Commission. Biggar followed this expedient in 1874 with the intention of winning the Fenians over to Home Rule, even joining the IRB Supreme Council.

83 *Proceedings of the home rule conference held at the Rotunda, Dublin, on the 18th, 19th, 20th and 21st November 1873* (Dublin, 1874).

84 *Freeman's Journal*, 20 Nov. 1873.

85 *Ibid,*. 22 Nov. 1873.

86 Sullivan, *New Ireland*, pp. 383

87 *North British Daily Mail.*, 22 April 1873.

88 *Freeman's Journal*, 21 Nov. 1873.

89 *Glasgow Herald* 18 March 1873.

90 *Ibid,*. 18 Aug. 1873.

91 E. W. McFarland, 'Marching from the Margins: Twelfth July Parades in Scotland 1820–1914,' in T. Fraser (ed.) *The Irish Parading Tradition, Following the Drum* (London 2000), pp. 60–77.

92 NLI, Butt MSS 8695, J. Ferguson to I. Butt, 1, 9 Sept.,10, 23 Dec. 1873.

93 Ibid., J. Ferguson to I. Butt, 9 Dec. 1873. The main rivalry was between Dundee and Glasgow.

94 Sullivan, *New Ireland*, pp. 384.

95 *Glasgow Herald,* 27 Jan. 2 Feb. 1874.

96 *Ibid.,* 18 March 1873.

CHAPTER FOUR

Introducing Mr Parnell

The 1874 election had ended Irish Liberalism as a political force, ensuring that the most significant division would now be between supporters and opponents of Home Rule.[1] In March, the home-rulers resolved to constitute themselves into a separate party, distinct from the Liberals and Conservatives, with the object of obtaining self-government. Unfortunately, the subsequent conduct of this new bloc proved much less decisive. This reflected the dubious calibre and commitment of the Home Rule representatives – many of whom were opportunistic liberals, much as Ferguson had feared. Nor were these faults remedied under Butt's benign and ineffectual leadership. The Conservative-dominated House listened unmoved to his magnificent oratory. Soon the new dawn had degenerated into 'tea-party politics'.

> When some earnest-minded person protested to him that there was indignity in the spectacle of Irishmen vainly asking the English for consideration of their country's troubles, Mr Butt would open wide his arms and exclaim in his rich, honied, abundant voice, 'My dear boy!' . . . When English society had been thoroughly permeated by Irish charm and Irish reasonableness, then, said Mr Butt, the revolution in Ireland would take place without the effusion of anyone's blood or the fracture of a single friendship.[2]

Instilling backbone

Disillusion was swift and Ferguson was adept at reading the signs. From the beginning of 1875, he was to become one of first public advocates of a more determined parliamentary strategy.[3] At St Patrick's day in Airdrie, in the presence of Biggar, now MP for Cavan and pioneer of aggressive tactics in the House, he reasoned:

> It was the policy of Irish members at every stage to weary out the House of Commons by all the tactics they could avail themselves of . . . (Great Cheering). And he could tell them that if the Irish members did not fight well in the coming struggle, a considerable number of Irishmen would loose faith in parliamentary agitation (Renewed Cheering) and a large number of people would secede from constitutional agitation altogether . . .[4]

After months spent raising expectations, Ferguson was understandably frustrated. In the first place, relations between the HRCGB and the HRL were deteriorating. The creation of a cohesive movement on the mainland had encouraged British-based Home Rulers to regard themselves as more than a mere auxiliary of the parent National League. Yet their criticisms of HLR policy grated, given the financial assistance that they received from its funds. This placed Ferguson in an embarrassing position, since, as a prominent Confederation member, he had been elected onto the HLR Council precisely to avoid these communication problems. Instead, he became personally embroiled in a tortuous wrangle over subscriptions, which rumbled on for the whole of 1875, causing him great distress.[5]

Secondly, the fragile unity of the Glasgow home-rulers and his own leadership role were equally coming under threat. The first strike came from the Catholic clergy. Like its Dublin counterpart, the 1875 O'Connell centenary demonstration in Glasgow was marked by a struggle between the forces of Catholic solidarity and secular nationalism. The event had been organised by a broad coalition of Irish groups in the city and was originally intended as a display of unity, but the inclusion of a resolution in favour of the Amnesty movement suddenly resulted in a rival 'non-political' procession led by the Glasgow priests. At a public meeting on the eve of the demonstration, Ferguson called for a few patriotic songs while he tried to collect his scattered wits and 'make peace where there was some little strife'.[6] It was a thankless task. The next day, he came under personal attack from Father Tracy of Pollokshaws, who warned the Irish not to follow 'false Protestant leaders and renegades', but to turn to the priests, 'the natural leaders of the people'.[7]

In the heated correspondence which followed, Tracy pressed home the attack, branding Ferguson as a 'Protestant adventurer from Scotland', whose firm was profiteering from the Home Rule cause.[8] The refusal of a large section of the Irish to follow the clerical lead and the spirited defence mounted by Ferguson's colleagues emphasised the persistence of a robust and independent spirit among the Glasgow Irish. However, this outburst of 'Catholic Orangeism', as Ferguson termed it, illustrated the sensitivities which surrounded the community's politicisation. It also threatened his sensitive work in giving Home Rule an inclusive character, while compromising his own public position in the movement. He now resigned his formal Presidency of the Glasgow Association. Still smarting months later, he complained to Butt that: 'the clergy will not let us alone and if I chair again, a really serious row will be on between Priests and People'.[9]

As in the rest of Britain, a more insidious decline in Home Rule activity was also setting in. By February 1875, some local groups had already fallen into a state of apathy.[10] The employment position of the Irish made them vulnerable to local economic fluctuations, thus curtailing political activity, but Ferguson also worried that the Liberals were 'pressing our people hard by means of Trade societies to go in with them'.[11] One answer was more public meetings to keep up the spirit, but even Isaac Butt's visit on St Patrick's Day 1876 failed to have the desired effect. The audience was scarcely as large as usual, and Butt himself turned in a lacklustre performance. After moaning at length about his crossing, he remarked that he had 'nothing more to say' regarding Home Rule.[12]

The pattern of public parades was similar. These had become

unenthusiastic and straggling events, marking a sad decline from the high point of 1874, when the crowd had numbered 20,000 to 30,000. Resignedly, Ferguson now further rounded down his estimate of the Irish vote in Glasgow to 7–8000.[13] Indeed, the procession on 13 August 1876 marked a particularly worrying development. Not only were shots fired near the platform party, but a vital component of the city's Home Rule coalition was missing. The Fenian element who has publicly grouped around the Amnesty movement had decided not to attend. A ruffled Ferguson noted with regret that:

> ... the gallant band that were with them last year were not with them today, and said that he would have been delighted to see the black flag waving above them as it waved last year. But ... they were not there as representatives of sectarian politics, but as Irishmen of all creeds and kinds struggling for Home Rule ... He would be satisfied with Home Rule, but were the people of Ireland to demand separation, he would advocate separation tomorrow'.[14]

Their absence followed the visit of the doctrinaire IRB activist, Charles Mulcahy to Glasgow the previous month. He had succeeded in rousing the blood of an audience of 500 – 'most good honest men, but of divided allegiance'.[15] This tense situation reflected the divisions which were opening up over Home Rule at national level in the IRB as Butt's three year trial period drew to its close. At the Supreme Council meeting in May, John Torley had reported that great dissatisfaction existed in Scotland 'by reason of the H.R. movement'. On 20 August the Council, backed by Torley, resolved to withdraw their 'countenance' to Home Rule.[16]

There was only one escape from this thicket of local difficulties – the Home Rule party in Parliament must display some dynamism. The realisation that this would require new leadership was slower to crystallise. Although he had been among one of the earliest critics of Butt's parliamentary shortcomings, it was hard to break

from a man with whom he had worked closely for eight years.
Ferguson's initial response was to stiffen the old leader's resolve.
When Butt complained in December 1875 that Irish politics was
a jungle, he chided him that, 'we should be ready to stamp upon
instead of avoiding the snakes'. Evoking O'Connell's failures, he
pleaded that he weed out half-hearted Whigs and ignore the
taunts of Fenian irreconcilables:

> Young Ireland today wants to follow Isaac Butt. But he must
> be a bolder leader of he will not be followed. By 'bolder' I
> mean he must care less about men of position and more
> about the will of his Sovereign Majesty: the People . . .
> You could in a session of Parliament make yourself such a
> power that no man, but your friend could open his mouth
> in Ireland. As it is pretended friends and open enemies treat
> you with disrespect.[17]

When these strictures had little effect, it became clear to
Ferguson and his more practically-minded Fenian associates that
they must impress upon Butt the strength of their own support.
An ambitious public meeting to celebrate the centenary of the
American republic at Harold's Cross, Dublin on 4 July 1876 gave
them an early opportunity.[18] In the face of the ex-Liberal Home
Ruler Mitchell Henry MP's claim that a 'Republican meeting
'could not be held in Ireland, Ferguson asked that assembly to
declare itself a 'Republican meeting'. The demonstration resolved
to send a congratulatory address to President Grant, and he
bragged to Butt that he had been carried on the shoulders of the
people, 'with the American flag above us and *God Save Ireland*
around us'.[19]

This heady experience was followed in August by the HRCGB
convention, again held provocatively in Dublin. Its deliberations
remained dominated by the question of parliamentary policy,
but it was Butt's initial refusal to attend which drew Ferguson's
thunder. Again, he begged him put his trust in the resolute men
of the party:

More than once had you not acted as Barry and I wanted you would have regretted . . . If you attend we can get the danger over. If not the result will be felt in every constituency and you will not have thirty returned on Home Rule principles . . . My opinion is people have given up all faith in the League. You are still popular. We are now about to divide at last Whig Home Rulers one way and Real Home Rulers the other way. The people love Isaac Butt. I hope he will not desert them for 'respectability' and 'shopboyism'.[20]

For his part, Butt was unmoved, finding it melancholy and heartbreaking 'to know of all the wretched jealousies, petty ambitions and mean spites that distract our counsels'.[21] Ferguson made a further attempt to get him to recover his position by addressing a public meeting in Glasgow, but their working relationship was drawing to a close. It was time to seek out a new man and a new strategy.

Patron and protégé

The new man Charles Stewart Parnell. It was Ferguson who was first to acknowledge him publicly as the probable successor of Butt, for which he was immediately chaffed by his colleagues in the British Confederation who dreaded disunion.[22] However, in the pale, cool Parnell he had found his 'policy for fighting men'. When the young Wicklow squire entered parliament in February 1875, representing John Martin's old seat of Meath, he had seemed destined to be little more than a graceful adornment to nationalism, but within a year he had begun to personify the assertive and energetic stance which the advanced party had long believed was needed in parliamentary business. In recognition, he had been deputed by the Harold's Cross meeting to carry their address to America and shortly afterwards was elected one of the HGCGB's five Vice-Presidents – alongside Ferguson.[23]

Essentially, the tactic of obstruction which Parnell formulated in company with Biggar and a few allies, involved the delaying of English and Scottish legislation, while initiating Irish policy motions through the private member machinery. There was little novel about their techniques in themselves, but from 1877 these began to employed as part of a systematic campaign against the government.[24] Obstruction was never intended as an end in itself. Indeed, for Ferguson, as for the rest of the advanced wing, the contingency remained that Irish MPs might have to withdraw from the Westminster Parliament.[25] Like the concept of Home Rule itself, 'obstruction' held important symbolic value. It suggested resistance, sincerity and action, an attitude of mind which was calculated to win back what was threatening to become a lost cause.

Obstruction not only caused uproar in the House of Commons, it also led to an internal crisis for the party. When Butt refused to condone the policy and rebuked Parnell in the *Freeman's Journal* for his conduct during the South Africa Bill, Ferguson was at last given the opportunity to open up the national debate and secure Parnell's position by pledging the support of the expatriate Irish. Organising a meeting in Glasgow City Hall on May 28, he had Parnell and Biggar set out their stall to an audience which contained some of the city's most advanced nationalists. The former was received with acclamation, but it was Biggar, usually a poor speaker, who captured the spirit of obstruction: 'They held up their heads like men. They did not bow and beg, and pray and beseech the English people . . . All he asked the meeting now was to tell the Irish party to act like men . . .' [26] Ferguson was in no doubt of the significant of this occasion.

They were upon the eve of a new departure in Irish politics, which up to the present time had not been comprehended fully by him. They were on the eve of tremendous changes. He would not for a moment be a party to an attack on their distinguished leader Isaac Butt, but Isaac Butt must be taught that it would be absolutely necessary for even him to obey the will of the people.

The meeting was indeed remarkable. It firstly illustrated how Ferguson's Glasgow stronghold had become a platform for major policy announcements. One element of his public strategy had at least been achieved: the Glasgow Irish were now integrated into the wider national movement. His own speech again showed extraordinary foresight, marking one of the earliest public uses of the 'new departure' phrase, which was later to become associated with Davitt and the Irish-American Fenian, John Devoy.[27]

For the rest of the year, Ferguson and the British activists rallied support, for Parnell the man, as much as for his policy. Their efforts climaxed at the HRCGB convention in Liverpool on 27 and 28 August. At this meeting, Denvir suggests, it was originally hoped to retain Butt as the Confederation's figurehead out of affection, but the room for gallant compromise was fast disappearing. When he indicated he wished to sever his tie with the British organisation to allow him a freer hand in policy, Ferguson, without hesitation, proposed the election of Parnell as President in his place. He threw Butt a face-saving escape route, but the message was clear.

It is my intention to propose Mr Parnell as the head of the Confederation. At the same time I feel the greatest possible regret that our grand old chieftain who, in trying times, raised the Irish banner, who has so long guided us, and who has been with us in so many hard fights, is to retire from amongst us. We are grateful to Isaac Butt for leading us so far, but we are going to try a more determined policy, and Mr Butt holds views different from those we are determined to carry out.[28]

Butt left the meeting leaning on Ferguson's arm, assuring him, 'You and I are old friends . . .'[29]

By late 1877, Isaac Butt's project was at an end. The first Home Rule movement, created in Butt's image, was already ceasing to function as a political force. The transfer of power was not immediate. The leadership struggle entered a temporary stalemate, as Butt continued as the *de jure* leader of an increasingly moribund party, while Parnell began to build the system of alliances which would eventually ensure his status as *de facto* Irish leader. In speeding Butt's eclipse, John Ferguson had helped usher in the reign of Parnell. His own star was equally in the ascendant. The *Irish World* had already noted his eloquence and ability on land issues, and predicted his rise, along with Biggar, as one of the tribunes of the movement.[30] Perceived as one of Parnell's intimate friends, it seemed that Ferguson, ten years his senior and with greater political experience, could hope for continued influence at the highest level. Parnell was well aware of the difficult task which lay ahead in finding suitable parliamentary candidates who would pursue and 'energetic and national policy'.[31] By August 1877 John O'Neill Daunt, proprietor of the *Freeman's Journal*, was sure that Ferguson would be a worthy addition to the vanguard of obstructionists.[32]

In his own mind he was less certain of his future direction and in the next decade was to multiply the avenues for his activism. His critique of ineffectiveness of Butt's movement had consistently been informed by the credo of radical democracy. At the beginning of 1877, in a burst of temper with the Glasgow Irish who refused to take part in a Burns demonstration because 'they were Irishmen', he set out an alternative pathway:

> I and most men of the Confederation have the idea of serving Ireland by using all the advantages of British citizenship to enter into the municipal and political combinations of our day. As Ishmaelites we are useless. There is a party slowly evolving itself from Whig and Tory manipulation. It is the party of the people -the British democracy . . . If we aspire to nothing more that the position of 'aliens' or 'foreigners'

in this country, by all means let us display no sympathy with the social life around us. We shall thus make neither enemies or friends . . . and we will have just as much, and no more, political power to serve Ireland or ourselves.'

He proceeded to produce the blueprint for his mature political mission:

I shall give them [the Irish] my views of public policy so long as they appear to be of use, and should a time come when they are not valued, I can easily, if I wish for public life, cease to be at war, as I have been for years, with all my circle of friends and organisations and step into the ranks of my old friends, the British Radicals. Not being a Catholic there is no prejudice against me, except on account of what many call the 'Home Rule craze'. I often think I might serve the cause of Ireland as much in the ranks of the British reformers as in those of Home Rule, and I would like to see a fraternisation of the English and Irish Democracy that would enable a man to belong to both organisations.[33]

Notes

1 Thornley, *Butt*, pp. 195–204.

2 St. John Ervine, *Parnell* (London, 1925), p. 101.

3 *Nation* 6 Feb. 1875.

4 *Ibid.*, 18 Mar. 1875.

5 PRONI, D. 213, Letterbook of the Home Rule League, 16 Feb. 1857; NLI, Butt MSS 8697, J. Ferguson to I. Butt, 16, 21 Dec. 1875. As President of the Glasgow Branch, he had received 1000 National Roll Cards for 1874 to the value of £ 50, but the League had not been sent its portion of the revenue. The implication was that he had retained more than the quarter from sales of the cards which was the Confederation's due.

6 *North British Daily Mail*, 7 Aug. 1875.

7   *Ibid.,* 9 Aug. 1875.

8   *Ibid.,* 19 Aug. 1875.

9   NLI, Butt MSS 8698, J. Ferguson to I. Butt, 6 Mar. 1876.

10 Ibid., MSS 8697, J. Ferguson to I. Butt, 2 Feb. 1876; *Nation,* 6 Feb. 1876.

11 Ibid.

12 *Glasgow Herald,* 18 Mar. 1876.

13 *Ibid.,* 14 Aug. 1876.

14 *Ibid..*

15 NLI, Butt MSS 8698, J. Ferguson to I. Butt, 1 Aug. 1876.

16 Moody, 'IRB Supreme Council', p. 294–5. Of the active Home Rulers among its membership, Barry and Egan later resigned and Biggar and Power were expelled.

17 NLI, Butt MSS 8696, J. Ferguson to I. Butt, 21 Dec. 1876. Davitt was to recall this 'epistle of the Apostle John to the Prophet Isaac' in the days when he faced 'snakes' of his own in his struggle with Parnell and the parliamentary party: TCD Davitt MSS 9328/179, M. Davitt to R. McGhee, 21 Jul. 1883; NLI, Butt MSS 8696, J. Ferguson to I. Butt, 21 Dec. 1876.

18 *Irish World,* 29 Jul. 1876.

19 NLI, Butt MSS 8696, J. Ferguson to I. Butt, 12 Jul. 1876; *Freeman's Journal,* 5 July 1876.

20 Ibid., J. Ferguson to I. Butt, 20 Jun. 1876

21 T. De Vere, *The Road to Excess* (London, 1946), pp. 328–9.

22 Denvir, *Old Rebel,* p. 192.

23 *Nation,* 7 Aug. 1876.

24 Thornly, *Butt,* p. 300.

25 NLI, Butt MSS 8698, J. Ferguson to I. Butt,12 Jul. 1876.

26 *Glasgow Herald,* 29 May 1877.

27 Davitt, *Fall of Feudalism*, p. 124.

28 Denvir, *Old Rebel*, p. 192–3. This is probably the most accurate account as Denvir kept the official account of the Convention; R. B. O'Brien's version has a tearful Butt stunned by the election: *Parnell* , vol. i, pp. 143–5.

29 This was Ferguson's recollection: *Glasgow Observer*, 22 Dec. 1894. A sad coda to their friendship was played out when Butt desperately tried to discredit Ferguson in the minds of Irish Catholics by begging friends to dig up details of a meeting of the Glasgow Home Rulers which the atheist Bradlaugh had addressed: Butt MSS 6997, P. Callan to I. Butt, 10, 12, Sept. 1887; F. Finday to I. Butt. 7, 13 Sept.

30 *Irish World*, 3 Nov. 1877.

31 NLI, Dillon Papers, C. S. Parnell to J. Dillon, 25 Jul., 6 Aug. 1877.

32 *Glasgow Herald*, 20 August 1877.

33 *Nation*, 6 January 1877.

CHAPTER FIVE

The Banner of the Rights of Man

Perhaps it was because he had originally embraced the Irish cause through an idiosyncratic route of self-education and cultural redefinition, that Ferguson remained particularly receptive to linking the nationalist narrative of the 'imagined people' with a broader agenda for human progress. One issue stood out as the junction point between his nationalism and radicalism. Just as land represented the basic means of subsistence without which human life was impossible, land reform was a principle so great that it transcended mere national demands. This, he believed, was also a concrete struggle that could win over his fellow Ulster Protestants to nationalism.[1] Not surprisingly, from the late 1870's, the revolution in land ownership came to join federal Home Rule as his beckoning utopia.

In terms of practical politics, this stance presented two challenges. The first line of attack was to convince Parnell, not only that he must maintain the momentum of Irish land agitation, but also that he should broaden his strategy to encompass a democratic alliance with progressive forces on the British mainland. The way ahead seemed clear: Ferguson had chosen this 'Young Napoleon' as a man of action and an instinctive rebel. On mature reflection he would have done well to heed Joe Biggar's plaintive query, 'I wonder what Parnell's politics are?'[2] A social conservative at heart, Parnell's national career in the early 1880s was to be built on brokering and, whenever necessary, repudiating competing local and sectional interests. In time, John Ferguson and his 'great principle of Irish democracy' was to become just such an interest.

The battle had also to be joined in Glasgow. Here too he appeared to hold the initial advantage. During the early 1870s, he had established a powerful local machine, winning the admiration of the most politicised sections of the Irish community. After a decade, however, it was far from inevitable that Glasgow Irish would continue to accept the direction of this 'political Baal'. The test would come if Ferguson's policy ran contrary to the will of the Irish Parliamentary Party. The latter was an increasingly disciplined body, whose own leader was attracting the trappings of infallibility. Would the Glasgow Irish, like Parnell, begin to outgrow their mentor?

New departures

One of the most important encounters in John Ferguson's life took place in London on the night of 19 December 1877. As part of an official deputation, he was introduced to Michael Davitt on his release from Dartmoor Prison, where he had already managed to read some of Ferguson's articles on land reform.[3]

The returning hero cut an impressive figure. Thirty-two years old, with a heavy black moustache, his romantic, soldierly appearance was enhanced by his missing right arm, the result of a childhood accident in a Yorkshire mill.[4] Seven years of penal servitude for treason-felony had also enhanced his moral authority even among constitutional nationalists. Despite their contrasting family backgrounds and experiences of migration, both men were drawn together by nationalism and agrarian radicalism. More than mere ideologies, these were the social languages of the day through which they defined their personal identities and found meaning for their feverish political activism. They also shared similar strengths and weaknesses of character. Determination, probity, courage and idealism were tempered by pride and impulsiveness. Inevitably, differences were to reveal themselves over specific tactics, but both remained acutely sensitive to changing political situations and willing to grasp new opportunities. Ferguson's eloquence could be overwhelming, while his tendency to act without consultation sometimes caused Davitt pained embarrassment.[5] These squalls aside, their friendship survived over thirty years. In his book on the Land

War published towards the end of his life, Davitt paid a double tribute to his collaborator. He was a man of 'fearless nationalism', a connecting link in the roll call of Irish Protestant champions from Molyneux to Parnell. But he was also an intellectual leader on land and social questions, who stood, 'among the foremost thinkers and advocates in Great Britain'.[6] For his part, Ferguson could always guarantee his friend a sympathetic platform when the tide turned against his radicalism in the official Irish party. Davitt became the darling of Glasgow Irish audiences, but always found a haven from his demanding touring schedule at Benburb.[7]

Ferguson had prophesised on the day of Davitt's release that this was the man who would bring together the warring nationalist parties.[8] Typically, the first fruit of the Dublin meeting was an invitation for the newest Irish hero to make a public appearance in Glasgow. In April 1878, he delivered an address in the City Hall on his prison experiences, but also took the opportunity to condemn sectional interests in Irish politics and express his desire to bring harmony to his countrymen wherever he found them.[9] The event was chaired by the IRB's John Torley and capped by a peroration from Ferguson, indicating that the demarcation between Fenianism and Home Rule could no longer be rigidly drawn in the city.

Practical co-operation of the type witnessed in Glasgow was soon to become the accepted model for nationalist politics. By 1878, both the revolutionary and constitutional movements were in rebellion against the policy of negativity.[10] The dynamics of what Moody has termed 'the second new departure' are well documented.[11] The traditional separatist dream of an armed rising had been dispelled for all but IRB ideologues. Meanwhile, the rise of Parnell had further polarised the parliamentary party into two hostile wings. To clinch the ascendancy and to have this confirmed by the Irish electorate in the next general election, Parnell required to broaden his power base. His original inclination in 1877 had been to get advanced men like Ferguson beside him in Westminster, but it became increasingly clear that extra-parliamentary assistance would be also have to be secured. This support had already enabled Parnell to capture the presidency of the Home Rule Confederation, but Torley's view, forcibly expressed at the Davitt meeting, that, 'Ireland's independence must be won outside England' contained an unavoidable truth.[12]

During January and March 1878, cautious negotiations had taken place between Parnell and representatives from the IRB and the *Clan na Gael*, the most prominent Irish-American republican organisation.[13] By May, Davitt also claimed to have pressed a stronger policy of collaboration on Parnell. This would leave a small conspiratorial body intact, but cast the constitutional movement as the first line of defence, capable of placing immediate issues before the people, including 'a war against landlordism'. [14] Events now moved quickly, also driven on by John Devoy, the most able of the Irish-American militants. Encouraged by Parnell's re-election to the presidency of the HRCGB at their convention in Dublin on 20 and 21 October, Devoy made the highly publicised offer of an 'Irish new departure'.[15] Its essential feature was an interim working agreement between the advocates of physical force and of constitutional agitation. For the Fenians, this would 'nationalise' Irish public opinion and prepare the way for a new Irish state. For the constitutionalists, it would mean increased support as long as their demands in parliament assumed a 'dignified and manly stance'.

Ferguson may have reflected on the irony of the situation. A few months before, Devoy had savagely lambasted the HRCGB's support for Parnell and obstructionism, a policy which Ferguson had signalled in own 'new departure' speech of May 1877.[16] Equally impudent was Devoy's demand that Parnell drop Butt's federalist scheme in favour of a general declaration for self-government, arguing that its insistence on a subordinate legislature implied England's right to rule Ireland. Yet the new offer contained important counterweights. Its call to exclude all sectarian issues from the platform harmonised with his own inclusive view of the nationalist movement, while it also gave a central role to vigorous agitation on the land question. Here indeed was a 'broad and comprehensive public policy' which a man of principle and restless enthusiasm could support.

From Home Rule to Land League

The frictions surrounding the new departure demonstrated Irish nationalists' infinite capacity for personal manoeuvering and abstract disputation. However, it was the unfolding of a real catastrophe, external to their highly-charged world, which was to dictate the future course of Irish history. Scottish contemporaries were in little doubt that the late 1870s marked the end of an era of prosperity, as losses in foreign investments and credit restrictions reacted on prices, production and employment.[17] But nowhere was despair more acute than in the Irish countryside. The harvest of 1878 proved to by the least profitable of any raised in Ireland for thirty years and the disastrous weather conditions promised even worse for the following season.[18] By early 1879, eviction figures were already on the increase and a wave of rural distress began to sweep across Ireland, which when set against recent historical memory, was widely believed to herald a return to the blackest days of the Famine.

Bitter hardship would be the reality for thousands on the land, but these were momentous times for John Ferguson. His years spent studying the land question left him better equipped that most of his contemporaries to grasp the significance of unfolding developments. Almost haphazardly, his opportunity to shine came at the HRCGB's convention in October 1878. According to his own account written in the 1890's, he had not expected to make a contribution, but on the way to the hall for the evening sitting, a thoughtful Parnell, who had previously heard him speak on land reform at a rally in Sunderland, urged him to use the same speech to test the impact of the land question on Irish urban opinion. The Dublin Rotunda was packed with waiting speakers when Parnell whispered to the chairman to call Ferguson.[19]

For the next forty minutes, he poured forth the radical doctrines which Butt had begged him to suppress. His *tour de force* called for a root and branch reform of the land system, involving 'the disestablishment of the landlords and the return of the right of property to the peasant', but he also delighted his 3000–strong audience by combining economic theorising with more orthodox nationalist fulminations on the superiority of the Irish people – 'missionaries when the British were painted savages.' Land reform was thus part of a wider call to national regeneration:

> . . . it may be our destiny yet, at the close of the nineteenth century, to repeat that which was our part in earlier days – it may be our proud privilege to uplift upon these shores the standard of a newer and nobler civilisation, when that of England shall have dissipated in a whirlwind of depravity.[20]

As he resumed his seat, Parnell assured him that he had found the question which could be used, 'to rouse all Ireland for Home Rule once more'.[21] The public impact was indeed immediate. Opponents were shocked by Ferguson's 'rank communism', but Patrick Ford's *Irish World* hailed his contribution as 'the speech of the era', expressing surprise that 'the new Irish creed' was delivered not by Parnell or Biggar, but by a Glasgow bookseller.[22] In Ferguson's recollection, the greatest impact was on Davitt who was then in America and still, 'taking no part in constitutional action'. Reading the *Irish World* account, he suggested, 'the interest it excited in him and throughout the country suggested the formation of the Land League'.[23]

This was a heroic, if rather hyperbolic, claim. Davitt was certainly ready to acknowledge Ferguson as his 'guide, philosopher and friend', but a complex range of influences and personalities was also at work to encourage his ideological shift during 1878.[24] While in America, for example, he had fallen under the influence of John Devoy, who had been openly advocating the abolition of landlordism as the prerequisite of independence from September of that year. Indeed, Devoy's 'new departure' telegram with its call for 'vigorous agitation on the land question' had been published in the New York press on 25 October, while Ferguson's speech did not appear in the *Irish World* until 16 November. Nevertheless, on his return to Ireland in December, Ferguson was one of the first colleagues to whom Davitt turned as he sought to formulate a rapid response to agrarian crisis.[25] Agitation was already getting underway in Mayo and he was anxious to lend assistance in order to make this local initiative into a movement of national importance. The outcome was the historic meeting at Irishtown on 20 April 1879. Organised as a protest at local evictions by a Catholic clergyman, its underlying aim was to give a voice to the general grievances of tenant farmers and to demand a reduction of the rent. The platform comprised of a number of prominent radical land reformers. There was a strong Fenian representation with John O'Connor Power, Thomas Brennan and the local IRB activist, John Daly of Castlebar in attendance, but it was Ferguson who represented Davitt, having allegedly missed his train.[26] He recalled it as a defining moment:

> At Irishtown the banner of the rights of man was uplifted. The morning was as dreary as the nation's prospect; but men who believed in the immortality of Truth spread her light that day before the people, and a living blaze has been kindled over the island of which the whole world has heard. Doctrines hitherto known to be true in halls of learning only, became accepted in the cabins of Connaught, and the truths of Economic Science have given new hope to the Irish peasant.[27]

In fact, few contemporaries grasped the significance of the proceedings. The agitation was more than an outgrowth of the traditional agrarian secret societies. Its novelty lay in its role as a popular front for fundamental social change. The cooperation of local and national politicians was matched by the solidarity of town and countryside, evidence of their growing mutual dependence. The principal doctrine promulgated was 'The Land for the People', but, as Sullivan sourly suggested, the speeches featured 'a great deal of "wild" talk and raw theorising'.[28] Indeed, there was little agreement over the nature of the land problem, much less its solution. As Davitt recalled, there were at least three positions represented by speakers on the day.[29] First, following the historic positions of James Fintan Lalor and John Mitchel, land agitation for Fenian activists like Brennan was a bridge to separatism. Essentially, their attack on landlordism and advocacy of peasant proprietorship contained an element of transitional demand, as they believed that no British government could ever grant such a measure.[30] Also represented in the speech of O'Connor Power was the 'parliamentarian' approach. Displaying greater faith in the efficacy of enlightened public opinion, this still viewed the land question in political terms, advocating the radical remedy of peasant proprietary.

Ferguson's platform performance stood out on two counts. First, he adopted a 'strictly economic treatment' of the land question, emphasising that it was worthy of settlement on its own merits.[31] Peppered with references to John Stuart Mill and his beloved 'highest authorities', even Sullivan was forced to admit that his contribution contrasted favourably with the other speakers of whom it could be said that, 'a little learning is a dangerous thing'.[32] Secondly, he had evidently shifted from the conventional nationalist pieties, which had flavoured his Rotunda speech of 1878. Ferguson now set out his belief that land agitation was of universal significance to oppressed 'producers', arguing that the principle of solidarity should be extended beyond mere national boundaries.

He pointed out how the land question has thus become one of vital interest to the artisans and working-men of the great manufacturing towns of England, and he said that

the time had arrived when it was the duty of Irish tenants
and English working-men to demand such a settlement of
the land question as will bring about the prosperity and
happiness of the people.[33]

Indeed, Irishtown set the pattern for Ferguson's future
involvement in the land campaign. His expertise in land
economics continued to inform the movement, but he was
unwavering in his belief that the question was a social rather than
a political one and that, 'the lines on which it was fought over
the water were the same as were laid down here'.[34] While this
interpretation was eventually to prove contentious, the severity
of the crisis was then sufficient for participants to swallow their
differences. By the middle of August, it was clear that throughout
two-thirds of Ireland the harvest was utterly gone.[35] The 'material
for victory', in Lalor's phrase, lay at hand with to build a well-
organised and sophisticated mass movement that would cement
the latest new departure.

Irishtown had been followed by a larger rally at Westport in
June at which Parnell was persuaded reluctantly to attend. On
18 August, the Land League of Mayo was founded and with
this organisational infrastructure in place the 'war against
landlordism' began to spread. Ferguson threw himself into
the work, addressing meetings in the South and East during
September in the company of Louden, Brennan, Biggar and
Parnell.[36] Even now, the rising star of parliamentary nationalism
remained cautious over agrarian agitation. Davitt had again to
urge him to accept the leadership of the Irish National Land
League (INLL), calling an inaugural meeting in the Imperial
Hotel, Dublin on 21 October 1879.[37] His diffidence – which stood
in such stark contrast to Ferguson's emotional enthusiasm –
seemed to stem from a desire to test the opinion of the clergy
and strong farmers before committing himself to a potentially
uncontrollable populist movement.[38] A more basic motivation
may also have been his political divergence from the aims of
the leading Land Leaguers. Rather than a revolution in property

relations, he hoped that the land question would create a stable relationship between enlightened gentry and a satisfied peasantry.[39] Such a 'new deal' would advance the nationalist project while rehabilitating his own landlord class. Parnell's belated recruitment was undoubtedly a triumphant step in the construction of pan-nationalist movement, but it also introduced a further competing emphasis in the direction of the land campaign

Ferguson was one a handful of prominent Irishmen resident in Britain who received Parnell's invitation to the Dublin meeting. Unable to be present, he failed initially to find a place on the seven-man Executive, which became a Fenian-dominated body, with Davitt, Egan and Brennan in the vanguard. He was, however, included in the Committee of fifty-four persons which represented a broader range of nationalist opinion.[40] Within months, he was also drawn into the enlarged executive, or 'governing council', in the company of Dillon, Thomas Sexton and other leading parliamentary nationalists.[41] His influential role, and his growing relationship with Davitt, were confirmed under the League's revised constitution of November 1880. He now became a member of the new executive council of fifteen members in which complete control of the League was entrusted.[42] Ferguson's residence in Scotland meant that his attendance at the central body's fortnightly meetings was probably less frequent than he would have wished, but where possible he managed to combine his sales trips on behalf of Cameron & Ferguson with League business.[43]

Besides his credentials as an activist, Ferguson's colleagues also recognised his ability to employ the theories of radical political economy in the service of the League. His early contributions on tenure reform and the free market in land showed that his spirit of intellectual enquiry was still unflagging. The focused quality of Mill's theory of utility and his scheme of land taxation continued to attract Ferguson, but his old mentor Cliffe Leslie's book, *Land Systems and Industrial Economies of Ireland, England and Continental Countries*, published in 1870, was another profound influence.

His eclectic reading and command of French and German also opened up the world of continental thought on the land question. In Europe the upheavals of the preceding decade had convinced radicals that revolutionary excesses could be tempered and 'true democracy' achieved only by promoting small peasant and artisan property. [44]

Mastering copious evidence to support his arguments, Ferguson was able to offer practical guidance to the INLL on specific policy issues, such as land purchase or the role of graziers. [45] This was a position he jealously guarded, later expressing contempt for the League's paid workers who strayed into his territory, on the grounds that, 'some of them were qualified to be organizers, but not light spreaders or educators'. [46] His efforts as a theorist also buttressed the claims to moral authority which became a characteristic of League propaganda. In a period when it was struggling against charges of lawlessness, Ferguson's public appeals to 'the principles of John Stuart Mill and Herbert Spencer' placed it within the mainstream of constitutional reform, while his quasi-religious faith in the laws of political economy instilled confidence that its cause rested on 'educated authorities' rather than mere 'Irish sentiment'. [47]

Hailed as 'the father of all the Irish land reformers', several Irish constituencies by 1879 had already expressed their desire to elect Ferguson if he would consent to stand. Unfortunately, the quality of mobility, which he had previously used to his advantage in his political life now turned against him. The constant attention needed for his dispersed business affairs meant that six months in Westminster would require too great a personal sacrifice. [48] Perhaps there was an alternative. He had already used his Glasgow power base to influence the leadership struggles of the Irish party. If he were to represent a Glasgow constituency, he also might be able to harmonise parliamentary duties and business concerns, while enhancing his grip on his local supporters.

A prophet without honour

In the counsels of the Glasgow Home Rulers expectations of imminent victory had given way to a more realistic discourse of struggle and endurance. As Ferguson was forced to admit, 'the battle . . . was a slower one than they had thought it would be six or seven years ago.'[49] Much of his energy remained channeled into smoothing over rivalries that stemmed from personality as much as policy.[50] In more positive vein, Ferguson persisted in his attempts to enhance the community's political leverage. As in the early 1870s, this involved painstaking work in building up the Irish vote. He also hoped that his emphasis on the electoral independence of this block would provide the more advanced sections of local Liberalism with a 'political education' in Irish priorities.[51] His efforts received the strongest public endorsement with Parnell's visit to Glasgow in March 1879.

The arrival of an Irish politician of Parnell's charisma and status gave Ferguson the opportunity of testing his strategy by boldly inviting many of the leading local Liberals and Conservatives to hear his speaker.[52] Although most declined, he was comforted by the appearance of, 'the more intelligent Scotsmen . . . as these were men who would probably play a part in the coming struggle of the people'. What they heard was intended to alarm. Parnell used the platform, to launch his own version of the 'new departure', articulating his belief in the new line of cooperation between constitutional and physical force nationalism.[53] He also supported Ferguson's electoral tactics, arguing that a show of power from the Irish in Scotland would bring both British parties to their door as supplicants. In local meetings Parnell was more ready to gratify his Glasgow audience's appetite for the strong meat of nationalist rhetoric, assuring them with reference to the Fenian military campaign in Britain in 1867 that, 'had these sacrifices been made sooner, they would have been in a more fortunate place than in that town'.[54]

Parnell was at least consistent in returning the compliment of Ferguson's early confidence. As part of his general desire to resuscitate the mainland movement and prepare for the forthcoming election, he presided at a conference of the Scottish District of the HRCGB held on 19 March at White's Hotel in Candleriggs. Here a local branch network of organisations was set up to implement the conference's policy at local level, 'where ever materials exist or circumstances are favourable'. Ferguson's own position was assured in a unanimous resolution which pledged the movement, 'to support most strenuously his efforts to score a victory for the Home Rule cause whenever and wherever he hoists the flag'.[55]

This was impressive mandate, but Ferguson's attempts to implement it were to result in a personal loss of face. A persistent problem was the nature of the Liberal Party in Glasgow. Despite internal tensions between traditional Whigs and dissenting radicals, the party shared enough common doctrines and antipathies to block the political advance of the Irish.[56] After more than a decade in the city, Ferguson had little time for the 'Whiggish shopboyism' of the Liberal establishment who seemed impervious to either intimidation or appeals to reason. Even now, as the Whigs were being eclipsed by issue-driven politics, he looked in vain for the emergence of a broad-minded radicalism after his own heart. In its place he found a strongly 'theological' radical perspective, focusing on questions of individual liberty, temperance and church disestablishment. This seemed far removed from with the practical 'civic gospel' of the English industrial cities, whose radical MPs seemed alive both to the justice of the Irish cause and to wider social and economic questions. The local party hierarchy was unwilling even to censor anti-Irish sentiment in their own ranks, a fact which Ferguson discovered when he was greeted by the hoots and groans of Liberal working men at public meetings.[57]

Relations were brought to crisis point in July 1879 when the new Liberal candidate for Glasgow, Charles Tennant of St Rollox, announced his intention to vote down any enquiry into the Irish case for Home Rule.[58] This was the wrong time for Alexander McDougall, Honorary Secretary of the Glasgow

Liberal Association to invite Ferguson to become a member. He responded by excoriating 'Scotch Whiggery' as narrow and insolent and promised to do his best to ensure that his friends, the Irish electors, would add 8000 votes to the Tory candidates. [59]

There the matter might have ended had not Ferguson's hubris attracted the scornful eye of press. The *Glasgow Herald*, which had long repented the politicisation of the Irish, firstly homed in on his extravagant claims for size of Irish vote – 8000 'men of buckram' – a figure he had arrived at by apparently doubling the actual vote at the 1874 General Election. It also questioned his own ability to exercise 'politico-mesmeric influence' over the direction of the vote. The spectacle of 8000 voters running after Mr Ferguson, 'like so many sheep after a bellwether', it mischievously suggested, was hardly credible given the extent of clerical influence in the community. [60]

More visceral was the attack from the *Bailie,* a Tory magazine which specialised in heavy-handed satire. In an illustrated profile, laced with much stage-Irish 'humour', Ferguson was shown in waistcoat and britches and wielding a shillealigh. [61] The accompanying commentary was equally unflattering :

Wirra, wirra; huroo, musha; hev at ye Pat Murphy; och, och; bedad – and all the rest of it. When the BAILIE read Misther JOHN FERGUSON'S bould bit ov writing in the *Herald* of Thursday, why he concaived that he was nowhere else that in the House of Commons on the College Green of swate Dublin city, and that a parliament ov pathriots was in full blast. All the ould ruction was goin' on. The mimbers were busy callin' one another names; or they were sellin' their votes to the highest bidder, or they were gethin' gloriously drunk on 'Jamieson' or 'Kinahan'. The humour of Mr FERGUSON'S communication is too amazing for this generation . . . No one but an Irishman could have written it, and as there are Irishmen and Irishmen, its author, as can be seen at a glance, must belong to the more amusing section of his countrymen. [62]

For a man who placed a unique value on his intellectual standing, such treatment was deeply wounding. The *Bailie* was always ready to hand out rough treatment those who stood outside the local Tory camp, and the squib was intended as much as a sideswipe against the Glasgow Liberals as the Irish. Yet it was also an explicit reminder of the barriers that faced Ferguson in being respected as a serious political force in the city. For all his Protestantism and mercantile credentials, the 'Home Rule chieftain', was, by his own definition, 'Irish' and thus subject to the full complex of historical prejudices which jaded editorialists and humorists could muster.

Ferguson's immediate response was to continue his policy of electoral independence. It was soothing to find his position as a 'virtual MP' confirmed at the HRCGB's Convention at Crystal Palace where he shared the platform with other Irish parliamentary notables, such as Biggar, O'Gorman and O'Donnell. He urged successfully that Irish votes should be committed to neither of the major political parties. After seven fruitless years at Westminster, he argued, pressure must be placed directly on the mainland constituencies, forty of which were vulnerable to the Irish votes where 'most of the Home Rulers were radicals and he was a most determined one'. [63]

By the end of the year, he had switched his attention to the more pressing task of rallying support for Irish land agitation. Indeed, the Glasgow Home Rulers could hardly avoid the limelight, since Davitt, who was to have been one of the principal speakers at a meeting at the City Hall on 24 November, was arrested by the Sligo magistrates on a charge of using seditious language only days before.[64] Ferguson discharged fusillades in all directions. Members of HRCGB, he promised, would tour Ireland repeating the very same words as the arrested men. Scottish supporters must organise funds to resist the government tactic of breaking the Land League by expensive prosecutions. The support of 'thousands of kind-hearted English radicals' was assured.[65] In this electric atmosphere, his platform rhetoric brought out some less engaging traits. Still smarting from his handling from Scottish journalists, his intellectual arrogance was matched by his contempt for opponents who were clearly less 'enlightened'. An unsuspecting audience from the Irish National Foresters Benefit Society benefited from his reflections that:

> The manufacturers of Glasgow and Manchester were but babes in political economy, and floated like corks and bubbles down the stream, not one having sufficient brain or power of education to turn upstream like an active living force.[66]

By time of Davitt's triumphant re-appearance in the city in December, Ferguson was still on the offensive against the citadels of Whiggish Liberalism, reviving the prospect of an alternative 'democratic' alliance between radicals and Home Rulers.

> He had written to Gladstone as representative of a great organisation which could prevent his return to power or which could return him to power . . . He hoped they would rally the democracy of England and Scotland, and carry the flag of land reform to victory under the leadership of W. E. Gladstone. He was determined that the Liberal Party should in the fullest and frankest manner, so far as the organisation in Scotland would support him . . . come to equal terms, for the people of Ireland would never go crouching to them to solicit assistance. If the bad influences of Scotch Whiggery constrained Mr Gladstone in this matter, so much the worse for Mr Gladstone and his party.[67]

The response which the great man drafted to this impertinent missive was curt in the extreme. While thanking Ferguson for his kind personal comparisons, he dismissed his threat that Irish voters were preparing to 'punish' the Liberals, reasoning that this ungrateful constituency could not possibly punish the party more severely than it had already been punished since

1874, following its generous settlement of the Irish church and land questions.[68]

The flimsy basis for Ferguson's attempts at brokerage was underlined even more publicly by the outcome of the 1880 General Election campaign. Although one Glasgow candidate – the remarkably inept Sir James Bain – did attempt to appeal to both Orangemen and Home Rulers in his bizarre campaign, more orthodox Tories had already protested their unwillingness to become part of Ferguson's balancing act.[69] Instead, they remained more comfortable in attempting to win over moderate Liberals, holding even their Orange allies in disdain. Lord Beaconsfield's national manifesto, threatening the renewal of coercion in Ireland, removed any lingering basis for tactical voting. The Glasgow Home Rulers lined up behind Liberal candidates, their contribution unsolicited and unrecognised, amid a sweeping national victory.[70]

Notes

1   See for example, NLI, Butt MSS 8698, J. Ferguson to I. Butt, 2 Mar. 1876.

2   Davitt, *Fall of Feudalism*, p. 654.

3   *Special Commission*, vol. iii, p. 285. Irish and American newspaper had occasionally reached him during 1876–7. For Ferguson's prominent role in Davitt's official reception committee in Ireland see, *Freeman's Journal*, 14 Jan. 1878.

4   H. M. Hyndman described him as possessing 'the face of a humanised and benignent raven': *The Record of an Adventurous Life* (London, 1911), p. 40.

5   On one occasion, Ferguson attempted to organise a national subscription on Davitt's behalf in the belief that he was about to leave Ireland through lack of money. In fact, he was only embarking on an extended lecture tour: *Tipperary Herald*, 9 May 1884, in TCD, Davitt Papers 9603.

6   *Fall of Feudalism*, p. 714.

7 Anna Ferguson remembered the exhausted campaigner throwing himself into a seat at their fire side with a sigh of relief and content, before turning to gossip and plan with her father: *Glasgow Observer*, 15 Mar. 1913.

8 *Glasgow Star*, 14 Apr. 1903.

9 *Glasgow Herald*, 30 Apr. 1878; TCD, Davitt Diaries 9527, Dec. 1877–8. He was impressed by the Glasgow turnout. There were 2000 at the 29 April meeting and a further 380 at Govan on 1 May.

10 *Fall of Feudalism* , p. 111.

11 T. W. Moody, 'The new departure in Irish politics, 1878–9', in H. A. Cronne, T. W. Moody and D. B. Quinn (eds.), *Essays in British and Irish History in Honour of James Eadie Todd* (London, 1949), pp. 303–33.

12 *Glasgow Herald*, 30 Apr. 1878.

13 Lyons, *Parnell,,* pp. 74–5.

14 *Fall of Feudalism* , p. 112–3. His biographer was sceptical that elements of this conversation may have involved Davitt 'projecting back' the social programme he later adopted: Moody, *Davitt*, p. 208.

15 *Nation*, 26 Oct., 16 Nov. 1878.

16 *The Irishman*, 18 Dec. 1877.

17 James Mavor, *My Windows on the Street of the World*, vol. 1 (London, 1923), p. 57.

18 Lyons, *Parnell*, p. 84.

19 *Glasgow Observer*, 22 Dec. 1894.

20 *Irish World*, 16 Nov. 1878.

21 *Glasgow Observer*, 22 Dec. 1894.

22 *Irish World*, 16 Nov. 1878.

23 *Glasgow Observer*, 22 Dec. 1894.

24 *Ibid.*, 8 Oct. 1893.

25 *Special Commission*, vol. iii, p.192.

26 *Ibid.*, p. 284; Sullivan, *New Ireland*, p.434. The latter account is, however, disputed by Moody: *Davitt*, p. 288–9. Ferguson's own version shifted over time. In 1903, he claimed to a Glasgow audience it was Parnell who had telegraphed him to attend with the message, 'You are to open the ball at Irishtown on Monday morning': *Glasgow Star*, 11 Apr. Again, this may have been a creative reworking of events given Parnell's well documented hesitancy on the issue – the Irishtown meeting was actually on a Sunday – but communication between them at this stage over a future land campaign is possible. See also, Davitt, *Fall of Feudalism*, p. 147.

27 *Land for the People*, p. 17.

28 Sullivan, *New Ireland*, p. 435.

29 Davitt, *Fall of Feudalism*, pp. 148–50.

30 P. Bew, *Land and the National Question in Ireland* (Dublin, 1980), pp. 230–1.

31 Davitt, *Fall of Feudalism*, p. 148.

32 Sullivan, *New Ireland*, p.435.

33 Davitt, *Fall of Feudalism*, p. 150.

34 These were his remarks from the chair at the Dublin Rotunda Land Conference: *Glasgow Herald*, 31 Oct. 1880. See also his comments and the Land League Executive meeting: *Glasgow Herald*, 3 Feb. 1881.

35 Sullivan, *New Ireland*, p.441.

36 *Freeman's Journal*, 1, 22 Sept. 1879.

37 *Ibid.*, 22 Oct. 1879.

38 *Fall of Feudalism* , p. 151.

39 Bew, *Parnell*, pp. 28–9.

40 Besides Parnell, he was the only Protestant among the INLL's 'foundation members': TCD, Davitt MSS 9369 RR (2).

41 *Fall of Feudalism,* p. 240.

42 *Freeman's Journal,* 22 Dec. 1880; TCD, Davitt MSS 9398/1500 for Davitt's copy of the constitution.

43 *Special Commission,* vol. iii, p.286. He managed seven out of sixty-eight meetings of the Central League between December 1879 to February 1881 and a further five before the INLL was proscribed, fewer than Dublin-based colleagues such as Brennan, but more that either Parnell or Biggar: TCD Davitt MSS 9635; see also Moody, *Davitt,* pp. 141–4, 571–6.

44 A. Offer, *Property and Politics* (London, 1981), p. 150. A typical authority was the Belgian agrarian economist, Laveleye who argued that inevitable progress towards the ideals of equality must put the very concept of private property in peril where a small number of great families enjoyed a monopoly of land.

45 For example, *Freeman's Journal,* 13 Sept. 1879.

46 *Special Commission,* vol. iii, p.288.

47 *Ibid.,* 8 Dec. 1880.

48 Davitt, *Fall of Feudalism,* p. 240. See C. C. O'Brien, *Parnell and his Party* (London, 1958), pp. 42–3.

49 *Glasgow Herald* 20 Mar. 1879.

50 On St Patrick's Day 1878, the Glasgow Irish had excelled themselves in holding two sets of celebrations, both with Major O'Gorman billed as the main attraction – an arrangement from which the valitudarian MP stirred himself to escape in an extraordinary burst of energy: *Ibid.,*19 Mar. 1878.

51 *Ibid.,* 19 Aug. 1878.

52 *Ibid.,* 19 Mar. 1879.

53 M. Davitt to J. Devoy [Feb. 1879], in W. O'Brien and D. Ryan, *Devoy's Post Bag 1871–1928* (Dublin, 1948), p. 301.

54 *Glasgow Herald.*, 20 Mar. 1879.

55 *Ibid.*, For similar attempts in London see, O' Day, 'Political organisation', p. 202.

56 Hutchison, 'Politics and Society', p. 219.

57 *Glasgow Star* 2 April 1906 for Arthur Murphy's recollections; *Glasgow Herald*, 17 Jan. 1879. In retaliation, the disruption of Liberal meetings became a sport for Home Rulers for the next few years.

58 *Ibid.*, 15 Jul. 1879.

59 *Ibid.*, 31 Jul., 1 Aug. 1879.

60 *Ibid.*, 31 Jul. 1879; 4 Aug. 1879.

61 It was an ironically combative pose in which the magazine had previously depicted Joseph Biggar: *The Bailie,* 22 Aug. 1877.

62 *Ibid.*, Aug. 6 1879.

63 *Glasgow Herald*, 11 Aug. 1879.

64 Moody, *Davitt*, pp. 350–1.

65 *Glasgow Herald*, 21, 22 Nov. 1879.

66 *Ibid.*,

67 *Ibid.*, 2 Dec. 1879.

68 British Library, Gladstone MSS Add. 44461, W. E. Gladstone to J. Ferguson 16 Dec. 1879.

69 *North British Daily Mail,* 5 Nov. 1879; McFarland, *Protestants First*, p. 166.

70 *Glasgow Herald* 17 Mar. 1880; Ferguson had some compensation at the election when his backstage dealings jockeyed Andrew Kettle out of the candidature for Cork and forced his associate, Rev Isaac Nelson,' the old eccentric

Presbyterian minister', on the local Catholic bishop: Kettle, *Material for Victory*, pp. 37–8. Nelson, however, proved a poor protege who refused to become a regular parliamentary attender.

CHAPTER SIX

Radicalism and Religion Join

John Ferguson had lost face in Glasgow, but for Parnell the 1880 General Election was a personal and political triumph: sixty-four Home Rulers had been returned of whom twenty-four were definite 'Parnellites' – matching Ferguson's estimate of twenty or thirty.[1] 'The Organiser of Victory' was narrowly elected leader of the Irish Parliamentary Party on 17 May. Now friend and foe alike would come to recognise that quality of icy determination which had won him Ferguson's support. Typically, the *Bailie* was repelled yet fascinated by this man who seemed:

> ... the very impersonation of crude aggressive vanity. Cold, and watery-blooded, his vanity is the mainspring which keeps all his faculties – such as they are – in play. There is besides a certain animal fixity of purpose about his character which prevents him, when he has once taken up with a subject, from ever letting it go.[2]

Parnell had previously harnessed the power of the land campaign to his own advantage, but now a new phase of engagement had begun. Balancing the adherence of his 'left' supporters, with the need to gain ground in terms of 'respectable' public opinion, he became increasingly sensitive to the destabilising potential of rural protest. His response over the next four years was an attempt to subordinate the INLL to the larger political goals of a revitalised parliamentary party.[3] By December, Parnell was already attempting to persuade the parliamentary committee to act as a 'cabinet' of the party, directing policy and tactics, but beyond this signal the drift to moderation was not immediately apparent.[4] On the contrary, there was little intimation during 1880 of Ferguson's future struggles with the parliamentary mainstream. Distress in the Irish countryside, coupled with rising evictions at the beginning of the year, had recast the League as a national relief organisation, representing the mass of the tenantry. Again, he relished the work, touring Queen's County in February beside an exhausted Davitt.[5] Both also remained anxious to broaden the struggle beyond Ireland.[6] In February 1880, they had represented the League at the inaugural conference of Charles Bradlaugh's Land Law Reform League at St James Hall, London.[7] Later that evening, to the strains of the London Secular Union singing, *The Song of the Lower Classes*, Davitt proceeded to declare all landlordism 'a conspiracy and a robbery'.[8] At the March INLL executive meeting, Ferguson was successful in securing modest financial support for the fledgling League, a more radical body than its Irish counterpart, but one with whom he believed they should make common cause.[9]

In a satisfying swipe at his Scottish critics who patently refused to recognise his vital role in Irish political life, he was among the platform party who addressed an audience of over 30,000 in Phoenix Park, Dublin.[10] He was also chosen to chair the land conference which met at the city's Rotunda on 29 April.[11] Here delegates from all over Ireland renewed the League's popular mandate to agitate on the basis of peasant proprietorship, fighting off a moderate attempt to substitute the old Irish Tenant League platform of fixity of tenure, fair rent, and freedom to sell. The League's policy, Ferguson reasoned 'was improperly called extreme', but was 'scientifically true'.[12]

However, at the very moment at which Ferguson was presiding over this restatement of INLL orthodoxy, his own views on the land question were evolving beyond either peasant proprietorship or 'the three Fs'.

A social messiah

There was a protean quality to Ferguson's philosophy and principles, just as there was to his political career. He was a radical intellectual striving to put philosophy into practice, while

testing new ideas by their political utility. It was through this
process that Henry George, the most articulate evangelist of land
nationalisation, came to join Ferguson's intellectual pantheon.
Born in Philadelphia in 1839, George had followed a colourful
career which included typesetting, gold prospecting and a spell
as Inspector of Gas Meters for the State of California, before
making his unique contribution to economic and social theory
with his defining work, *Progress and Poverty*.[13]

Ferguson was far from alone in his admiration. George's book
was political phenomenon rather than a dry, scholastic treatise,
selling well over 100,000 copies in Britain alone during the
1880s.[14] As one of his greatest admirers, Richard McGhee recalled,
it seemed unique in its combined address to, 'the senses, the
feelings and the intellect'.[15] Its style was messianic, loaded with
metaphysical imagery. Its argument was refreshingly simple: the
root cause of poverty was private ownership of land. On one
level, as Offer indicates, the argument was merely an extreme
form of Cobden's political creed, with George arguing that, the
fundamental antagonism of interests lay between labour and
capital on one hand and land ownership on the other. Capital
constituted, 'but a form of labour, and its distinction from
labour is in reality but a subdivision, just as the division of
labour into skilled and unskilled labour would be'.[16] Ferguson's
other intellectual heroes were present here. Mill's justice and
expediency of a peculiar tax on rent sat alongside Spencer's
demonstration of the invalidity of landed titles. George's journey,
however, took him beyond liberal political economy to revive the
Rousseauist doctrine of 'natural rights' as a challenge to utilitarian
conceptions of the inviolability of property. The land of a country
was 'a natural agent' which, he argued, belonged to the people
as much as the air and sunlight. To secure these rights, the cure
was as straightforward as the diagnosis. Land should be taxed to
its full value, exclusive of improvements, thus obviating the need
for all other taxes. The landlord's unearned increment would be
abolished, along with speculation in land, and absolute free trade

would reign. This was more than a matter of fiscal readjustment, but offered a message of spiritual rebirth, for the tax on rent would ultimately reverse urbanisation, end man's alienation and inequality, and bend human nature towards nobler vistas:

> It is the Golden Age of which poets have sung and high-raised seers have told in metaphor! It is the glorious vision which has always haunted men with gleams of fitful splendour. It is what he saw whose eyes at Patmos were closed in a trance. It is the culmination of Christianity – the City of God on earth, with its walls of jasper and its gates of pearl! It is the reign of the Prince of Peace.[17]

While some critics later dismissed it as 'brilliant high-class journalese', this pellucid text was remarkably in tune with the mentality and mission of a generation of British radicals.[18] Its personal attraction for Ferguson was also apparent. His eclectic reading had already prepared him for national ownership doctrines, as well as George's broader scheme of painless social revolution. The emotional intensity of the work and its application of moral reasoning to social themes sat easily with his utopian tendencies and deeply-held religious beliefs, yet it also proposed a concrete strategy, 'upon severely scientific lines', which accorded a major role to intellectual activity in shaping human destiny.[19] There was a resonance too between the moral issue of the disparity between wealth and need, neatly captured in the book's title, and Ferguson's own experience of material advance in the midst of Glasgow's urban misery. A successful businessman, championing an economically marginalised community – here indeed was George's 'House of Have' meeting 'the House of Want'.

The impact of George's land nationalisation theories on Ferguson's politics is more difficult to specify. In the first place, such approaches were hardly new to him. From his earliest days among the Glasgow democrats, he had been exposed to Chartist views on private property in land which stated that land should be held by the state for the benefit of the whole community, with government expenses defrayed by 'economic rent'.[20] The picture is also complicated by the time lag between private conversion and open evangelism.[21] George himself suggested that Ferguson, along with Davitt and Brennan, had wanted to make land nationalisation part of the Land League's policy at its formation.[22] Ferguson, for his part, claimed that he had advocated ground rates as the true and only source of taxation from the time of Butt, challenging 'Manchester bourgeois ideas' in the process.[23] He also boasted that George had sent him two unsolicited copies of *Progress and Poverty* in the late 1870s. This would imply that he was one of the few Britons to be favoured with the author's edition, published in August 1879.[24] Alternatively, given Ferguson's faulty memory for dates, he may actually have been among the second wave of recipients during 1880. Davitt had previously pledged the Land League to help in pushing the book and other prominent Irish land activists were targeted with copies.[25] Whichever chronology is correct, Ferguson stayed publicly loyal to the official policy of peasant proprietorship during the first phase of the land agitation.[26] It was not until later in 1880 that he began to employ Georgite terminology, typically flattening Davitt's proposal of a 'House League' against rack-renting as committing the cardinal sin of contradicting 'educated authority'.[27]

By 1881, George's ideas were campaigning slogans rather than mere debating points. Cameron & Ferguson had already signalled the shift by publishing a cheap edition of *Progress and Poverty*.[28] Ferguson was now less abashed at posing peasant proprietorship and land nationalisation as alternatives, claiming that at Irishtown the programme was 'the Land for the WHOLE PEOPLE' not just for the peasants. Nationalisation of the land was thus the 'especial object of the Land League to teach'.[29] Accordingly, at the massive Land League demonstration held in Glasgow in August 1881, with Parnell's sister, Anna as star attraction, he urged the passage of resolutions which drew on the pure nectar of *Progress and Poverty*: that natural agents are the property of the state; that the possession of a natural agent as private property by a class or individual is an injury to the community; that the right either to use the unearned increment or the natural agent as private property should be denied.[30]

The radicalisation of Ferguson's views during these critical months was not only the product of his engagement with theoretical developments, but was also in tune with the escalation of the Land War. Agrarian crime which in 1879 had been 25 per cent of general crime, had reached the level of 58 per cent by 1881.[31] In January 1881, Chief Secretary, Forster introduced his long-feared coercive legislation, the Protection of Person and Property (Ireland) Bill, which gave government the power to suspend the ordinary law in Irish districts where this was deemed necessary. As parliamentary warfare broke out, Ferguson privately attempted to use his network of radical contacts, via Bradlaugh and John Bright, to induce Gladstone to withdraw the Bill.[32] On 2 February, as the Speaker intervened to close the House of Commons debate, Ferguson chaired a grave meeting of the central Land League. Reaffirming his belief in its role as 'a great social movement', he spoke of the 'terrible position' into which the League was moving and which they must face 'as serious, thoughtful men, without passion, without temper, but with determination'. In addition, he warmly supported Davitt's proposed address to the English and Scottish people for, 'as soon as the principles of the Land League were made known . . . they would find the number of their supporters increase'.[33]

His appeals seemed in vain. The next day Davitt was re-arrested, following the cancellation of his ticket-of-leave. An all-out intensification of the land campaign appeared imminent, with radicals in the movement arguing for dramatic action in the form of secession from parliament and a general strike against rent.[34] While Davitt believed the crisis held real revolutionary potential, Parnell committed himself to intense parliamentary activity. With his usual poise, this policy of moderation and realism was balanced by a leftwards gesture. Parnell suddenly announced his support for 'deepening the lines and widening the area of our agitation' by appealing to the great masses of the population of England and Scotland', who though currently 'much less represented in the House of Commons than the masses of Ireland,' would soon acquire greater electoral power through franchise reform.[35] This was precisely the measure which Ferguson and Davitt had urged on the League only days before.[36]

Hardly a stranger either to organising the expatriate Irish, or to cultivating British opinion, Ferguson now discovered that his cherished ideal of a democratic alliance had the sanction of his leader. In reality, this was to prove tactical manoeuvre rather than a genuine conversion. Nevertheless Parnell's will was rapidly given institutional expression in the formation of the National Land League of Great Britain (NLLGB). The new body was inaugurated on 25 March, under the leadership of Justin McCarthy, vice-president of the Parliamentary Party. Presiding over its launch, Parnell assured his audience that while the English land question was not ripe for settlement, anything achieved in Ireland would benefit the labouring masses in England and Scotland.[37] Despite the garnish of new enthusiasts, the League not only used the organisational infrastructure of the old HRCGB, but also continued to rely on familiar vanguard of Ferguson and John Barry for its grassroots operations.[38]

Ferguson was to remain in touch with the developing themes in Henry George's work. From 1879 onwards, George himself had become increasingly engaged with the Land League's campaign, cemented by his meeting with Davitt in New York in November 1880. A significant outcome was Cameron & Ferguson's reprint of his pamphlet, *The Irish Land Question* in March 1881.[39] In it he applied the main doctrines of *Progress and Poverty,* in an attempt to place the Irish crisis in its full international context, thus merging Irish and British social issues. The Irish land system, he argued, was not 'peculiarly atrocious', but was merely a specific manifestation of a universal abuse of 'natural rights'. The answer was uncompensated land nationalisation rather than Parnell's policy of peasant proprietorship. For the latter would be class legislation which would fail to attack the offending principle of private land ownership and deliver nothing to 'the laboring and artisan classes'. In contrast, by creating a mass movement which included the proletariat, the Land Leaguers would seize the 'radical ground' and attract the support of their 'natural allies' in the British working class. This was necessary as it was in Britain, not Ireland that the battle would be won. 'If the Irish leaders are wise', he suggested, 'they may yet avail themselves of the rising tide of English democracy. Let the Land Leaguers adopt the noble maxim of the German Social Democrats. Let them be Land Leaguers first, and Irishmen afterwards'.[40]

The Land for the People

It was time for Ferguson to set out his own thoughts on the land question and its place in broader social reform. The result was his pamphlet, *The Land for the People. An Appeal to All who work by Brain or Hand.*

On the simplest level, this was an intervention into the debate over how the Land League should respond to the 1881 Land Bill. The intricate provisions of this measure had occupied the House for fifty-eight sittings between April and August. Its introduction suggested that following Parnell's reigning in of insurrectionary responses to coercion, the initiative had again passed to the British government. Gladstone was well aware that the spiralling crisis in the Irish countryside threatened to undermine British policy, designing the legislation to derail the momentum of the agitation by buying off rank and file supporters. Essentially, its provisions were intended to control rent by the creation of land courts to arbitrate between landlord and tenant. Fixity of tenure was also guaranteed – where rent was paid – and tenant was also given the freedom to sell his right to occupancy at market value.

For Ferguson, the INLL by 1881 was a reform movement in danger. Early success had meant that swarming in the League's ranks, and even officering its forces, were, 'tremblers and doubters, who stood afar and mocking the enthusiasts'.[41] This element were now pressing for the Bill to be given a fair trial. However, since the measure was designed to perpetuate landlordism by mitigating its ferocity, it ran contrary to the League's central principle of the total abolition of the landlord system. In a rather confusing formula, he went on to argue that was not for the League to accept or reject the Bill. The Irish people should use it to their best advantage. Any good to come from it would be the result of League action, 'but woe to the Irish people, if, as in 1871, they settle down in fancied security'.

Yet the work was of deeper significance than a statement of policy. After a decade of intense political activity, it was also a benchmark of Ferguson's personal and intellectual development. The combative and forward-looking hallmarks of his personality are deeply imprinted on its pages, with his distinctive platform style transferred to exhortative prose – indeed large sections of the work were included in his fighting speech to the Glasgow Land League in August 1881.[42] Like most of his writing, it was suffused with a burning optimism, confident in the inevitability of change and the triumph of reasoning humanity. As always, the language was highly emotive, studded with pungent imagery and Latin aphorisms, despite his claim to have little use for the Classics. His arguments were buttressed not only by a wealth of international comparisons which stretched from the Rhine Provinces to America, but also by constant appeals to an array of authorities – 'the highest in economic science and continental philosophy'.

Indeed, *The Land for the People* also provides a glimpse of how his theoretical perspectives on the land issue, as much as his practical politics, had still to settle into a coherent mould. Although he proclaimed in the *Freeman's Journal* that he was, 'in perfect harmony on the Land Question with Mr George', he was hardly the man to swallow any philosophy whole, however inspiring.[43] What emerges from the *The Land for the People* is that the new messiah had been grafted on to his accustomed 'highest authorities' rather than supplanting them.

The pamphlet initially suggests Ferguson's continuing debt to the 'Free Trade in Land' literature, which identified primogeniture as the root of all evil. His starting point was the traditional Benthamite proposition that, 'the greatest happiness of the greatest number should be the object of all government – *salus popula suprema lex est.*[44] Following Leslie, Mill and Macaulay, he then argued that Gladstone's Bill was an 'unscientific and impracticable compromise', attempting to promote peasant proprietorship while leaving primogeniture, entail and settlements as law. The great estates would be left untouched by the measure and the possession of land would be left carrying a value other than a commercial one. In the course of time, the process of concentration would wipe out small freeholders, while British agriculture would remain undercapitalised and stagnant since tenants would have little incentive to improve their holdings under the flawed tenurial system. The first step was to destroy the feudal land laws and the archaic system of conveyancing, making the registration of sales of land compulsory, cheap and convenient after the continental model.

Yet he went further than his mentors in classical economics. The manner in which, he believed, '1,000,000 cultivator-owners' could to be created in Ireland signalled that his conception of 'peasant proprietary' had developed along quite different lines from Parnell's. While Bentham had advocated law reform to reinforce private property rights and *laissez faire*, Ferguson employed the Georgite theory of natural agents, advocating a key role for government in revolutionising land ownership. Land, he contended is either the property of the people, to be used for and by the people in the way conductive to the greatest happiness of the greatest number, or it is the property absolute of certain persons, 'be they 30,000 or 1,000,000'. If it is the latter:

> then stop whining about evictions, down on your knees and
> ask the landlords to permit you to live in this land of theirs;

you are the intruders the land is theirs. But if the former cease this babblement of words about the rights of landlords. they can have no rights that conflict with the public good and the people's will.[45]

Degenerative diseases required sharp remedies: hence the state would be required to step in and dispose of the land of the nation to the people who wish to purchase it, securing to the feudal lord, 'whatever compensation it may please the country to give him'. In addition, a first charge of 'perhaps ten shillings' an acre should be imposed upon the nation's land for the services of the whole community. Such an imperial tax would really reduce the landlord's interest in the land, whilst the sweeping away of the feudal monopolies would put practically the whole 80,000,000 of British and Irish acres onto the market. [46]

Ferguson's impatience with the fine detail of such schemes was revealing.[47] A much grander vision called him. The 'bloodless Social Revolution already underway' must be channelled and economics must be pressed into the service of morality. The clearest sign of this in *The Land for the People* was found in his desire to reconcile the dichotomies apparent in the social thought of his day. This was a position which sat easily with his own bridging role between Protestantism and Irish nationalism, but also echoed his reputation as a conciliator in the fractious world of nationalist politics.

His 'healing mission' had three aspects. First, the case of Ireland is consciously embedded in broader social and economic questions of land reform. What was good for Ireland, argued Ferguson, was good for British commerce and the British working man. In both societies wealth was increasing as man was decaying. They shared Pauperism as a festering sore which could not be healed 'so long as the Upas tree of feudalism casts its poisonous influence around':

Destroy it, and you solve the labour question, for then the labourer will work upon the land of others with that

diligence he acquires working on his own . . . Destroy it, and
you solve the land question by making every man's industry
the measure of the security of his tenures . . . Destroy it, and
the product of Irish and English acres will be trebled in a few
years, and the cities and towns will abound with industry.[48]

With Ireland and England, 'dying from the same cause', it was
not his intention to raise national or religious hatreds. On the
contrary, he now held 'Humanity to be above the nation', teaching
'nineteenth-century philosophy in alliance with the old world
doctrine that all men are brethren'.[49]

The developing role of 'the religion of humanity' in Ferguson's
thought was also evident in his refusal to let social revolution
degrade into class warfare. Capital and labour as natural allies,
but an artificial and unnatural system had organised them
into hostile camps. This placed the country and the whole
social edifice in danger, when, in fact, the real social division
was between wealth producers and, 'two non-producing and
economically worthless classes, feudal landlords and legal
conveyancers' – or, as he later preferred to label them – 'loafers'.
He resisted 'communistic' charges against land agitation, claiming
to be 'no leveller', as inequalities of position must exist. He only
urged that such inequalities should be natural, not artificial, and
that distinctions of society should be the result of useful services,
not the accident of birth.[50]

Thirdly, *The Land for the People* followed both Cobden and
George in rejecting any opposition between the interests of town
and country. Land reform was essential for their well-being, for
their fates were intimately connected. The crux of Ferguson's
argument was that by the early 1880s Britain was paying the
price for the historic feudal monopoly on land. This had led to
the undervaluing of her productive agricultural population. As
that population diminished the home market for British goods
declined with it. Migration had taken place to the towns, but
in the longer term the industrial labour supply would also
be exhausted, 'as man deteriorates under urban conditions of

life'.[51] The first educational effort of the Land League had been to enlighten the peasant, but now 'trumpet-tongued' it must call to the masses of the cities to win back the heritage their fathers lost. Indeed, nowhere more evident were the malevolent effects of urbanisation than among the Irish in Britain:

> I have walked through the slums of Glasgow, Liverpool and London, and in broad daylight at the corners I have seen crowds of horrible-looking women, all decency gone, dirt and drink visible in their features, and the language of infamy upon their tongues, and those tongues were Irish, and around me were hundreds and thousands of Irish men and women who lived by crime. These were the children of the deserted village . . . [52]

The final hope which Ferguson set before his readers in 1881 was of a new dawn for mankind – without any of the painful effects which usually attended such a transformation. It would come because the doctrines underpinning it were true: 'Mighty is Truth, and it will conquer':

> It is a revolution of the brain, not of the barricade; it is a revolution in which Radicalism and Religion join, and the weapons of their warfare are passive resistance to tyranny and the ballot for reform. Its soldiers shoot ideas into people, not bullets; it seeks to expand men's brains, not scatter them; it abhors violence both in a Government and a people. Its prayer is –
> When thou shalt help the people, Lord,
> O God of Mercy, when?
> Not kings, not thrones, but nations,
> Not chiefs, not lords, but men-
> God Save the People.
> Thine they are, Thy children as the angels fair,
> Save them from misrule and despair-
> God save the People.[53]

Notes

1 *Ibid.*, Sullivan, *New Ireland*, p. 447.

2 *Bailie*, 27 Oct. 1880.

3 See A. O'Day, *The English Face of Irish Nationalism* (London, 1977), pp. 32–41.

4 TCD, T233, Journal of the Irish Parliamentary Party, 27 Dec. 1880.

5 *Irish World*, 27 Mar. 1880. See also, *Special Commission*, vol. iii, pp.286, 290–1.

6 Note Davitt's plan in December 1879 for 'land clubs' to be established in the main centres of Irish population in England and Scotland: TCD, Davitt MSS 9398/1499.

7 *Irish World*, 13 Mar. 1880.

8 Darcy, 'Charles Bradlaugh', p. 247; D. Tribe, *President Charles Bradlaugh MP* (London, 1971), p. 187.

9 *Freeman's Journal*, 25 Mar. 1880. While the Association had a more ambitious policy of land nationalisation, it did have a greater respect for the efficacy of the parliamentary process than the INLL.

10 *Ibid.*, 14 Mar. 1880.

11 Healy, *Letters and Leaders*, vol. 1, pp. 92–3.

12 *Freeman's Journal*, 30 April 1880.

13 *The Bailie*, 20 Feb. 1884; Henry George Jr., *The Life of Henry George* (New York, 1949); C. A. Barker, *Henry George*, New York, 1955. For a recent reappraisal see, J. R. Frame, 'America and the Scottish Left: the Impact of American Ideas on the Scottish Labour Movement from the American Civil War to World War One' (University of Aberdeen PhD Thesis, 1998), pp. 77–118.

14 E. P. Lawrence, *Henry George in the British Isles* (Michigan, 1957).

15 *Land and Liberty,* Nov. 1922

16 Offer, *Property and Politics,* p. 184; George, *Progress and Poverty : an Inquiry into the cause of Industrial Depressions and of Increase of Want with Increase of Wealth: the Remedy* (London, 1883), p. 144.

17 *Ibid.,* p. 392.

18 Hyndman, *Adventurous Life* p. 281.

19 John Ferguson, *The Taxation of Land Values. A Retrospect and a Forecast,* p. 2.

20 *Forward,* 18 Jun. 1910.

21 Davitt's case was similar, see: Moody, *Davitt,* p. 413.

22 *Nation,* 1 Jul. 1882.

23 *Glasgow Observer,* 5 Dec. 1903.

24 Chamberlain, Spencer and Gladstone were among this group: New York Public Library (NYPL), Henry George Correspondence, J. Chamberlain to H. George, 5 Jan. 1880.

25 Loc. cit., H. George to E. R. Taylor, 20 Nov. 1880. It is also possible that G. B. Clark had sent him the book. He had met George in San Francisco and had been entrusted with twenty copies to get the work reviewed in the English press: *Forward,* 13 Aug. 1910.

26 *Glasgow Herald,* 16 Aug. 1880.

27 'A house is a chattel, or almost; land is a natural agent': *Freeman's Journal,* 8 Dec. 1880.

28 *Irish World,* 1 Oct. 1881.

29 *Ibid.,* 10 Sept. 1881.

30 *Glasgow Herald* 29 Aug. 1881.

31 Lyons, *Parnell,* p. 144; See Clifford Lloyd, *Ireland Under the Land League: a Narrative of Personal Experiences* (London, 1892).

32 Kettle, *Material for Victory,* p. 42.

33 *Glasgow Herald,* 3 Feb. 1881.

34 For the internal debate on 'concentration ' versus 'dispersal' see, Lyons, *Parnell* pp. 146–9.

35 Davitt, *Fall of Feudalism,* pp. 306–8; O'Brien, *Parnell,* pp. 62–3.

36 Lyons, *Parnell,* p. 153.

37 *Glasgow Herald,* 26 Mar. 1881.

38 See also Davitt, *Fall of Feudalism,* p. 227–8: he was in prison at the time of its foundation which he dates to 1880.

39 NYPL, Henry George Correspondence, H. George to F. Shaw 28 Apr. 1882.

40 *The Irish Land Question: What it Involves and how it can be Settled. An Appeal to the Land Leagues* (Glasgow, 1881).

41 *Land for the People,* p. 18.

42 *Irish World,* 10 Sept. 1881.

43 *Freeman's Journal,* 5 Jul. 1882. George had suggested to him that they discuss their points of difference on 'capital as a factor in production and the population question with Michael Davitt as umpire': *Glasgow Echo,* 1 Sept. 1894.

44 *Land for the People,* p. 8.

45 *Ibid.,* p. 26.

46 *Ibid.,* p. 16.

47 See G. Himmelfarb, *Poverty and Compassion* (New York, 1991) for a more general discussion on this aspect of land nationalisation.

48 *Land for the People.* ,p. 11.

49 *Ibid.,* p. 20.

50 *Ibid.,* p. 29–30.

51 *Ibid.,* p. 5.

52 *Ibid.,* p. 29.

53 *Ibid.,* p. 31. Not a Ferguson original, but the verses of the 'Corn Law Rhymer', Ebenezer Elliot.

CHAPTER SEVEN

Early Retirement

Given the sound and fury of *The Land for the People*, Ferguson's actual response to the passage of Irish Land Act in August 1881 was a something of an anti-climax. At the National Convention in Dublin the following month he was received with cheers as he delivered a speech in which he attempted to face both ways, suggesting that, '. . . without lowering the flag of 'The Land for the People', it is still possible to work with the Bill'.[1] On this occasion, the pragmatist in his nature had triumphed over the visionary. Like Parnell, he had grasped the difficult dilemma that now faced the League. Agitation would be necessary to ensure the most favourable terms for tenants from the Act, yet continued rural unrest ran the risk of an immediate onslaught from an impatient government, resulting in the loss of moderate and clerical support in Ireland.

The act had another significance which to have a direct bearing on his future. The Fenians who had originally dominated the Land League had hoped that the demand for peasant proprietary would lead to independence for Ireland. Their reasoning had been that only an independent parliament would grant such a measure. But now Gladstone, as Parnell privately admitted, had done enough to meet the demands of key sections of the Irish tenantry. In so doing he had detached enough support to make the grand gesture of withdrawal from Westminster impossible. In challenging one of the main ideological tenets that had linked the land campaign and the national question, the new legislation seemed to prepare the way for land reform to be addressed as a major social issue in its own right.[2] This was a position which Davitt was quick to grasp, but which Ferguson had argued from the outset of the Land League agitation. Nevertheless, both were in agreement that the democratic alliance should be placed at the heart of their project.

Setting the heather ablaze

Building solidarity in Scotland firstly required a more informed position on 'Scottish' issues. Only a few years before Ferguson had been airily dismissive of Scotland's constitutional position, claiming that the Scots had 'independence' from England as they enjoyed independence of jurisprudence, religion and financial institutions.[3] Now he applied himself to analysing the legal intricacies of English writs in Scotland, arguing that not only were these detrimental to business, but an encroachment on Scottish rights.[4] Private study was complemented by public activity. During 1881, an increasing number of Scots appeared on League platforms in Glasgow, including figures such as the radical land reformer, J. Shaw Maxwell who was to play an important part in Ferguson's later political career. Anxious to reduce the 'otherness' of Irish agitation, Ferguson was also proud to boast that half the Glasgow Land League Council were 'Scotchmen', while the majority, counting himself, were Protestants – a tribute to 'Irish Catholic chivalry'.[5] In one contemporary's view, this development reflected the prevalent 'anti-imperialist views' of the time and the tendency of some progressive Scots to regard the Irish question as 'an economic question', bound up with the current debates over land ownership.[6] More candidly, Maxwell admitted that Irish meetings also offered rewards often lacking in conventional city politics:

An assemblage of Irish men and women forms, perhaps the most sympathetic audience a speaker could possibly have . . . Less phlegmatic that the Scots, and less emotional than the French, the great mass of them are always in such accord with the hero of the hour that every part of his speech is a 'palpable hit'.[7]

Another 'hit' with League audiences was the veteran Highland radical, John Murdoch. Born in Islay in 1818, his years as an excise employee in Dublin had brought him into contact with Young Ireland's ideas on land reform.[8] His newspaper the *Highlander* had been one of the few sources of support in Scotland for Irish Home Rule and the Land League.[9] It appeared that the compliment would soon be reciprocated. In *Land for the People,* Ferguson had already singled out the mania for deer forests as an indictment of absolute property in land.[10] Now it was the mounting land crisis in the north of Scotland, particularly in the north west Highlands and islands, which, he believed, presented an early opportunity to put the democratic alliance into practice.

The City Hall meeting of April 1881 had rallied 'the Irish and radicals of Glasgow' with a call to action. Parnell's presence ensured that the hall was filled to suffocation to hear Ferguson proclaim that:

> Irishmen were neither narrow clansmen nor narrow nationalists, but were broad-minded nationalists, as ready to give a helping hand to the men of Scotland or England that their own countrymen when the land question was at stake. Whilst all Irishmen cherished in their hearts the ideals of national autonomy, they came forward when asked . . . to show themselves politicians, and to bring with them the doctrines of John Stuart Mill and Richard Cobden, and not those of Irish agitators. They had come with the doctrines of educated authority from all over the world . . . the Land Leaguers of Glasgow had reason to be proud that night . . . for the whole nation was moving on the lines laid down by Glasgow ten years ago.[11]

He was followed by 'Mr White', who asked the audience to support a resolution expressing their abhorrence of the threatened evictions on Skye and elsewhere in the Highlands.[12] Setting out the plight of the eight-two souls at the mercy of the 'factorial hydra' on Captain Fraser's estate at Valtros, he only regretted that the Highlands had been so long in appreciating the services of the Land League.

Rhetoric of this variety was to cast a warm fraternal glow over Land League meetings in Scotland for years to come. There were immediate similarities in the conditions of the two rural populations. As the lowland press informed its audience, 'amphibious' communities of Highland crofters and fishermen – if anything more isolated than the Irish peasantry – lived in conditions of poverty and insecurity.[13] The problem was more complex than mere backwardness. Traditional livelihoods were threatened both by agricultural depression and by the cumulative effects of uneven economic development. In areas such as Skye, for example, new methods of land management clashed with the semi-feudal practices of common pasturage and even the performance of labour dues. Both material standards and popular expectations had risen in the decades following the 'Great Highland Famine', but these gains proved as easily reversible as those won by Irish tenants. As Devine suggests, successive poor harvests in the Western Highlands in the seasons 1881–2 removed the supports of a delicate economy, sending over 24,000 people to seek poor relief.[14]

Spontaneous contact had begun in 1881 when some Skye fishermen landed at Kinsale Co. Cork and became exposed to Land League doctrines – apparently communicated through the shared medium of Gaelic.[15] As the Highland land struggle intensified during the early 1880s, these encounters were to be matched by more formal attempts at organisational and propaganda work among the crofters. In later years, Ferguson's widow proudly remembered, 'the Crofter movement . . . which Mr Davitt and my husband started'.[16] From his own recollection, his involvement had began after an invitation from 'a Highland gentleman' to help organise the Valtros rent strike.[17]

The subsequent grassroots work was spearheaded by his young associate, the Tyrone-born Edward McHugh, who undertook a fact-finding and a missionising tour of Skye with Murdoch during 1882.[18] A sum of fifty pounds to pursue this project had been voted by the League's Dublin Executive after a speech by

G.B. Clark. He had assured the Irish that conditions in Scotland were as bad if not worse than in Mayo and that the people of Skye were beginning a rebellion, which he hoped would spread.[19] According to Ferguson, the message McHugh carried was not the official policy of peasant proprietorship, but the 'social gospel' of Davitt.[20]

The success of these efforts to extend the scope of the League's work was far from guaranteed. Murdoch was already well aware of how overlapping personal and doctrinal tensions might impair the 'bond between the sister Celtic countries'. While Davitt was to hold him in the highest regard as a staunch ally, his pan-Celtic enthusiasm and faith in the regenerative powers of Gaelic had failed to avert the chill of Parnell's disapproval when he toured the USA in his company at end of 1880.[21] There were also structural constraints. Despite similarities in the broad contours of resistance and in the social composition of agitation, the exportation of Irish tactics and ideology to Scotland had to be delicately handled. The 1881 Irish Land Act was an inspiring example, but the crofters' demands were for a greater share of land in addition to fixity of tenure and fair rents, a position which reflected the largely pastoral basis of their agriculture and their historic loss of land to sheep farming and deer forests.[22] More importantly, in order to achieve these objectives the Highlands lacked an equivalent tradition of agrarian violence to the Irish. This was a point quickly grasped by one correspondent to the *Glasgow Herald* as early as February 1881, who argued that, 'Mr Parnell may suit our more fiery brethren on the other side of the Channel, but we require a class of leader greatly different from him'.[23] Behind the greater violence and intensity of the Irish agitation, lay differing levels of politicisation and a much stronger link between land issues and national aspirations in the Irish case.[24] The nature of landlord-tenant relationship had left distinct historical memories, with the result that subtle but important differences also existed in the way in which the rural distress of the early 1880s was interpreted. For the Irish, the emphasis was on continuity, linking the present crisis with seven centuries of oppression. 'Landlordism' was the nexus of economic, political and cultural struggle – the instrument of rule of an alien, governing class, forcibly imposed upon the Irish nation. In the Highlands, the quasi-paternal relations between landlord and tenant had begun to be eroded from the beginning of the nineteenth century, as the land of the great chiefs and the smaller estates began to fall into the hands of 'strangers'. The new owners, often southern-based trusts, symbolised the penetration of impersonal capitalist relations into the Highlands rather than the perpetration of 'historic wrongs'. Anti-landlordism in the Highland thus failed to reach the vitriolic pitch of Irish Land League propaganda, with its imagery of 'cormorant vampires'. Crofters could at least employ the rhetoric of a vanished past when religion and lineage had been a common bond, before kinship had been replaced by commercial principles. This also suggested that it might be possible to accommodate Highland grievances within existing political and constitutional frameworks, if attempts were made to restore to crofters a measure of economic security. The distinction was one which Ferguson had himself groped towards in 1880, when he traced the practical and emotional divide in Irish rural society to the historic experience of conquest and dispossession:

> ... the landlords of England and Scotland were not robbers, but the Irish were. Scottish landlords had never forgot that they owed a duty to the state and to the people of the state ... Irish landlords had received land for military service, shuffled of that responsibility, but still put rents in their pockets.[25]

Of course, it was not only the crofters in their Highland fastness that he sought to draw into his political net. As suggested by the City Hall meeting, he was also aware of the potential of the Highland community in Glasgow and the West of Scotland for supporting joint agitation. The tradition of labour migration was well-established, with lowland industrialisation providing a vital safety valve from economic and demographic pressures which Ireland lacked. By 1871 20,000 of Glasgow's population was Highland born, supplemented by growing numbers of second and third generation Gaels.[26] Yet 'common cause' was still far from automatic. Highland migrants were more materially secure than their Irish counterparts, enjoying better housing and a stronger representation in skilled employment. While some struggled to maintain an ethnic subculture, their collective identity tended to be weaker. Indeed, they had less need of defensive solidarity than the Irish because they attracted less hostility from the host society. They were Scots, for the most part Protestants, and bearers of a culture which lowlanders had increasingly romanticised and adopted as part of their own 'national' heritage.[27]

Just as these Highland overtures commenced, opposition to Ferguson's leadership re-emerged from within the Irish community. Lurking under the pseudonym 'Orion', his adversary confined his attack to the letter columns of the *Herald*.[28] The first charge was that the Glasgow League was run by Ferguson's 'tail', a clique of faithful henchmen, like McHugh and Martin Clarke, who did as they were bid. For a politician who shouted for a democratic popular front, he was singularly undemocratic in his dealings with his followers who were treated like children. Secondly, his advanced views and penchant for 'peculiar movements' were accused of dividing the community, scaring away from League meetings the respectable Irishmen of the city and the clergy'. Here, Orion's assault contained a disturbing echo of the clerical attack on Ferguson as a 'false Protestant leader' that had split the 1875 O'Connell celebrations. Ferguson was a man whom 'the Irish could pull down whenever they liked':

He is one whose apparent mission is to throw ridicule on whatever he seeks to advocate, whose erratic behaviour has made him the laughing stock of the city . . . The Irish cause is travestied by him; whenever he opens his mouth or drafts a bill, his arguments are insults to reason and sense . . . It is for the Irishmen of Glasgow to say how long Mr Ferguson's licence to stultify them is to run. So long as it does, Irish politics in Glasgow will be a mockery and a sham.[29]

Before the year's end he had more pressing concerns than Orion's poison pen. As the Land League continued to spur on agitation in Ireland, the government swooped. On one of his periodic Irish trips, Ferguson found himself reluctantly in the thick of events. Sharing a platform with Parnell at Wexford on Sunday 9 October, he warned him that, from the evidence of Gladstone's speech in Leeds the previous day, the premier intended to deal him 'a deadly blow'.[30] Parnell had dismissed his concerns with his customary cool, but Ferguson was soon vindicated. On 13 October, he was in at the Imperial Hotel in Dublin awaiting Parnell's arrival to hold an executive meeting, when he heard the news that his leader had indeed been arrested.[31] A warrant was also produced for Ferguson's arrest, but as the round up of other League leaders continued the next day, he quickly left for Belfast and from there sailed to Scotland, afraid to return to Ireland for months. This was a dramatic departure whose memory was to linger in nationalist circles, with to charges that John Ferguson had 'scuttled out the back door'.[32]

Back in his Glasgow base, his difficulties mounted. The arrests had provoked an outburst of feverish activity among the local Irish.[33] Still shaken by his own narrow escape, Ferguson wielded his personal authority to keep indignation within the bounds of legality. In his speech to an excited meeting of Glasgow Leaguers on 16 October, he was anxious to defend the INLL against charges of violence and intimidation and restate its policy of moral force. The League remained for him, 'a sacred trades union to end feudal landlordism'. He warned his audience not to rise to provocation, but instead they were to follow the example of the recent Dublin Convention:

They were to work by steadily persevering on the legal and constitutional lines of the most representative assembly Ireland had ever seen. This was not a time for weak language, for violent language was always weak language, but a time for strong argument.[34]

This message of restraint was not universally welcomed. Two days later, the crisis deepened with the issue of a 'No Rent' Manifesto signed by the arrested leaders in Kilmainham, with the names of Egan and Davitt appended. For Ferguson, the manifesto was, 'right in principle – wrong in time'. As a League insider he knew that the lack of preparation for such a campaign made defeat certain.[35] As he feared, this measure took the INLL to the brink of open rebellion and hastened its suppression on 20 October. Again Ferguson pressed the Glasgow Leaguers to withhold support from the fateful manifesto for fear that the British organisation too might be proclaimed. But the Glasgow Irish were far from being the docile flock imagined by Ferguson's enemies. After an agonising debate which spanned three Sundays, the most outspoken activists, now organised in the 'Michael Davitt Branch', pledged their support regardless.[36] The branch was punished by expulsion from the British section of the Land League.

Battlelines

Whether as an exotic incubus or a political missionary, Henry George burst in person onto the British stage in 1882. After a lecture in Belfast in January, he met Ferguson, who at once impressed him as a strong ally of Davitt, communicating his candid criticism of the failure to reconstitute the suppressed Land League under another name.[37] In return, Ferguson invited him to address the St Patrick's Day Irish National Demonstration in Glasgow, where in a quirky lecture which ranged from Irish cows to Druid priests, he informed his audience of the honour given to Ireland to lead the in the van against worldwide landlord oppression.[38] In another striking example of expanding radical solidarity, Ferguson joined him a few days later at a 'great public meeting' of the Democratic Federation in the city's Grand National Halls.[39] The Federation, which later became the Social Democratic Federation (SDF), had been established in early 1881 as 'a really democratic party'.[40] From the outset, its policy included opposition to Irish coercion, quickly establishing a deputation of enquiry which toured Ireland during the following months. At the Glasgow event, Ferguson and George shared the platform with J. S. Mill's stepdaughter, Helen Taylor, and the Federation's founder, H. M. Hyndman who was also an executive member of the NLLGB.

Moving beyond Ferguson's progressive redoubt, however, George had grasped that the Irish parliamentary leadership in London were more inclined towards a policy of having neither 'any cooperation with, or aid from Englishmen'.[41] With the sceptical eye of an outsider, George sensed the element of opportunism that had been implicit in Parnell's call for democratic solidarity. He also identified the battlelines liable to divide the national movement. In this conflict, Ferguson had outlived his usefulness to Parnell, and not even the eloquence which attracted his leader's public admiration could save him from defeat.[42]

They had been friends once. On private visits to Ferguson's home, Parnell had enchanted his children with his kindness and gentleness. The unguarded family atmosphere had even allowed him to display his playful nature, racing Ferguson's son to the gate of Benburb.[43] The wonder was that the two men had stayed in political harness together for so long. Parnell, one biographer suggests, had entered politics almost accidentally, from 'a combination of boredom and disappointment'.[44] He had risen through his strength of character and determination, rather than through self-acquired knowledge, preferring the company of dogs and horses to *Progress and Poverty*. Even so, their estrangement was a gentlemanly one. Ferguson may have found closer intellectual companionship in Michael Davitt, but he remained captivated by Parnell.

Both 'the uncrowned king of Ireland' and 'the father of the Land League' began 1882 in prison. In neither case was experience of confinement unduly severe, but whereas Parnell in Kilmainham kept in touch with political developments through a constant tide of well wishers, Davitt's months in Portland Prison were spent in solitary reflection and study. From a rich jumble of reading one familiar authority emerged. Steeping himself in *Progress and Poverty* for the fourth time, he was fully ready to embrace the doctrines of national land ownership and the taxation of land values.[45] He emerged from Portland as a public ally of Henry George, armed with the zeal and the blueprint to make the doctrine of 'the land for the people' a reality.

Unfortunately, just as Davitt's vision of social change was expanding beyond occupying ownership, Parnell's was contracting. This reflected the quiet improvement in his political capital during his imprisonment. In the absence of open political organisation, spasmodic violence had ruled the Irish countryside during the winter of 1881. Gladstone now turned to his erstwhile adversary as a force for stability, recognising beneath his splendid fighting rhetoric, a basic willingness to make the most of the Land Act. The compromise which resulted, the so-called Kilmainham 'treaty', was precisely a recognition of their shared interest in reigning in agrarian agitation. 'Suspects' would be released and the issue of rent arrears satisfactorily addressed, while outrages would be curtailed.[46] Beyond this, Parnell was determined to recast the febrile populism of the Land League into a disciplined national movement. Absolute loyalty must be secured for the League's original goal of peasant proprietorship, as part of a general strategy which restored the initiative to the parliamentary party under his personal leadership.

Released within days of each other in early May 1882, both men were drawn together momentarily by their shared horror at the Phoenix Park murders, but destructive public jousting over Davitt's new doctrine could not be avoided, following its public baptism in speeches at Manchester and Liverpool. The danger for radicals was now that theoretical innovation might be interpreted as a challenge to Parnell's leadership at a critical juncture. The latter's condescending cynicism over the scheme threw Davitt onto the offensive as he tried to rally support among Irish Americans. For his part, Ferguson struggled valiantly to reconcile the positions of two figures whom he still had good cause to consider his political heroes. In July, he wrote to the *Freeman's Journal* defending Davitt, claiming that he had suggested to him that he avoid using either of the terms 'peasant proprietorship' or 'land nationalisation' in his Liverpool speech. As one, he believed, would inevitably lead to the other, he felt entitled to argue with a Jesuitical flourish that, 'nationalisation as advocated by Michael Davitt is precisely the same as peasant proprietary of Charles Parnell'.[47] A further letter to the National Irish Land Conference in Dublin dug him deeper into the conceptual mire. Still searching out a common platform for proprietors and nationalisers, he claimed that the real differences arose out of verbal ambiguity: 'peasant proprietorship' had been invoked by the Land Leaguers for want of a better term, while he regretted the use of 'land nationalisation', as it carried a 'German Socialistic meaning', not intended by Davitt. Both schemes shared the same object – 'limited ownership which alone any individual can exercise over a natural agent limited in supply and belonging to the whole nation'. Where they differed was in means – was the ferocity of landlordism to be mitigated through the Land Courts, or torn up it up by the roots by removing its feudal legal props? For Ferguson, the answer was to work together in spreading the light: 'let him who is surest in his principles have the largest toleration, and thus show he has faith in the ultimate triumph'.[48]

This soothing balm was hardly enough to reconcile the differences now widening over the future direction of the land campaign, the conduct of the parliamentary party, and the relationship between these two wings of the nationalist movement. The hostility towards Davitt and his supporters within Ireland was intense, with suspicions that he had deserted nationalism to become, 'some kind of internationalist and socialist'.[49] During August, he attempted to win Parnell over to the revival of land agitation, but found him lacking in 'backbone' and determined to obstruct every one of his plans and proposals.[50] His fear that he wished, 'complete control over everything' was confirmed by the national conference on 17 October held in the Antient Concert Rooms in Dublin which inaugurated the Irish National League (INL). Controlled by a three-man executive with undefined powers, the new body was as oligarchic at heart as its predecessor, but with the key distinction that its chief purpose was to serve as an electoral machine for the parliamentary party. Above all, its objectives were to be national rather than agrarian, for as Davitt had foreseen, the INL would 'run' land policy rather than being run *by* it.[51]

While Davitt was sickened by the 'name-worshippers' who assisted in Parnell's coronation, Ferguson was equally disappointed in the fate of a movement for which he had been so energetic a publicist.[52] His *Land for the People* had been intended to seize the moment offered by the land campaign to make the triumph of the people complete. Now that triumph was postponed indefinitely. Bridge-builders rather than dissidents by inclination, neither man was willing to force an open breach with Parnell. The compromise appeared straightforward. The campaign for radical democracy would be waged on a British rather than Irish stage. Solidarity with British democratic forces would be promoted, matched by a public commitment to the national movement and its leader. As long as these boundaries were not transgressed, the battle might yet be won.

Within days of the Dublin national conference, the first blow was struck by Davitt's tour of Scotland. At the initial meeting in Glasgow on 25 October, Davitt sighed inwardly as Ferguson from the chair embarked on his accustomed 'eternal verities speech', but had to admit rather guiltily that the result was 'good, forcible and logical'.[53] Indeed, Ferguson's delivery was a powerful blend of conciliation and determination. He read a loyal memorial to Mr

Parnell, while assuring his audience that:

> ... there was no split or dissention in the national ranks ...
> Yet there would be no sacrifice of their independent opinion
> or their right to express it. At present there were two
> parties in the movement – a conservative and a democratic.
> Those present represented the democratic party, and were
> prepared to cooperate with the conservative party until they
> succeeded by force of argument in bringing the conservative
> party to regard the thing as they regarded it ...

This gathering was inspiring in its decisive declaration for land
nationalisation – or 'national peasant proprietorship' as it was
now cautiously termed.[54]

The rest of his tour aimed at a wider audience than the local
Irish. Davitt relished the large number of 'Scotchmen' in his
audiences in Greenock, Aberdeen and Edinburgh and even in
Dundee – where his meeting had been chaired by 'a stupid priest-
worshipper'.[55] Yet it was the situation in the western Highlands
that most energised him. Views on the impact of McHugh's
mission there earlier in the year had been divided. Initially, the
prospect of 'this *brute*' going about the island and 'peddling his
vile doctrines' had been an outrage to officials who were already
inclined to link the tempo of local agitation with the state of
Ireland.[56] By July 1882, however, intelligence from some of the
townships on Captain Fraser's estate suggested that his Roman
Catholicism and his status as a paid agitator might be telling 'very
much against his cause', with his meetings poorly attended and
crofters isolating on his visits to their homes.[57] McHugh himself
was in no doubt of his contribution, informing his audience at
the NLLGB's annual convention in August 1882 that, 'the Scotch
Highlanders were ripe for the cry of the Land for the People'. This
optimistic view was later supported by Ferguson who offered a
romantic picture of his young colleague spreading the light over
glen and mountain, 'until the Land League became a Highland
warcry'.[58]

Wherever the balance of truth lies in these reports, McHugh had at least done enough to establish a foothold for Davitt. His visit was also well-timed. On the day before his arrival in Scotland, agitation had again flared up in Skye after an attempt to serve interdicts.[59] This built on the open resistance of the previous spring, when crofters had petitioned for the return of traditional grazing rights. The 'Battle of the Braes', as the press dubbed it, involved a rent strike on the Irish model and disturbances which ultimately required police intervention. Despite public denials that the tour of the Highlands was merely to see conditions and not encourage a stand against landlords, the question for activists like Davitt and Ferguson was how the momentum from such localised episodes could be channeled into a sustained land campaign.[60] Here they pinned their hopes on the rising generation of crofters whose folk memories invoked the evictions of the 1840s, while sparing them their directly demoralising influence.[61]

Visiting Inverness on 4 November, Davitt's optimism seemed confirmed.[62] Despite the local press campaign against an 'ex-felon, Fenian . . .', he found the most advanced doctrines heartily cheered. He was delighted by those he met, communicating in Gaelic and finding them, 'much better specimens in every way than the lowland Scotch'.[63] In the more educated Highlanders, he had discovered 'just the class of men to start a land movement on the right basis. All read Kay, Arnold and some George [and] promise to keep the ball rolling in the Highlands'.[64] As he rested with the Ferguson family at Benburb, he was still intoxicated by the good work he had done, breaking down, 'a good deal of Scotch prejudice against the Irish land movement, and [carrying] the banner of the land for the people into the Highlands.'[65]

'A platform of truth and justice'

As with Butt, Ferguson became not only Davitt's 'compere', but also his publisher, rushing out two pamphlets, based on his original Manchester land nationalisation speech and the lectures

from his Scottish tour.[66] Yet the days when he could use Glasgow
to launch men into the vanguard of the Irish national movement
were already passing.

The creation of the INL has been described as 'the Thermidor'
of the Land War.[67] The effective departure of the left now
stimulated Parnell to buttress his own position in the country
and strengthen the parliamentary grouping in anticipation
of the next general election. During 1883 and 1884, the latest
new departure in Irish politics gathered pace, resulting in
a rightwards turn in policy and a more centralised political
organisation. One symptom was the deteriorating relationship
between Parnellism and the amorphous body of parliamentary
radicalism. These two groupings were hardly the natural allies
which many contemporaries assumed – even Ferguson had
warned that he 'would vote against any English radical not
broad-minded enough to take on board the cause of Irish Home
Rule'.[68] His reservation touched the heart of the problem, as
many of his fellow radicals viewed an enlightened Irish policy
precisely as a bridgehead against self-government. It had been
easier to remain allies while the Liberals were opposition, but
now tensions had increased following general radical support
for coercion in 1881.[69] Eager to conciliate the Roman Catholic
clergy who would prove indispensable in electoral terms, the
Parnellites by 1883 had developed a more determined strategy
of 'decontamination'. Typically, Ferguson's old ally, Bradlaugh
who in 1880 had received Parnell's support for his attempts to
enter parliament as a declared atheist, was now abandoned in
deference to Catholic sentiment.[70]

Another casualty of the new politics was even closer to
Ferguson's heart – Irish political organisation on the British
mainland. Briefly adopting the new title the National Land
and Labour League of Great Britain, the British Home Rulers
had stopped short of supporting land nationalisation, but
nevertheless provided a useful conduit for radical ideas.[71] This
organisation too was now brought under firm parliamentary
control. The convention in Leeds in September 1883 inaugurated

a new body, the Irish National League of Great Britain (INLGB).[72] 'Smart work' was Davitt's bitter comment, as the former representative executive was replaced by a new appointed executive of parliamentarians.[73] The post of president was assumed by the Parnellite loyalist, T. P. O'Connor, who had made an opportunistic conversion from radicalism to Home Rule only three years before.[74] The League's primary function was clearly defined from the outset as the work of voter registration, providing loyal assistance to the Irish cause when called upon in national and local elections.[75]

Tim Healy could later be candid that the political goal of these years as, 'to efface and blot out every local distinction and recognise only the interests of the country at large'.[76] Yet this was a strategy which threatened Ferguson's qualities of independence and initiative, just as the Glasgow situation seemed to demand them.[77] The city had been shaken literally in January 1883 by a series of dynamite explosions, as 'Skirmishers', inspired by the maverick nationalist Jeremiah O'Donovan Rossa and funded from America, hit a number of prominent targets.[78] Recalling the 'Fenian Fever' of the 1860s, Ferguson feared that the actions of the dynamite party would result in an anti-Irish backlash. Accordingly, the St Patrick's Day demonstration of 1883 was one of his most uncomfortable. In a sign of the times, he was first forced to listen while F. H. O'Donnell MP, who been one of Bradlaugh's main tormentors, enthused over the 'new vigour' which had possessed the Irish movement under the leadership of Parnell.[79] His own martial rhetoric did not prevent him firmly repudiating the unwelcome intrusion of physical force nationalism into his local base. He firmly warned the Irish-American nationalists who were about to gather in Philadelphia:

> ... the tactics of the dagger and dynamite are calculated to retard, if not to utterly destroy, the friendly feeling of interest which was growing rapidly between the working classes of Great Britain and Ireland under the influence of

the teachings of Mr Henry George and Mr M. Davitt, and out of which the Irish race had every thing to expect.[80]

Indeed, the dynamiting episode, coinciding with the trials of the Phoenix Park murderers early in 1883, seemed to confirm the Irish movement's violent and lawless reputation. As James Mavor recalled, a suspicion had now been planted in the minds of even those who sympathised with Ireland's plight that an element existed in her population 'averse from order of any kind, and that even under Home Rule the strongest measures would have to be taken to deprive this element of the power of mischief.'[81]

While financial contributions towards the Highland land agitation could not be overlooked, concerns over too close an association with the Irish had already been voiced by cultural activists such as John MacKay, a member of the Gaelic Society of London, who found it, 'lamentable to see Highland grievances taken up by Irish members'. [82] These sentiments were ultimately to feed into the formation of the Highland Land Law Reform Association (HLLRA) on 31 March 1883. The new body was determined to enter Highland politics in its own right, developing a distinctively radical land reform manifesto that demanded security of tenure and a fully functioning Land Court. It rapidly established a framework of branches in the north-west and by the summer of 1884 could boast a membership of 5000.[83]

In helping to erode the localism of Highland protest, the Irish had perhaps done their job too well. The crofters' cause had begun to attract a broader range of external supporters. The majority of the mainstream press and regional papers like the *Oban Times*, for example, gave their agitation favourable publicity which had been denied the Land League.[84] The Highland societies in the lowland cities were also mobilised, with influential members, such as John Blackie, Professor of Greek at Edinburgh University, lending their support.[85] The longstanding Liberal engagement with land reform secured further political sympathisers, both in the inner counsels of government and among leading Glasgow Liberals.

This basic fund of goodwill was to expand with the opening of the government's Napier Commission in May 1883, offering an additional focus for sympathetic campaigning on the crofters' behalf.[86]

In slipping from Irish tutelage, it may have been the effectiveness of the crofters' coalition that convinced Ferguson that he too should continue to cultivate a wide range of allies closer to home. If the initial Irish input into the crofters campaign was flagging, relations with individual Glasgow radicals, such as Shaw Maxwell, had at least survived both the dynamiting episode and the ill-judged sneers of visiting Irish parliamentarians.[87] In familiar language, Maxwell's imaginative, but short-lived weekly, the *Voice of the People* called for a united front against the common enemy of the 'land class':

> Men of Great Britain and Ireland! Grasp the hand of fraternal friendship, and as, you have often done on the battlefield abroad against enemies so-called, range yourself shoulder to shoulder against more insiduous, more deadly enemies at home![88]

For Ferguson, working from within the local Liberal party organisation was obvious strategy to build on this enclave of radical support. Despite his fury at the government's Irish coercion tactics, he shared the fervent personal admiration for Gladstone already widespread in Scotland.[89] He was also acutely aware of the new voices that were being raised in the local constituencies against the prevailing business ethos of the city's Liberal establishment. This younger, radical element was a constituency that could be taught to have confidence in Irish Home Rule.

After a decade in which he had consistently advocated a position of tactical independence in party contests, Ferguson's new course was signaled in late October 1883 by his appearance at the National Liberal Federation Conference in Glasgow on behalf of the newly-formed Irish Electoral Committee.[90] His speech in support of a land law reform resolution was an uncharacteristic – and rather disingenuous – model of restraint. While full of his growing belief that, 'the battle must be fought in the towns, by the mercantile classes in the ranks of the Liberals', the convinced Georgite claimed to favour free trade in land as the solution and 'nothing artificial'. Such moderation was in vain, as the *Herald* immediately seized on his presence as evidence that Ferguson was spreading division and attempting to convert radicals in the Glasgow Liberal Association to Home Rule.[91] The Association's wounded response suggested that 'Scotch prejudice' had not receded as Davitt had hoped. The legacy of disrupted meetings and platform abuse still weighed heavily on its executive who had instinctively found the Irish claim to representation at the conference 'shady' – indeed Ferguson had only secured an invitation by the circuitous route of an approach to the radical Birmingham Liberal Federation.[92]

The controversy did nothing to deflect Ferguson's strategy of rapprochement with the Liberal battalions. Indeed, national developments in the shape of Gladstone's Third Reform Bill encouraged him to brush aside faint hearts. This measure at last faced up to demographic realities and sought to extend the household franchise from the towns to the counties.[93] The overall impact when the Bill was eventually passed in December 1884 was to double the number of Scottish voters and triple the electorate in Ireland to just under three-quarters of a million voters. While Parnell feigned indifference, chaffing over the possibility of dissention which this legislation might sow in Irish ranks through the creation of a labouring and small farmer vote, Ferguson was strengthened his conviction that the tide of progress was setting in.[94] As he struggled to consider the implications of the Bill for his own position as 'a member of that great trading community', his speech from the chair at the St Patrick's Day celebrations was striking. Also on the platform was William Forsyth, President of the Scottish Land Restoration League (SLRL), a body which had been formed on 24 February 1884 in association with Henry George's visit to Glasgow.[95] Ferguson was anxious to offer some observations, which would be 'useful in relations between the Irish and the Scots and English'. His rhetoric had a chiliastic flavour betraying a growing awareness of class-based allegiances as a force for conflict and change:

> They were on the eve of a change in the balance of political power. They were on the eve of a social revolution which would be great, or greater in its effect that any of those revolutions through which the empire had passed. He was thoroughly satisfied that when the industrial classes once got the extended franchise they would give society a shake which would make everyone think. How was the genteel society, the commercial class, prepared to meet the coming extension of the franchise? If they were prepared to meet it in a spirit of kindness and of generosity then the industrial classes would meet them in the same spirit . . . but if the industrial classes were met with jeer and gibe, and stern refusal to grant them their rightful demands, the mercantile and other classes would be taught a lesson which they would not soon forget . . . They were on the eve of a great crisis, a great victory . . .[96]

Far from rallying 'the democracy', this spirited piece was greeted with greeted with cat-calls. The immediate source of hostility was his opposition to Parnell's plan for an extension of party control over the selection of parliamentary candidates, a measure which was intended precisely to head off any radical challenge to the Parnellite hegemony in rural Ireland from franchise redistribution.[97] In a last ditch attempt to regain the initiative, Ferguson and Davitt had reasserted the power of the constituencies, hoping to mobilise local Land League cadres and return agrarian radicals at the next election. They were to be decisively out-gunned, as Parnell underlined in his speech at Drogheda on 14 April. With wounding sarcasm, he dismissed, 'the great wave of English democracy which is coming over here to poor Ireland to assist the Irish democracy. The poor Irish democracy will have, I fear, to rely upon themselves in the future as they have had to do up to the present'.[98]

Their failure on the selection issue had merely confirmed the impulse towards centralised nationalism. In March, Parnell had already intimated that candidates would be required to subscribe to, 'a pledge to sit, act and vote with the Irish party' – a measure first implemented at Dungarvan under the baleful gaze of Tim Healy.[99] After the exhilaration of the Land War, the frustration for radicals was overpowering. Henry George, for example, confided to Davitt that the whole Irish movement seemed dead, killed by the parliamentarians' conservatism.[100] In Davitt's own view trying to instill spirit into the Land League, with the parliamentary party on its back, was like, 'twisting ropes of sand'.[101]

By June, Ferguson too was in despair and again it took the cautious counsels of Davitt to pull him back from a public breach with Parnell. Davitt's argument was partly pragmatic, appealing to Ferguson's abiding fear of splitting Irish ranks, a development eagerly awaited by the Irish authorities.[102]

It will be wise in my opinion to allow the country to wake up of *itself* to the knowledge that men who have been masquerading as Land Leaguers are now invidiously apologising for landlordism. There can be no danger to the principle of the true reform for our adoption of a watch and wait policy. There is great strength in well-regulated silence, particularly where ideas are ripening in the popular mind, side by side with increasing evidence of a reactionary propaganda [sic] by opportunist politicians.

Our course continues plain and clear. Do nothing to *create* division, but let it come through a defection for *principal* on the other side. Continue to *preach ideas and not men* and wait for the victory of the Franchise.

On these lines the future is ours – that is, it will be won by a platform of truth and justice.[103]

Ferguson's restraint was short-lived. He was elected as president
of the Glasgow Home Government Branch (HGB) the following
month, but a chapter was closing.[104] On Friday 19 September 1884,
an astonished *Evening Citizen* announced that John Ferguson had
retired from active politics, aged forty-eight. The announcement
had, in fact, been made on 25 August, at a public meeting chaired
by Joe Biggar at Derrylin, County Fermanagh. Still constrained by
the prospect of a general election, Ferguson's first concern on this
emotional occasion had been to prevent a full-scale nationalist
schism. In a fighting speech he explained that:

> Although he had retired from public life after twenty years
> earnest struggling, let it not be understood . . . that he
> had retired from the principles of his life. The principles
> of the Irish national democracy, the principles which had
> produced a great and powerful Parliamentary Party . . . he
> belonged to a party who would have no disunion, for if
> Mr Biggar wanted to quarrel with the party to which he
> belonged, they were round the corner at once. They would
> have no fight with them, but when he saw them in the thick
> of the fight with the common enemy, they would be back to
> help them.[105]

The *Citizen's* editorial noted the development with a mixture
of relief and smug satisfaction. It was certain that Ferguson had
moderated his opinions over the years, 'living as he did in an
atmosphere of Scottish tranquility . . . and exposed to a daily
inoculation with the pride with belongs to association with a
mighty empire rather than a limited province.'[106] Its image of
a Butt-type constitutionalist alienated by dangerous extremists,
such as Sexton and Healy, was woefully short of the mark, yet
underlined the bemusement which Irish politics still created
for mainstream Scottish opinion. In fact, the rightwards shift
of the national party and its enhanced grip of on local decision-
making now seemed inexorable, dissipating the early gains of the
Land League campaign. As he explained to the *Citizen* reporter,

Ferguson could either attempt to enter parliament and fight the new course as a party maverick or withdraw.[107] Political and financial realities made the first step impossible and the second inevitable.

Ferguson's position in the national movement was compromised all the more by his faltering relationship with sections of the Glasgow Irish. Developments in the community's politics were of a long-term nature and thus less immediately obvious than the party's policy shifts, but they were equally threatening to his personal hegemony. If Ferguson had transcended narrow nationalism, there were those in the Irish ranks who felt that they had equally outgrown his idiosyncratic leadership. The community had developed in terms of size, ambition and social complexity in the thirteen years since he had first established the Glasgow Home Rule Association. Swollen by the effects of agricultural depression, 13.2 per cent of Glasgow's population was Irish-born by 1881. While frustration persisted that they had not achieved the representation that their numbers deserved, the proliferation of organisations, such as the Young Ireland Society, the Irish National Foresters, and the Irish Electoral Union and Mutual Improvement Association was testament to a rising spirit of self confidence and an improved infrastructure for political activity. The Electoral Union, for example, had grown out of an early attempt by the Irish to contest a municipal seat in 1882, with Ferguson delivering its inaugural address. After three years of educational work and attentive canvassing it had increased the Irish vote in its ward by a third and recast itself as the 'O'Brien' branch of the INLGB.[108]

The city's other INLGB branches were also enjoying good health, with the rising prestige of the national Home Rule movement tempting new and younger members into their ranks.[109] Parnell's rapprochement with the Catholic clergy also meant that, unlike the Father Tracy episode, it was more difficult to demarcate between the 'politicised' section of the Glasgow Irish, and those who instead chose to follow their traditional clerical leaders. Typical of the new guard was the Gorbals taylor, Owen Kiernan, who had only joined the movement in 1881, but quickly rose to become the controversial organiser of the INLGB's northern district. These men were often removed in sympathy and experience from Ferguson's pioneering role during the stormy days of the early 1870s.[110] Indeed, Ferguson's blend of secular nationalism and radical democracy now appeared rather anachronistic to those who took unqualified pride that Catholicism was the defining feature of their identity in Scotland.[111] The element who had always felt uneasy with Ferguson's Protestantism were equally vindicated and could dress their essentially sectarian stance in the proprietorial pride which the Glasgow Irish felt towards Parnell – after all another 'Protestant leader' – whose career had received a decisive boost in their city. In the previous decade, Ferguson could draw disparate strands of Glasgow nationalism together, now he had become part of the problem.

Parnell's Drogheda speech had now signaled an open season for 'dissidents', no matter how distinguished their previous service to the movement. As Davitt protested, it was 'the first law of political puppyism . . . that when a big dog barks at you, all the whelps and curs of the neighbourhood must follow suit and pursue you with their yelping attentions . . .'[112] Ferguson's tormentors found their mouthpiece in a short-lived weekly, *Exile*. The paper was under the editorship of the ambitious Paddy Sheils, and was warmly endorsed by Kiernan as 'advancing the Catholic interest in this Protestant, but once Catholic, country and for stern and unswerving support of Irish nationalism'.[113] Its inaugural edition on 30 August 1884 sympathised with 'the hardy sons of the Highlands' – now a commonplace for those aspiring to progressive credentials – but it was on more familiar ground when it pronounced the latest Parnellite orthodoxy of a strictly nationalist platform, which could only be secured by refusing to join or identify with either of the main British parties. In October of the previous year, the leader's mandate had been delivered to Glasgow by one of his young lieutenants, M. J. Kenny, MP for Ennis, infusing a spirit of independence among the people and healing the sore which, the *Exile* believed, was, 'eating into the heart of the Irish effort, and had almost paralysed their political actions'.[114]

This cryptic reference was to Ferguson's continuing work to build links with the Liberal camp. He had been eager to involve the Irish in the approaching franchise demonstration which was being organised by the Glasgow Liberal Association, in cooperation with the SLRL.[115] For the *Exile*, this was bred of a desire create divisions among the Irish which contrasted with, 'the dignified reliance on the London executive' of his Parnellite opponents. It thundered against this breach of 'the clear and distinctive policy of the League . . . that the Irish people should not attend Liberal conferences or public meetings in a representative capacity', adding that, 'if any Irishman wished to join a Liberal association, by all means let him do so, and the Irish party would be well rid of him; but he would not be allowed to drag the Irish people after him'.[116]

For all his obsessive hesitancy over dividing nationalist forces, Ferguson's retirement prompted new burst of partisanship and faction fighting in the local Glasgow branches. The burning issue was how his political withdrawal could to be squared with his desire to become the HGB delegate to the INLGB's September convention in Dublin. The anti-Ferguson party, led by Kiernan, commented that, 'it was funny that every time Mr Ferguson's name was mentioned it led to uproar – and so long as it was mentioned it would lead to uproar.'[117] Despite their opposition on the grounds of his disloyalty, Ferguson's candidature was decisively carried. Motions of censure and counter-censure ensued over the next week, but begrudging permission was granted for him to attend, with 'the freedom of his own will' to speak and vote.[118] The defeated officebearers now left to form their own 'Glasgow Branch', but a bitter Kiernan delivered his own parting shot with a letter to Parnell's *United Irishman*, explaining that the branch had selected Ferguson as a delegate, 'not for love of the man, but for sheer hatred of some of the individuals who led the opposition'.[119]

Ferguson's attendance in Dublin was something of a Pyrrhic victory. He persuaded his audience to choose Glasgow as the next venue for their annual convention, but shortly after his return he confirmed his formal resignation as president of the HGB.[120] Whilst superficially polite, his letter contained some thinly veiled barbs against the neophyte nationalists who were taking over 'his' movement:

> ... I now beg to say, with deep regret, that my official relation to your branch terminates, and I have only to wish you all prosperity and happiness. The national cause is no longer a despised one. It is no longer down in the dust and ashamed to be seen. It has now position, honour and honest pay for those who serve it, and crowds of men are rushing to serve it. One man, more or less in its ranks now matters little . . .[121]

Ferguson's 'retirement from active politics' lasted little over six weeks. By November he was chairing a SLRL-sponsored meeting, addressed by Davitt in the City Hall.[122] Yet the episode marked a turning point in his political career. Like Davitt, he now became a 'freelance' nationalist, paying little heed to the constraints of party. The political fluidity of the early 1880s had been crucial in sharpening his political thought and deepening his engagement with the forces of social radicalism. While maintaining a local base among the Irish was difficult without support from the Parliamentary Party, he had grown closer to an alternative democratic element in Glasgow politics which he believed could be usefully cultivated. His involvement with Henry George's theories had invested his attacks on private landed property with moralistic, yet practical, overtones, bringing him into the forefront of the movement for the taxation of land values. The campaign to extend the franchise presented him with the spectacle and power of 'the democracy' in action, as the streets of the city were commanded by a massive demonstration of Liberal and trade associations.[123] Yet doubts as to whether traditional Liberalism was capable of realising the potential for social justice offered by franchise reform were to open up a new career as an advocate of the claims of labour.

He was determined that the Irish would not be left behind again. Keenly resenting charges that he had abandoned a 'national policy', the issue was how such a policy was to be defined. The machinery of INLGB might have been captured by the Parnellites, but not all of the Glasgow Irish were attracted by the abstract quality of their nationalism. The bulk of the community were also part of the urban labour force who might be persuaded that the goal of legislative independence for Ireland need not be raised over material needs in their city of adoption. This was to be Ferguson's new audience. Well aware that 'Home Rule' concerned more than mere constitutional change, his mission now became to weld the narratives of 'the nation' and 'the people' in a social reform movement which aimed at bringing the Irish in to the mainstream of the struggle for democratic rights in Scotland.

The first task would be to shift the balance of the land question from historic wrongs to present politics.

Notes

1 *Freeman's Journal,* 16 Sept. 1881.

2 Bew, *Land and the National Question,* p. 230.

3 *Glasgow Herald,* 11 Aug. 1879.

4 *Ibid.,* 25 Mar. 1882. He drew on his experience as a trader to cite the costs of defending legal action in English courts.

5 *Glasgow Herald,* 13 Jun. 1881; *Irish World,* 10 Sept. 1881.

6 Mavor, *My Windows,* vol. 1, p. 164.

7 *Voice of the People,* 10 Nov. 1883.

8 *Ibid.,* 4 Jun. 1882.

9 See for example, *Highlander,* 17 Oct. 1879.

10 *Land for the People,* p. 26.

11 *Glasgow Herald,* 19 Apr. 1881.

12 This was probably Henry Whyte, a Glasgow Gael who wrote for the *Oban Times*: under the pseudonym 'Fionn': see ULL, J. B. Glasier Papers GP 1/1/262, H. Whyte to J. B. Glasier, 24 Feb. 1894.

13 *Glasgow Herald*, 20 Apr. 1882; *Scotsman*, 22 Apr. 1882. See, C. Withers, 'Rural Protest in the Highlands of Scotland and Ireland, 1850–1930', in S. J. Connolly et al. (eds.), *Conflict, Identity and Economic Development* (Preston, 1995), pp. 172–188.

14 T.M. Devine, *The Great Highland Famine* (Edinburgh, 1988), p. 296; for a general overview see, R. Douglas, *Land, People and Politics. A History of the Land Question in the United Kingdom* (London, 1976), pp. 60–75.

15 NAS, Lothian Papers, GD/40/16/32 fo. 21 ff. (McNeill's Report).

16 TCD, Davitt MSS 9375, Mrs Ferguson to Mrs Davitt, 13 Jan. 1908.

17 *Irish World*, 30 Apr. 1887. He had guaranteed their passage to America if they were evicted.

18 He was accompanied by John Murdoch. For constrasting views on McHugh's role see, Davitt, *Fall of Feudalism*, p. 228; *Scotsman*, 22 April, 6, 7 Dec. 1882; NAS, GD 36/1/16/2, Police Report, Glendale, 6 July 1882.

19 *Forward*, 18 Jun. 1910.

20 *Irish World*, 30 Apr. 1887. He also claimed the sum dedicated to this work was £200.

21 Davitt, *Fall of Feudalism*, pp 228–9; *Devoy's Post Bag*, p. 520–30: according to Devoy a 'course Irishman' had spoiled things by asking Dillon, '. . . what the devil does Parnell want by bringing that bare-legged Scotchman around with him for?' Note also, NYPL, Henry George Correspondence, H. George to P. Ford, 27 Apr. 1882. For Parnell's disinterest in

matters Gaelic see, Healy, *Letters and Leaders,* vol. 2, p. 401.

22 J. Hunter, 'The politics of highland land reform 1873–1895', *Scottish Historical Review,* vol. LIII, (1974), p. 50.

23 *Glasgow Herald,* 11 Feb. 1881.

24 E. Cameron, *Land for the People? The British Government and the Scottish Highlands, c. 1880–1925,* p. 5.

25 *Glasgow Herald,* 16 Aug. 1880.

26 T. M. Devine, *Clanship to Crofters' War. The Social Transformation of the Scottish Highlands* (Manchester, 1994), p. 242.

27 *Ibid.,* 248–9; W. Sloan, 'Religious affiliation and the immigrant experience: Catholic Irish and Protestant Highlanders in Glasgow, 1830–1850', in Devine, *Irish Immigrants* , pp. 67–90.

28 *Glasgow Herald,* 12 Feb. 1881.

29 *Ibid.,* 12 Feb. 1881.

30 *Glasgow Herald,* 10, 11, 17 Oct. 1881.

31 *Special Commission,* vol. iii, p.291–2.

32 *Glasgow Observer,* 12 May 1894. Such accusations were unfair as Parnell had apparently communicated that as many leaders as possible were to 'clear out' for the sake of the movement.

33 The Ladies Branch, for example, launched itself into a fundraising drive to supply comforts for the prisoners and their families: *Glasgow Herald,* 17 Oct. 1881.

34 *Ibid.*

35 University of Birmingham, Joseph Chamberlain Papers, JC 8/6/3G/1 J. Ferguson to Cameron, 8 Dec. 1881; *Glasgow Observer,* 2 Oct. 1886. It was to be the end of the year before he contemplated visiting Ireland again despite the fears of his friends that 'Tory magistrates' were waiting for him.

36 *Glasgow Herald,* 14 Nov. 1881. *Glasgow Observer,* 27 Jul. 28 Nov., 1885.

37 NYPL, Henry George Correspondence, H. George to P. Ford, 4 Feb. 1882.

38 *Glasgow Herald,* 18 Mar. 1882.

39 *Ibid.,* 21 Mar. 1882.

40 Hyndman, *Record of an Adventurous Life.* pp. 223–6, 246–9; Ferguson was also present at George's farewell dinner at Gresham's hotel in Dublin in the select company of Davitt and T. D. Sullivan: *Freeman's Journal* , 2 Oct 1882.

41 NYPL, Henry George Correspondence, H. George to P. Ford, 13, 28 Dec. 1881, 4 Jul. 1882; 3 Aug. 1882.

42 *Freeman's Journal,* 18 Dec. 1890.

43 *Glasgow Observer,* 15 Mar. 1913. (My thanks to Mairtin O Cathainfor this reference).

44 Bew, *Parnell,* p. 10.

45 Moody, *Davitt,* p. 504.

46 See Bew, *Parnell* pp. 55–8; Lyons, *Parnell,* pp. 196–207.

47 *Freeman's Journal,* 5 Jul. 1882.

48 *Irish World,* 18 Nov. 1882.

49 This was the veteran Fenian, John O'Leary's later view: M. Brown, *The Politics of Irish Literature: from Thomas Davis to W. B. Yeats* (Washington, 1972), p. 100.

50 TCD, 9535 Davitt Diary 3 Aug. 1881; see also entry 17 Aug.

51 Ibid., 17 Oct. 1881. See also *Fall of Feudalism,* 377–8; O'Brien, *Recollections,* pp. 466–7.

52 TCD, 9535 Davitt Diary 17 Oct. 1881: 'When the Irish people learn to follow *principle* and cease to worship names they will win – but not till then – no never'.

53 Ibid., 25 Oct. 1882.

54 Davitt's next experience in Glasgow on 29 October exposed him to the shabbier side of local Irish politics with which Ferguson was well acquainted. He was taken to a meeting which he had been led to believe was an ordinary weekly meeting of the errant 'Michael Davitt Branch of the Glasgow Land League'. Instead he found an immense gathering for which admission had been charged, and was forced to give an impromptu ten minute speech. Deeply wounded, he lashed out in private at 'Dirty work by dirty-minded people': Ibid., 29 Oct. 1882.

55 Ibid., 26, 28, 30 Oct. 1 Nov,. 1882.

56 NAS, GD 36/1/1/4/35 and 38, Ivory Papers, N. Macpherson to W. Ivory, 21 May 1882; P. Spiers to W. Ivory, 31 May 1882.

57 NAS, GD 36/1/16/2, Police Report, Glendale, 6 July 1882.

58 *Freeman's Journal*, 14 Aug. 1882; *Glasgow Observer*, 9 Jan. 1892.

59 *Glasgow Herald*, 25 Oct. 1882.

60 *Ibid.*, 27 Oct. 1882 .

61 Devine, *Clanship to Crofters' War*, pp. 222–3. For a contrary view of the problems of deference see ULL, J. B. Glasier Papers, J. Murdoch to J.B. Glasier 17 Mar. 1885.

62 *Glasgow Herald*, 6 Nov. 1882.

63 He also noted that the Highland ladies were 'much better looking than those of Glasgow': TCD, Davitt MSS 9535, Diary 4 Nov. 1882.

64 Ibid., 5 Nov. 1882.

65 Ibid., 6–7, 9 Nov. 1882: see also, TCD, Davitt MSS 9602.

66 *The Land League Proposal: a statement for honest and thoughtful men* (Glasgow and London, 1882); *Land nationalisation*

*or national peasant proprietary, Michael Davitt's lectures
in Scotland: the principles of radical reform in the land laws*
(Glasgow and London, [1882])

67 Lyons, *Parnell*, p. 237.

68 *Glasgow Herald*, 11 Aug. 1879.

69 O'Day, *English Face of Irish Nationalism*, p. 92.

70 TCD, Journal of the Irish Parliamentary Party, 21 Jun. 1880;
F. Callahan, *T. M. Healy* (Cork, 1996), pp. 116–7.

71 *Freeman's Journal* ,14 Aug. 1882.

72 *Ibid.,* 1 Oct. 1883.

73 The agrarian left viewed the work of 'political jackasses'
like Healy as part of a more general tendency which saw
'. . . the principle of representation being sat upon whenever
Mr Parnell sees an opportunity for doing so . . .', see TCD,
Davitt MSS 5536, Diary 29 Sept. 1883.

74 See, L. W. Brady, *T. P. O'Connor and the Liverpool Irish*
(London, 1983), p. 20; O'Day, *English Face of Irish Nationalism,*
pp. 87–9.

75 O'Day, ' Political Organisation', pp. 188–90.

76 *Freeman's Journal*, 16, 19 Feb. 1900.

77 TCD, Davitt MSS 5536, Diary 28 Dec. 1883

78 *Glasgow Herald*, 22, 24 Jan. 1883; see also K.R. M. Short, *The
Dynamite War – Irish American Bombers in Victorian Britain*
(Dublin, 1979), pp. 104–5.

79 The *Bailie* dismissed O'Donnell as a Colorado beetle,
'sprung into notoriety in virute of being simply a pest': 22
Aug. 1877.

80 *Glasgow Herald*, 20 Mar. 1883. See also Davitt's comments
on the City Hall resolutions. He considered the dynamite

campaign 'war against *the democracy of England*' : TCD, Davitt MSS 9399, M. Davitt to J. Ferguson, 25 Mar. 1883.

81 Mavor, *My Windows,* vol. 1, p. 165. See also: J.B. Glasier Papers, University of Liverpool, M. Clarke to J. B. Glasier, 27 Oct. 1883.

82 Davitt had sent £150 for the cause: TCD, Davitt MSS 5536, Diary 1 Feb. 1883. National Library of Scotland (NLS), MS 2634, Blackie Papers fol. 315, J. Mackay to Blackie, 12 Aug. 1882.

83 Hunter, 'Politics of Highland land reform', pp. 50–3.

84 Devine, *Clanship to Crofters' War.* pp. 225–6.

85 J. G. Duncan (ed.), *The Life of Professor John Stuart Blackie* (Glasgow 1895), pp. 81–96.

86 Despite its compositon, Davitt, for example, believed the Commission at least shed light on the 'odious system' of landlordism: TCD, Davitt MSS 9328, M. Davitt to R. McGhee, 22 May 1883.

87 *Voice of the People,* 10 Nov. 1883 for Thomas Sexton's comments.

88 *Ibid.,* 17 Nov. 1883.

89 See, for example, Walter Freer, *My Life and Memory* (Glasgow, 1929), p. 47.

90 *Glasgow Herald,* 31 Oct. 1883.

91 *Ibid.,* 1 Nov. 1883.

92 *Ibid.,* 20 Nov. 1883.

93 It also liberalised the burgh franchise, breaking the link with poor law rates and removing the prohibition on those in tied accomodation: M. Dyer, *Capable Citizens and Improvident Democrats. The Scottish Electoral System 1884–1929* (Aberdeen, 1996), p. 11.

94 Lyons, *Parnell*, pp. 266–7.

95 *Glasgow Herald*, 17 Mar. 1884; *Christian Socialist*, Jul. 1884.

96 *Ibid.*, 18 Mar. 1884. Ferguson's enthusiasm for franchise extension outstripped Henry George's who assured his Glasgow audience that, 'the suffrage was a lesser goal than control of the land and the end of landlordism'.

97 *Freeman's Journal*, 25 Mar. 1884; Callanan, *Healy*, p. 98.

98 *Irish Times*, 15 Apr. 1884; see also Davitt's furiously annotated copy: TCD, Davitt MSS 9640; O'Brien, *Parnell*, vol. ii, pp. 34–6.

99 *Freeman's Journal*, 29 Mar., 21 Aug. 1884.

100 TCD, Davitt MSS 9332/245, H. George to M. Davitt, 9 Jan. 1883.

101 TCD, Davitt MSS M. Davitt to R. McGhee, 21 Jul. 1883.

102 Dublin, INA, Proceedings of the Land League and Irish National League, Police Report, 18 Jul. 1884.

103 Ibid., 9375, M. Davitt to J. Ferguson, 25, Jun. 1884. He had given similar advice to McGhee who was also straining at the leash to attack. He argued that exposing the inconsistency of a man they had recently 'preached up' would not win converts. The answer was to ignore 'little minds' and go on preaching 'the Land for the People': 9328/180/5, M. Davitt to R. McGhee, nd. [15 Apr. 1884].

104 *United Irishman*, 13 Jul. 1884.

105 *Freeman's Journal*, 26 Aug. 1884.

106 *Evening Citizen*, 20 Sept. 1884.

107 *Ibid.*

108 Handley, *Irish in Modern Scotland*, p. 275; see *United Ireland*, 25 Feb., 17 May 1884 for the Union's weekly meetings.

109 *Exile* , 30 Aug. 1884: the INLGB now had five branches in the city.

110 TCD, Dillon MSS 6788/65–8.

111 Their willingness to defend their rights as Catholics was evident, for example, in the campaign to secure representation on the school boards in 1882. The leading figure here was Father Murphy, one of Ferguson's associates, but already the *Herald* believed that the politicised Irish no longer owed Ferguson sole allegiance: *Glasgow Herald,* 27 Mar. 1882.

112 TCD Davitt MSS 9238/ 180/5, M. Davitt to R.McGhee, nd.[15 Apr. 1884].

113 *Exile* , 30 Aug. 1884.

114 *Ibid.*

115 *Glasgow Herald,* 19 Aug. 1884.

116 *Exile* 30 Aug. 1884.

117 *Ibid.*

118 *Exile,* 6 Sept. 1884.

119 *United Irishman* 6 Sept. 1884. The HGB censured him for this step, *ibid.,* 27 Sept., 4 Oct. 1884; *Glasgow Observer,* 8 Oct. 1887.

120 *Ibid,* 13, 20 Sept.1884.

121 *Exile,* 20 Sept. 1884.

122 *Glasgow Herald,* 12 Nov. 1884.

123 *Ibid.,* 8 Sept. 1884.

Plate 1. The *Bailie*'s view of Ferguson's battles with the Glasgow Liberals in 1879 (Mitchell Library, Glasgow).

Plate 2. From firebrand to city father: Ferguson on his elevation as a Glasgow Bailie in 1899 (Mitchell Library, Glasgow).

Plate 3. This 1877 cartoon of Joseph Biggar captures his pugnacious spirit (Mitchell Library Glasgow).

Plate 4. An unfamiliar, clean-shaven Charles Stewart Parnell on his visit to Glasgow, 1879 (Mitchell Library, Glasgow).

Plate 5. Henry George – 'a man of great copiousness and strength of language' (Mitchell Library, Glasgow).

Plate 6. This sheet music for the concertina was part of Cameron
& Ferguson's 'Songs Series'. Their range also included Christy's
Minstrels' music, sacred songs, and comic and burlesque pieces.

Plate 7. One example of cheap digests of 'wit and wisdom' produced by Ferguson's firm for over thirty years – usually priced 3d.

CAMERON & FERGUSON'S
SIXPENNY LIBRARY
OF
ROMANCE AND ADVENTURE.

。 The Publishers will forward the Works named below, or others of their Publications, free by post, to any address in the United Kingdom, on receipt of Stamps to the required amount.

。 Containing first-class Reprints and Original Works of an interesting character. The titles will show that there is variety to suit most readers, and all cannot fail to derive pleasure from their perusal. Each volume is complete in itself, contains 128 or 160 pages Crown 8vo, printed on good paper, done up in handsome illustrated coloured covers. This series supplies a want long felt, of Books which do not weary by their length, but sustain the interest throughout, by their stirring narratives and powerfully portrayed characters. Price 6d. each, or Free by Post for 7 Stamps.

1. THE SCOTTISH CHIEFS, by Miss JANE PORTER.
2. THE OUTLAWS' REVENGE; or, The Lost Heir of Rookelyn.
3. THE SHRIEK OF FREEDOM; or, Warsaw's Last Champion. A Romance of the Polish War.
4. THE WARRIOR BROTHERS; a Romance of Love and Crime.
5. THE INSURGENT CHIEF; or, the Pikemen of '98. A Romance of the Irish Rebellion.
6. THE CHAMBER MYSTERY; or, The Nun's Daughter.
7. THE PIRATE OF THE SLAVE-COAST; or, The White Lady of the Island.
8. THE SHAWNEE FIEND; or, Nick of the Woods.
9. RIPPERDA THE RENEGADE; or, The Siege of Ceuta.

10. THE ARKANSAS RANGER; or, Dingle the Backwoodsman.
11. NEVERFAIL; or, The Children of the Border.
12. THE WHITE QUEEN AND THE MOHAWK CHIEF.
13. PAUL THE ROVER; or, The Scourge of the Antilles.
14. THE WITCH OF THE WAVE; or, The Rover's Captive.
15. THE HEIR AND THE USURPER; or, The Ducal Coronet.
16. THE MYSTIC TYE; a Tale of the Camp and Court of Buonaparte.
17. THE TURKISH SLAVE; or, The Dumb Dwarf of Constantinople.

A NEW VOLUME ISSUED EVERY MONTH.

CAMERON & FERGUSON'S
AMERICAN FOURPENNY LIBRARY,
CONSISTING OF
TALES, LEGENDS, ROMANCES, AND EXCITING ADVENTURES.

。 This Series embraces the Choicest Works of American Authors, giving pictures of Life in the Great Western Continent, full of intense dramatic and personal interest, new to most British Readers. Each volume is a novelty, and presents a Complete Tale or Romance certain to command attention. The size is large octavo, double columns, clear type, and covers elegantly printed in colours. Travellers by rail, road, sea, or river should not go on a journey without them. Price 4d. each; or, Free by Post for 5 Stamps.

1. THE YANKEE SCOUT; or, Haps and Mishaps of the Border.
2. THE CROWNING REVENGE; or, Fight Fire with Fire.
3. RUBE, THE HUNTER; or, The Captive of Crow Village.
4. THE YOUNG RANGER'S LIFE MYSTERY; or, The Frontier Scouts.
5. THE TRAITOR'S DOOM; or, The Heiress of Bella Vista.
6. THE SECRET SHOT; or, The Rivals of Misty Mount.
7. THE BORDER SPY; or, The Beautiful Rebel Captive.

8. A ROMANCE OF THE PAMPAS.
9. OLD HAL WILLIAMS; or, The Spy of Atlanta.
10. TRUE BLUE; or, The Writing in Cypher.
11. THE GUERRILLAS OF THE OSAGE; or, Loyalty on the Borders.
12. KATE SHARP; or, The Two Conscripts.
13. THE ORONOCO CHIEF; or, The Fortunes of a Diamond Locket.
14. THE CAVALRY SCOUT; or, Old Guess Markham's Adventures.
15. THE OLD FLAG; or, Home at Last.
16. OLD PEGGY BOGGS; or, The Old Dominion Inside Out.

The above Tales may be had of the Publishers or any Bookseller.

GLASGOW AND LONDON: CAMERON & FERGUSON.

Plate 8. As their catalogue from the 1880s suggests, the firm's novelette output was also prodigious and diverse. The *Pikeman of '98* has some strange company in the Sixpenny Library.

Bailie Maxwell said that "Mr Ferguson was an experienced deputationist, and on his visit to Limerick he called on the Mayor, and marched in triumphal procession to the particular factory. All that was wanted was a brass band to complete the procession."

Plate 9. The 'Boss' Deputationist. As a senior member of the Corporation of Glasgow, Ferguson was accused of abusing his position to indulge in political patronage. A Limerick firm's success in winning a lucrative clothing contract from the Corporation in 1905 was seen as linked to his visit to the city in 1905 (Mitchell Library, Glasgow).

Plate 10. The Weary Glasgow Deputationist. Local opponents were deeply suspicious of the frequent trips made to London by Ferguson and his Corporation colleagues on municipal taxation business (Mitchell Library, Glasgow).

Plate 11. Ferguson (front row, fifth from right) and his fellow councillors inspect Glasgow's first electric tram in 1898 (Strathclyde Passenger Transport Authority).

Plate 12. Benburb Villa, Lenzie. Ferguson's family home and political HQ (East Dunbartonshire Libraries).

Plate 13. Ferguson's grave in Old Aisle Cemetery, Kirkintilloch. The headstone – now rather forlorn – was raised by public subscription shortly after his death (East Dunbartonshire Libraries).

CHAPTER EIGHT

The Whole Sky was Brightening . . .

With his usual flippancy, Henry Labouchere summed it up as the search for 'the urban cow'. How could ideas of radical land reform be translated into urban terms? How could they be made relevant for the newly-enfranchised masses in the swollen cities? The same questions had confronted the Glasgow democrats as they embarked on their land campaign in the 1860s. On that occasion, their efforts had failed, but now John Ferguson believed he had found the true path. It was his belief that the Land War which had begun in Mayo held the key for future radical action and that land reform was only one part of a wider social revolution. An alliance between feudalism and capitalism, he argued, had been instrumental in shaping both Irish and Scottish economic destinies. Feudalism pushed and ejected the peasant, while capitalism sucked the dispossessed masses into an urban holocaust and left them at the mercy of utilitarian entrepreneurs. He pledged himself to challenge this unholy alliance of rural and industrial interests in the interests of the whole productive community.

In proclaiming the universal relevance of the Land League's principles of social justice, he was assisted by the economic depression which began to grip Scotland in earnest in the mid-1880s, confounding expectations of lasting prosperity and stability. The dislocation which had affected the rural economy of Britain and Ireland had now become an industrial and commercial malaise. Against this background, individualistic radicalism of the old school was losing its motive spring. Instead, it was Henry George's 'Single Tax' which seemed to offer a new remedy through the liberation of productive labour and enterprise from their historic burdens.

Ferguson later explained George's impact in Scotland as

testament to the Scottish mind's 'peculiar inspiration upon economics', but his success also reflected the inability of either of the main political parties to produce similarly concrete policies to address the crisis of trade and industry.[1] The franchise reform of 1884 had already created a more varied and unpredictable constituency, less conducive to the hegemony of a single party, while traditional political alignments were further slackened by Gladstone's embrace of Irish Home Rule at the end of 1885.[2] As debilitating divisions opened among the Liberal Party's elite, struggling over 'true' meaning of Liberalism, the end of the two party system was widely predicted.[3] The growing bitterness in public life during these years reflected shifting socio-economic interests and sharpening class antagonisms. Some of the worst exchanges were to take place as a radicalised Liberal Party jostled with the gathering strength of labour in a confused political arena. From the plethora of electoral contests in the next few years, Ferguson emerges less as a far-sighted 'apostle of labour' and more as a practical politician struggling to clarify own position in the light of uncontrollable new forces in society and politics. Many advanced Liberals shared the same dilemma, but his own position was infinitely complicated by the question of how the Irish should respond to these developments.

The *Glasgow Observer* had stated in its inaugural edition that the fulfilment of the programme of the Irish Parliamentary Party was, 'the only scheme which can accomplish the destinies of the Irish race'.[4] Although public rejection of this orthodoxy would have been political suicide, Ferguson had become convinced that interests of the Irish in Britain might not be identical with those of 'the Irish race' in their homeland. While embracing Parnellism had apparently allowed Irish migrants to transcend the limitations of the politics of locality, he grasped that blindly following the banner of 'the nation and its leader' could actually reinforce their minority status and particularism. The democratisation of the franchise had produced a more individualistic voter and a more uniform national electoral system. Now, he believed, the INLGB must move from single-issue, interest politics to become an integral part of 'the democracy' which had history on its side.

In his own mind, democratic politics and the demand for Irish Home Rule were of course perfectly compatible. Home Rule would lay the foundations for a more just society, while progressive politics must admit the justice of the Irish national cause. 'With the overthrow of class government', he wrote in 1885, 'many national prejudices will disappear. With the triumph of the democracy in England centralisation will give way to local self-government'.[5] It was his misfortune that political realities were a great deal more untidy. Some alternatives were already closed off. Despite his threats, he would never repudiate the Irish cause which was the cornerstone of his political identity. Now personally linked to the Liberal Party, he had to tread warily. Although the departure of much of its Whiggish element was to permit a stronger stand on land reform, the party still displayed a decidedly anti-democratic spirit in its candidate selection. He had nevertheless to balance his recognition of the claims of independent candidates with awareness that it was only from a Liberal government that an Irish parliament could be obtained.

This seemed a pragmatic, yet principled, position which maximised his independence of judgement. For his critics on left, it was at best indecisive, at worst cynical and manipulative. For his opponents in the Irish community, it represented a dangerous flirtation which threatened to undermine Irish interests. It was at least some compensation that he had a growing band of allies, particularly in the ranks of the HGB, who would continue to support him in the crucible of Scottish politics.

Ferguson's 'tail'

When the young Ulsterman, Alexander Bowman arrived in Glasgow in 1888, the opportunities for nationalist and democratic activism were very different to those encountered by Ferguson almost thirty years before. Not only was the Secretary of the Irish Protestant Home Rule Association (IPHRA) welcomed into a well-established structure of INLGB branches, he was also able to tap into elaborate organisational and personal networks, based around land agitation and Home Rule, which drew in both Irish and Scottish reformers.[6] Ferguson's personal contribution to this situation was significant.

The group whom 'Orion' had dismissed in 1881 as 'Ferguson's tail', he personally viewed as a new political force – 'Home Rule Radicals'.[7] If he had become alienated from the young journalists and lawyers who flocked round Parnell, he had done his best to encourage his own rising generation. While a few of his allies in the late 1880s were associates from the Democratic Hall days, most were younger men, born in the 1850s. They were far from dutiful satellites – Davitt was called upon on at least one occasion to smooth feathers – but as they pursued their independent political careers, they remained indebted to their Glasgow apprenticeship.[8] Displaying the greatest talent and longevity of the brood were: Hugh Murphy, Edward McHugh, Richard McGhee, and the Scottish radicals, John Shaw Maxwell and John Bruce Glasier.[9]

Ferguson's dignity did not allow the taking of liberties and he was apt to be short-tempered with those who disagreed with him, yet his iconoclastic reputation and impressive range of learning made him a natural focus for young men entering politics.[10] There were other points of connection between Ferguson and his new colleagues. Most were from humbler family circumstances than his own, but, with the exception of Maxwell who was born in Glasgow in 1856, all were migrants who had shared Ferguson's experiences of re-orientation and self-improvement in a strange city. McHugh had left Tyrone as a child to settle with his family in Greenock, moving at the age of sixteen to Glasgow in 1869; Murphy had left Newtownbutler in County Fermanagh, aged ten, also settling in the city in the late 1860s; McGhee, a Protestant from Co. Armagh, arrived in 1871, aged twenty; the teenage

Glasier had moved to Glasgow from Ayrshire two years later. There was even a common occupational thread: McHugh was a compositor, McGhee a commercial traveller in stationary and Maxwell was a self-employed lithographic designer who, like Ferguson, had faced a commercial boycott because of his political views. [11]

In their new surroundings they had sought out the fellowship of other progressively-minded individuals in the city's debating societies and discussion clubs – indeed Glasier and Maxwell originally met in the same Eclectic Institute, 'Freethought Hall', in which Ferguson had experienced his political baptism.[12] It was, however, the Irish branch organisation which the older man had built in Glasgow which provided a more sustained grounding in public affairs. On first acquaintance, Murphy, aged seventeen, was still pledged to physical force nationalism, but he was soon been won over by Ferguson's constitutionalist arguments, becoming a founder member of the HGB and presiding over some of its stormiest meetings.[13] Prior to his Highland missioning, McHugh too had been drawn into the HGB during the 1870s, eventually serving as its secretary. Maxwell was a future HGB Vice-President, while McGhee and Glasier also played a high-spirited role during the Land League period.[14]

The meetings of INLGB branches followed a familiar routine. Minutes and correspondence would be presented by the secretary, followed by the chairman's resume of the week's political events. This could be a tedious process. Secretaries occasionally read from the minutes the speech they had delivered the previous week, while discussion arising from correspondence sometimes took up the entire evening from four to seven or eight o'clock. More commonly, there would also be a speaker, a collection and a vote of thanks. For all the frustrations, these proceedings provided a disciplined training for young activists. In particular, they provided a test for tyro orators. After a meeting, members would immediately form in small groups and discuss the merits and otherwise of the speaker. While they hated having papers read, or anyone speaking extensively from notes, were ungrudging in their applause for those who could dispense with such aids.[15]

Of all the Glasgow branches, the regular Sunday debates at the HGB's Home Rule Hall provided probably the most stimulating platform. The branch had retained its independent and progressive reputation, with both Irish and Scottish social questions tackled an earnest and improving spirit. Indeed, as the decade progressed, it was to develop as a truly eclectic forum for progressive ideas, its guests ranging from the Russian anarchist, Prince Kropotkin to the Indian nationalist, J. N. Mukharji.[16]

The combative and emotional dimension of Irish cause was also an inspiration. Ferguson's colleagues naturally gravitated to the agrarian left of the party, with Murphy, Maxwell and Glasier defying him over their support of the 'No Rent' Manifesto in 1881. For the latter two activists, who came to the land question through this medium, the example of Ireland during the Land War, raised energising issues which domestic politics could not. The undercurrents of extremism and rebellion which still haunted the movement appealed to their romanticism and radical-self image. In later years, Glasier's wife claimed that he became disenchanted by the conspiracy surrounding the Phoenix Park murders, but his engagement with Irish agitation, in fact, survived this episode.[17] He assured the Paisley INLGB branch in 1885 that although he felt himself to be an intruder, 'if an earnest desire to see Ireland enjoying the freedom to which she was entitled gave one a right to be present then he thought he had that right.'[18]

Nowhere was the spirit of struggle and self-sacrifice better represented than in the person of Michael Davitt. His frequent visits to Glasgow meant he became a shared influence on the 'Home Rule Radicals', who were attracted not only by his qualities of leadership, but also by his 'moral grandeur'. McGhee became Davitt's close friend and life-long correspondent – his trusted *Advocato de Diabolo"* – while Glasier's response was a more conventional hero worship. The latter's poetic sensibilities were aroused in Davitt's defence, after he had been howled down by

Fenians at a public meeting in Oldham in 1883:

> They cannot bring his noble soul to bay;
> They cannot chain his fearless spirit down:
> But they can hiss at him, and yell like fiends, and drown
> In ghoulish clamour what his speech would say:
> . . . a war of ignorant and recreant rage
> Against the truest heart they have today.[19]

If Davitt was a unifying force for Ferguson's allies, the impact
of Henry George was more complex. He was another a figure
who tempted his Glasgow admirers into verse. Even if their
efforts were clumsy, they captured the messianic quality of the
man:

> We praise you, worker, thinker, poet, seer!
> . . . You on whose forehead beams the aureole
> That hope, a 'certain hope' alone imparts -
> Us have you given perfect heart and soul;
> Wherefore receive as yours our souls and hearts![20]

For Murphy, McHugh and McGhee, he did indeed offer
a 'certain hope'. All of them remained resolute Single-Taxers
throughout their political careers.[21] Murphy continued his
political work with the HGB, but also became a strong trade
unionist and member of Glasgow Trades Council. McGhee
and McHugh similarly carried their Georgite principles into
nationalist politics and labour organisation in Britain and
America.[22] Even at the height of George's popularity, however,
others viewed his doctrines as 'a stepping stone'.[23] The political
trajectories of Maxwell and Glasier, for example, took them
beyond single-tax radicalism and into the more systematic
embrace of socialism.[24] After years of growing impatience with
the Liberal Party, Maxwell became the first secretary of the
Independent Labour Party (ILP) in 1893, and later a Glasgow
councillor. Glasier's conversion came through the medium of
Morris' Socialist League, but after its failure he also helped in the

ILP's launch, becoming one its leading evangelists.[25] Socialism – involving 'socialisation of the heart', as well as of wealth – now became his new literary muse. In short, there could be few better illustrations of the ferment of ideas which faced Ferguson in the mid-1880s that his own circle.

Land and labour

Isolated from the nationalist mainstream, Ferguson's world seemed to shrink for a time. The battles of local democracy and land reform were fought out in miniature as he brought his campaigning might to bear on the attempts of his Lenzie neighbours to win new school and reclaim a traditional right of way. Both campaigns were successful, winning him genuine popularity in his local community.[26]

Small victories were to be cherished, but as he busied himself with the democratic rights of Lenzie, Parnell was moving towards the climax of his political career. The prospect of playing the Conservatives off against the Liberals in the pursuit of Home Rule had been a crucial strategic device for Parnellites. During the spring of 1885, as the prospect grew of a general election – the first under the new franchise – posturing became reality. Acute observers sensed Parnell quietly 'coquetting' with the opposition as early as February.[27] By May, the Irish party had combined with the Tories to bring down the Gladstone administration, serving notice that their support had become a negotiable asset. For the potential of this exceptional situation to be realised, the Irish vote in Britain also had to be kept free of entanglements and placed fully at the disposal of Parnell. Thus, the machine-like quality of Parnellism, as Ferguson and Davitt had feared, would be finally translated into local politics.

In Glasgow, the problem, as Hugh Murphy explained to the HGB, was how to get Irish Catholics to vote for the Tories, if required.[28] The response of the INLGB Executive was a softening-up campaign, importing a string of parliamentary favourites to prepare voters for just such a contingency. While the mellifluous T. P. O'Connor assailed his City Hall audience with charm, Joe Biggar preferred the bludgeon of common-sense. His message was one calculated to infuriate Ferguson. Addressing the Irish Electoral Union in May, he hinted that Tory alliance was not out of the question, as after all the Tories had not acted with any particular unfairness towards Ireland when in office. This was not wholly objectionable, as Ferguson had himself maintained the wisdom of a resolutely independent line in the past and even had flirted with supporting the Conservatives in 1879. It was when Biggar turned to the land question and to the issue of links with local radical candidates that the chasm between party dictates and local initiatives opened up:

> There was another set of politicians who were rather a noisy set at any rate (laughter)–he meant the advocates of the Land Restoration Society. Their principles were contrary to the policy of Mr Parnell (Cheers) ... these gentlemen who talked of land restoration spoke of something that did not exist in any country under the sun, and which there was no prospect of putting into effect. [29]

The object of Biggar's scorn, the SLRL, was exactly the type of organisation with which Ferguson believed the Irish should work in harness. It had been warmly welcomed by Davitt on its inception the previous year, and had already attracted McGhee and McHugh as founder members, with other Scottish allies like Maxwell, Glasier and John Murdoch in its executive.[30] Drawing on the support of 'rentier' interests, such as small businessmen and shopkeepers, the League accepted the full canon of Georgite teachings.[31] Its object was, 'the restoration of the land to the people by the abolition of all private property in land, the appropriation of rent thereof for public purposes, and the relief of the people there by from all Imperial or local taxation' – or as Maxwell succinctly expressed it, 'emancipation of the land from bondage'.[32] In the year since its foundation it had been active in propaganda work, attracting over a thousand members, and was now resolved to put forward six candidates in urban constituencies containing significant Irish, Highland and working class representation.

These 'land and labour' or 'land restorationist' candidates have been traditionally assigned an honoured place in the genealogy of independent labour representation.[33] Yet, the Glasgow campaign in 1885, and the significance of Ferguson's involvement in it, are probably best understood on their own terms as the product of a volatile local situation. While he viewed the alliance between Irish nationalism and British democracy as an article of faith, the 1885 contest also gave him the opportunity to restate his pre-eminence among the Glasgow Irish and reach out to Scottish working class audiences.

Candidate selection had become an increasingly divisive issue in the city, as the shift to single member constituencies had forced the various stands of Scottish Liberalism into open competition.[34] Dismissing the SLRL as 'a section of Faddists', the elite caucus in Glasgow were particularly anxious to shut out ambitious young radicals like Maxwell, who wished to democratise party organisation in working men's constituencies and make it more responsive to popular feeling.[35] These machinations also had an impact on official Liberal policy. Like the 'moderate' Home Rulers of the 1870s, Whiggish Liberals resisted attempts to limit individual members' autonomy by means of an official party line. The result, as evident on Glasgow election platforms, was a varied and haphazard approach to the land question and the trade depression which, while well-meaning, was devoid of specific remedies, not to mention Ferguson's vaunted scientific principles.[36] In his lexicon of contempt this was Liberal 'shopboyism' at its worst, contrasting with the SLRL's rigorous attempts to apply the Single Tax solution to the problems of poor housing and unemployment in the city.[37]

Having fought originally to maintain Liberal party unity,

Maxwell and his colleagues realised that the cost would be renouncing their political goals.[38] While their refusal to accept dictation from commercial interests mirrored his own experiences of Glasgow Liberalism, Ferguson had to be judicious in his support. His current lack of an official position in the INLGB was an advantage, but with rumours circulating that Davitt intended to field twenty or thirty radical candidates in opposition to Parnell, he was open to charges of rebellion.[39] Accordingly, his endorsement of the SLRL candidates was carefully targeted in constituencies such as Bridgeton and Blackfriars where his influence would be most telling.[40] William Forsyth was one beneficiary, but when he wobbled over Irish Home Rule, it was Shaw Maxwell, who received Ferguson's most enthusiastic support.[41]

The fluent and dapper Maxwell was close to his ideal as a candidate. Brimming with conversation and political energy, his tile-hatted figure had cut an incongruous dash at Irish League meetings. He had been prominent in the 'Davitt Branch' episode, where his political courage had contrasted with Ferguson's own circumspection. At the launch of his campaign in June, Ferguson seized the moment to expound his own theories on the commercial crisis.[42]

Despite his boundless optimism that social problems could be solved by good sense, his analysis increasingly involved an industrial 'system' – with landlordism at its heart – which was impeding social progress. From the outset of the SLRL campaign, his focus was on the crisis in Scotland's integrated economy. Changes in the manufacture of steel and the run down of natural resources had begun to affect the pig iron sector, which in turn undermined the coal sector. Paralleling this industrial downturn, was an assault on Scottish farming by cheap overseas imports.[43] For Ferguson, these were seminal developments, invoking both the evils of feudal tenure and rights of labour. He addressed an enthusiastic audience of Blackfriars electors:

. . . the great question of the moment was 'How should
the people live?'At the corners of the streets of the city of
Glasgow in recent years, they were all more accustomed
to meet people standing idle and asking for food to enable
them to live . . . If they wanted trade to improve, they should
bear in mind that it would only improve through sensible
men grasping the real facts . . . [44]

In his own case, he had grasped the 'real facts' through a
lifetime of study. The concept he used to apply his ideas of land
reform and land tax to industrial Scotland was 'loaferage', in
other words the royalties extracted by landowners for mineral
rights in the vital pig-iron industry:

'Loaferage' was the right name to apply to a tax of that sort,
for the man who received 5s. a ton on the pig-iron was,
economically, a loafer – (laughter) . . . In Belgium, however,
the ton of pig-iron paid only a royalty of fivepence or
sixpence, and this tax, in Belgium, was rightly called 'royalty'
because it was paid to the State. Bearing in mind that the
English ton of iron paid 5s. of 'loaferage' as against fivepence
or sixpence paid in Belgium for 'royalty' to the State – and
went therefore for the good of the whole community – was
it possible that the iron trade in England should compete
successfully with the iron trade in Belgium? (Applause).[45]

The cost of these unearned increments was borne by the people.
Yet their ultimate destiny was very different:

He was prepared to prove when the nobles, and the
capitalists and the manufacturers had done a useful part
in the history of the civilisation of the country. But the time
had arrived when all these classes must realise that there
was a third and greater entity than all to be taken into
consideration – and that was the people. (Loud applause).
Labour had never received its fair share of the profits of

trade: it had never received a share of the profits in anything like equal proportion to the sacrifices that labour made (Cheers).[46]

In this scheme of historical development, his guide was Mill rather than Marx, but his stance seemed perfectly compatible with labour's political claims. Indeed, he urged working men to return men of their own class to parliament, helpfully setting before them the wholesome example of the Irish party's parliamentary fund to pay the expenses of members.[47]

This was a powerful opening salvo, but as election campaign waxed and waned during the autumn, he could not ignore the strength of support for Parnell's independent line.[48] By October, Ferguson re-asserted his Home Rule credentials by publishing a recent exchange of letters with the radical icon, Joseph Chamberlain – a tactic which also served to distinguish the SLRL candidates from the uncertain record of the parliamentary radicals on Ireland.[49] This was at some personal cost as he had previously placed great faith in Chamberlain and his 'manly programme', and had desperately sought to avoid his breach with the Irish party.[50] It was perhaps also an indication of growing pressure, that he now muted his claim in *The Land for the People* that he held 'humanity' above the national community. Instead, he insisted that 'duty to the Ireland of our fathers must ever stand before that of our adoption', qualifying this by a classic Ferguson fudge, that, 'the two duties are not antagonistic in our case'.[51]

In fact, he seems to have travelled hopefully with the SLRL candidates in the belief that his support would make Parnell's 'exception' in their case a reality. However, his fatal flaw was to overstate his current standing with the national leadership. Events quickly overtook him. After a particularly elusive speech in Edinburgh, it was clear that Gladstone would refuse to better Salisbury's equally vague sentiments on Irish constitutional demands.[52] On 21 November, six days before the Glasgow poll, Parnell's long-awaited manifesto to the Irish in Great Britain was delivered.[53] It was an angry document – 'a publicity puff for the gallery' in McGhee's view – which recommended the Irish to vote for Conservative candidates when these were facing Liberals and radicals.[54] This was reinforced by a personal appearance from the party's rising star, John Redmond who carried the uplifting message that in Glasgow: 'it was their duty to support the Conservatives – at least three of whom were Catholics'.[55]

There remained one last hope. In Blackfriars, the Conservative candidate was certainly not a Catholic, but the prominent Orangeman, W. C. Maughan.[56] Even worse, the likely beneficiary of Irish support for Maughan was the anti-Parnellite renegade, Mitchell Henry – an old adversary of Ferguson's – who had been driven from his seat in Galway and was now standing as a Liberal.[57] The HGB telegraphed the League Executive asking for an exemption in the Blackfriars case, but this met with a haughty denial.[58]

The 1885 election was ideally suited for psephological inquests. Liberals, including the despised Henry, were returned for all the Glasgow seats, but, as the *Herald* suggested, their dominance had been shaken, with the Conservatives receiving a windfall both from Liberal divisions on disestablishment and from the discipline of Irish electors.[59] Contemporaries found the impact of Ferguson's public campaigning more difficult to determine, especially as he sought to reach both Irish *and* Scots working men. In Bridgeton, Forsyth's intervention, by splitting the vote, almost cost the Liberals the seat, while Maxwell's greater popularity with the Irish may explain an even more impressive performance in Blackfriars.[60]

While this was the conviction of loyal HGB members, for McGhee, who had been intimately involved with the campaign, Maxwell's result was a disaster.[61] The obvious villains were Parnell and 'The Porker' [O'Connor] for refusing to grant an exemption, a step which, he believed, was motivated by personal malice against Davitt and particularly Ferguson. But, he was also unsparing of the latter's tactical naivety which he identified as the immediate cause of the Irish vote being so heavily thrown against Maxwell. His juggling of support for the SLRL candidates alongside public assurances that he would personally vote as Parnell directed, merely confused the Irish electorate. When the promised exemption was not granted, the voters lacked the will to resist the official mandate, but used Ferguson's statements to justify their rejection of an old friend of the Irish movement.

As these squabbles in the 'Home Rule Radical' camp revealed, there were major lessons to be learned from this turbid campaign. Some Glasgow activists, like Kiernan, were delighted that Parnell had refused to make any exceptions in Scotland.[62] Yet, in rejecting Ferguson and Davitt's sweeping democratic vision, they were far from short-sighted in their political behaviour. On the contrary, they operated in accordance with their own conception of Ireland's unfolding destiny, placing the restitution of national rights at heart of their hopes and aspirations. Accustomed to the grind of voter registration, these men were unwilling to have their efforts hijacked for candidates who, whatever their personal or doctrinal merits, might prove inimical to the strategy of Parnell. Their arguments, powerful in their simplicity, were to reoccur repeatedly during Ferguson's career.

Wordy warfare

The outcome of the 1885 election nationally had left the Liberals equally balanced by the combination of Conservatives and Parnellites. Despite the political opportunities this offered, the new year opened with Ferguson's colleagues in low spirits. Davitt confided to his diary that Parnell's 'stupid support of the Tories' had cost them Home Rule in the immediate future, since Gladstone now had insufficient power to deliver a parliament.[63]

The mood among the Glasgow branches was rather different. Claims that the Irish vote in the recent election had exceeded 18,000, coupled with a thriving organisational base, had boosted confidence.[64] By 1886, the INL in Glasgow had ten branches, with expansion also evident in surrounding burghs, such as Maryhill and Kinning Park.[65] The HGB, with an estimated 400 members, was the largest branch, while the other locally-based branches had an average roll of 156.[66]

Fault lines persisted nevertheless beneath this impressive edifice. Some of the newer branches had a precarious existence. The St Rollox branch, for example, founded in October 1885, found it difficult to sustain momentum and expired in less than two years.[67] Meanwhile, the paper membership figures of the more established branches were often hotly disputed – an alternative reckoning of the HGB's total compliment was only 175.[68] Branches, however, could turn out much larger numbers for individual demonstrations. The audience at a 'monster' anti-coercion meeting addressed by Ferguson in 1887 was estimated as 4000, whereas an open air rally addressed by a major visiting speaker like Davitt could attract 20,000.[69] These public displays indicated the potential pull of the Home Rule cause, but it is sobering to remember that the INLGB's actual membership in the mid-1880s drew on only a minority of the Glasgow Irish, a community which according the *Exile's* generous estimate in 1884, totalled over 100,000.[70] Nationalist politics were largely a male sphere, although the HGB did welcome female members and had an active ladies' section.[71] The movement also struggled to broaden its class base throughout the 1880s. By 1889, the indifference of 'the majority of the well-to-do classes was still a source of regret, one theory being that the 'better class' of migrants were reluctant to mix with the 'common class' of their countrymen in Scotland.[72] Indeed, some of his supporters attributed Ferguson's longevity in the movement to precisely this restricted social profile. As one HGB loyalist commented in 1886: 'They had plenty of carpenters, shoemakers, and tailors, who could work the branches in detail, but they had not a leader, and who was so fit to lead them as the man who had led them fifteen years ago.'[73]

An even more disturbing tendency was for activists to engage in internecine squabbles. Although for some 'wordy warfare' was the lifeblood of the branches, it could also have a corrosive on Irish political culture and forms a neglected cross-current in relations with other political forces in Scotland.[74] The failure of the INLGB executive to give attention to Scottish League matters was one source of tension, with a separate Scottish convention even mooted, but a more common flashpoint was the relationship between the HGB and the other Glasgow branches.[75] The 'Boss Branch', as Davitt termed it, was a proud and independent body, which gloried in the *Glasgow Observer's* label of 'cranks', if this meant freedom from that newspaper's cloying clericalism.[76] While its size meant that it could provide practical campaigning support for smaller branches, its tendency to claim a leadership role in electoral and propaganda work could appear as presumptuous and bullying. The charge was ironic, since the HGB's own major grievance concerned centralised control by the INLGB's London-based executive. Inevitably, issues of policy and personality became hopelessly tangled, with much of the struggle against the executive being carried out in the form of a vendetta between the HGB's Hugh Murphy and the League's Scottish Organiser Owen Kiernan.[77] Although Ferguson kept aloof from the routine work of the HGB, he could not help being drawn into these wrangles – to the detriment of his reputation as a political mediator.

This destructive potential was amply demonstrated by a bout of feuding in the spring of 1886. The intriguing parliamentary situation bequeathed by the general election results seemed about to bear fruit. The lines of communication between Gladstone and Parnell had opened up in the beginning of the year, and during February and March, drafts of a Home Rule Bill and a Land Purchase Bill began to appear. As 'the hour of victory' beckoned, the Glasgow Leaguers fell out over whether John Ferguson should chair the next St Patrick's day demonstration.[78]

The astonished *Observer* struggled to impose a sense of proportion, as the unfolding dispute revealed how contentious a figure Ferguson had become in migrant politics. Much to his chagrin, he had not been the organising committee's first choice as chairman and only accepted after a consultation with Davitt.[79] Already frozen out by leading parliamentarians during the League's recent convention in Glasgow, the INLGB executive now warned that Irish MPs would not attend if he presided. The ostensible charge was electoral indiscipline, but the suspicion persisted that it was actually his 'very extreme views' on the land question and the personal enmity of the League's president, O'Connor, which lay at the root of the executive's hostility.[80]

The HGB, whose delegates had originally sponsored his chairmanship, were forced back on the defensive, as the other Glasgow branches accused them of flaunting Ferguson in their continuing war against the executive. As the argument ranged backwards and forwards, his supporters argued with legalistic fervour that he had not personally violated Parnell's mandate, as he had voted as instructed in his own constituency. His detractors were equally inflamed, one delegate retorting that putting Davitt and Ferguson in the same boat was like comparing Mr Parnell to 'Nero' – a fraudulent black preacher, who had recently been touring Scotland.[81] As the issue became framed as a test of loyalty to Parnell's leadership, the HGB delegates slid narrowly, but inevitably, to defeat. Sensing the talismanic quality which now surrounded Ferguson, it was James Simpson of the Northern branch who put the opposition case most robustly:

> They heard a great deal about the independence of mind of individuals and of the Glasgow Irishmen . . . that had been the ruin of the Irish National movement since the day when the English first planted their foot on Irish soil . . . They had arrived at a crisis in the history of their countrymen when individuals must be prepared to make sacrifices for the good of the cause as a whole, and he would throw a dozen individuals aside – no matter how big they were or might have been, or how brilliant their talents – in order to uphold the cause as a whole.[82]

After weeks of public dispute, Ferguson's mortification was palpable as he rose to address the HGB at the inauguration of their expanded premises.[83] Simpson's views were part of the developing nationalist common-sense and at least open to reasoned refutation, but what his pride could not suffer was to hear his good name associated with that of a notorious swindler. Acknowledging that his audience comprised of a younger generation of nationalists who were probably hearing his voice for the first time, he was forced unusually to depart from his prepared lecture to make one his periodic offers to retire from nationalist politics.[84]

Home Rule at hand

Despite this gesture, he knew that this was hardly the time to withdraw. On 8 April, Gladstone revealed his Irish proposals to Parliament.[85] Irish peers and members would be withdrawn and a parliament established in Dublin to take control of internal Irish matters. To protect minority rights, a 'first order' would be established, with a £200 property franchise for election. The measure was coupled with an ambitious Irish Land Purchase bill, permitting the issue of £50 million of new 3 per cent stock to buy out landlords who were willing to sell.

Ferguson's panegyrics of his political hero reached new heights. Although he was eventually to offer a more developed critique of the Home Rule Bill, for the moment he brushed aside apparently minor reservations over the voting powers granted to peers and landlords to hail a 'great and glorious bill'.[86] While he claimed to believe only in either a 'fair federation' or a 'fair separation', like many Irishmen, he also sensed the symbolic significance of Gladstone's measure. At last, the principle of national self-determination for Ireland had been admitted by a British political party, and if the Bill was not a full restitution of her rights, it was at least a large instalment. More than this, it was a personal vindication after almost two decades of struggle. From the mid 1880s, his public pronouncements began to look backwards as much as forwards. In front of a capacity audience at the City Hall in April, he saluted a day of pride for workers in the cause:

> The whole sky was brightening with Irish prospects. Twenty years ago they raised the flag of constitutional agitation under the guidance of the great Isaac Butt. They raised that flag with trembling hand and almost despairing courage . . . tremblers and doubters were in their ranks – scoffers who asked 'What good?' . . . The odds against them were tremendous, but they fought, as he had often told them, for the principle. Those who fought on the side of truth were pretty certain of victory. Well, there they stood that day, and who doubted now the success of the national movement. And yes it was a terrible struggle. At times it tried men's souls. They had, however, lived down contumacy and misrepresentation; and today the purest-minded and noblest English statesman who had ever guided the destinies of England has espoused their cause (Loud cheers).[87]

As he attempted to rally support, it was becoming apparent Gladstone's policy departure had produced a crisis in Scottish politics.[88] Dissident Liberals, drawn heavily from mercantile and professional interests, were already using Glasgow as a base for mobilisation against Home Rule. The minds of the competing factions were concentrated by the prospect of a general election which would place the constitutional issue before the people. The constituency Liberal associations again became war zones, with unionists and Gladstonians struggling for control. During May, the nucleus of the Liberal Unionist organisation was being hastily drawn together.

Gladstone's proposals were finally defeated at their second reading, followed by a speedy dissolution of Parliament in June. For the Irish camp, electoral campaigning that summer brought unaccustomed unity.[89] There had been a range of opinions in the branches on Gladstone's scheme, but the response was generally

favourable.[90] Moreover, the secession of the Liberal right had
permitted the party's radical element more room for manoeuvre.
Now that Home Rule was wielded as a metaphor for the struggle
of ordinary citizens against the arrogance of entrenched power,
even Maxwell and his SLRL colleagues rallied with a manifesto
of Liberal support.[91] At first sight, the new alignment of forces
may have resembled Ferguson's idealised democratic alliance,
although more sanguine analysis was to reveal that a number of
prominent Liberals, like the Celtic enthusiast, Professor Blackie,
had at best a 'dilettante' interest in Irish Home Rule, prompted by
their admiration for Gladstone.[92]

As INLGB branches threw themselves into constituency work,
Ferguson, as an Irish Protestant, secured his own niche in the
Liberal campaign.[93] The maverick of the previous year was
welcomed back into the fold, his presence badly needed as the
Liberals attempted to defuse fears of abuses of power by a ruling
Catholic majority. At the eve of poll demonstration on Glasgow
Green, organised by the National Liberal Federation of Scotland,
he was joined by Bowman of the IPHRA and the veteran Protestant
Home Ruler, J. G. Swift McNeil. Like them, he was convinced that
constitutional change could be sweetened for Ulster Protestant
farmers by a solid measure of land reform. Happily brushing
aside Protestant fears, he joked that his old friend McNeil was not
afraid that Catholics would cut his throat. With a shaky grasp of
demographic and sectarian realities, he reasoned:

> The 150,000 Protestants in Belgium would laugh if they were
> told that they suffered persecution at the hands of their four
> million Catholic fellow subjects. It was only in Ireland
> where the Protestants were in a majority that they were
> afraid of religious persecution. Where the Protestants were
> in a minority they had no fear (Cheers). The cause of Home
> Rule was in the ascendant . . . the principles of Michael
> Davitt had prevailed, and one touch of nature had made the
> whole world kin.[94]

This faith in brotherhood as a solvent of bigotry proved badly misplaced. His fellow Protestants on the platform were already becoming political curiosities with their organisation, the IPHRA, representing at best a fragmented and localised challenge to the might of the Unionist propaganda machine.[95] Ferguson was soon given a personal opportunity to reflect on this only weeks after his light-hearted remarks at the Liberal rally. Visiting Belfast in July, he toured the Falls and Shankhill Road areas in the company of Bowman. He found himself the thick of some of the worst sectarian riots ever witnessed in the city, with some fifty deaths and many injuries.[96] In future, he invoked, 'the red furnace of Ulster nationalist and religious bigotry', with rather more respect.[97]

Back in Scotland, the Home Rule crisis had administered a further check to the Liberal's easy dominance of political life. The new Liberal Unionist grouping had achieved success in nine out of the thirty western constituencies which they had contested. In Glasgow, where Gladstonians retained only four seats, the Conservatives had also established an unexpected bridgehead. The strength of opposition to Home Rule probably reflected enduring Scottish attitudes the Irish in their midst, as much as economic self-interest and fears of constitutional novelty.[98] Yet the Glasgow Leaguers were far from downhearted. The fate of the bill had been sealed as soon the scale of the Whig and Chamberlainite revolt had become apparent from late April, but Irish hopes were not to this single piece of legislation. As Ferguson explained, it was now impossible for any future government to ignore Irish Home Rule. It was merely a matter of the kind of Home Rule which was to be conceded – whether it was to be given by the Tories, which he doubted, or by the Whigs, but certainly, 'by a radical government headed by an advanced radical of some kind'.[99]

Some contemporaries later reflected on the 1886 defeat as 'a blessing in disguise' to their organisational work, encouraging more diligent attention to the building up membership.[100] Only

the over-enthusiastic attempts of the HGB to seize a coordinating
role in securing the Irish vote threatened to disturb the new
harmony.[101] With the destiny of the nation close to fulfilment,
the Glasgow Irish from 1886 onwards also turned to writing the
heroic narrative of their movement. In personal reminiscences
and histories of the individual branches, these constitutional
nationalists were confident enough to identify themselves with
the earlier exploits of the physical force men in the city.[102]

His personal goals achingly close to achievement, Ferguson
embedded the motif of 'twenty years of service to the cause' into
his mature public image. Interviewed by the *Glasgow Observer*
in October 1886, he reviewed his career in proud, philosophical
mood and considered how the movement might maintain the
constitutionalist momentum with their Liberal allies out of
office.

> Men who have grasped the root principle of a social problem
> see the future with prophetic eye. They see, 'God within the
> shadow, keeping watch above his own' . . . The men of mere
> expedient grow jealous of the men of principle, who they
> denounce as mere theorists. Strife arises thus between two
> classes of men, both of whom wish to do good.[103]

His self-belief was tempered by regret as he realised he was
no longer 'in any position in the National League to know its
power or plans'. This exclusion was all the more poignant, as
the movement was currently struggling to resurrect the spirit
of agrarian radicalism by replaying the heroic years of 1879–82
in the shape of the Dillon and O'Brien 'Plan of Campaign'.[104]
Ferguson offered qualified support for this familiar notion of a
tenants' combination, if the ground could be adequately laid to
resist impossible rent, but believed that the real axis of struggle
had moved beyond the Irish countryside. The first step, he argued,
was to take the landlords in the rear by 'rousing the British
democracy on the side of fair play'.[105] This tactic was only one

aspect of his prescription for the role of Irish issues in progressive politics. He returned to his concept of a division of labour within the nationalist movement with Parnell as 'the Irish Leader' and Davitt, 'the Irish Reformer'. For all the squalls of the early 1880s, it was Parnell who continued to fascinate him, recognising the 'personal charm about the man'.[106] If only this magnetism could be combined with his own scientific approach to social questions, Parnell would at last repay his early confidence in him and become a great democratic leader.

> He would be a power in Britain, second to Gladstone alone. He had two or three men in the Party who could use a British platform to Ireland's advantage – 'first rate' – and perhaps half a dozen most effectively . . . I admit other subjects other than '82, '98 and '48 would have to be talked about. Nor would Waterloo or Bannockburn be much better. How much the British workman with 10/- a week could be raised to 25/-, and how capital could obtain profits would be their required subjects. *Economics* and not history are now required – the common interests of the industrial classes, British and Irish, against ignorant talk of 'Protection'. These are 'social lines', but they are the lines on which victory is within Mr Parnell's grasp. I admit that it is easier to talk sentiment, and it is much easier to stand 'heckling' after the talk by avoiding the big question which go down to the root of society, but the bottom question must be fought and faced by those who would win a British audience.[107]

For the first time in over four years, Ferguson seemed in sympathy with the leadership of the nationalist movement. Bringing Home Rule to the centre stage of British politics they acknowledged as only part of task, the next step was to win over the British electorate. In practice, this meant consolidating the ad hoc cooperation between nationalist and Liberals. This strategy was evident during John Redmond's tour of Scotland in November 1886, when his platforms attracted local party notables with ease.[108] Ferguson too embraced the work. With a turn of the political kaleidoscope, another initiative which he had piloted – and which had originally earned him official censure – had now become party policy. If anything, he was at first over-zealous, balancing a visit to the Young Ireland Society, the redoubt of extreme nationalists in the city, with an effusive address to the former Irish Viceroy, Lord Aberdeen.[109]

The year ended for Ferguson as it had begun, with a messy dispute raging about his ears. Criticism of the Aberdeen ceremony indicated the immediate sensitivities which surrounded 'the Union of Hearts'. [110] A more absorbing question was whether the nationalists' new political partners could be persuaded to deliver, not only on Irish constitutional demands, but also on his own radical agenda of economic and social reform. Over the next few years, Ferguson was to discover that by cementing links with the Liberals, the Irish party had actually reduced his freedom of action.

Notes

1   Ferguson, *Taxation*, p. 2.

2   J. McCaffrey, *Scotland in the Nineteenth Century* (London, 1998), p. 73; Fraser, *Popular Politics*, pp.114–5.

3   *Glasgow Observer*, 14 Apr. 1888.

4   *Ibid.*, 18 Apr. 1885.

5   *Ibid.*, 3 October, 1885.

6   Bowman, *People's Champion*, pp. 108–9.

7   *Glasgow Herald*, 13 Aug. 1887.

8   TCD, Davitt MSS 9328/180/13, M. Davitt to R. McGhee, 12 Mar. 1884.

9   For Murphy see, *Glasgow Star*, 29 Sept. 1903 and Ferguson's obituary of him: 28 Oct. 1903. McGhee and McHugh, see *Dictionary of Labour Biography*, pp. 152–155, 156–59. Maxwell: *Bailie*, 7 Oct. 1885; *The Councillor*, 22 Jan. 1898; W. M. Haddow,

Socialism in Scotland. Its Rise and Progress (Glasgow, nd.), p. 10. Glasier: L. Thompson, *The Enthusiasts* (London, 1971); J. B. Glasier, *On the Road to Liberty: Poetry and Ballad* (Manchester, 1920). W. M. Haddow, *My Seventy Years* (Glasgow, 1943), pp. 167–70.

10 A feature which drew comment from his obituarists. See, for example, *Kirkintilloch Herald*, 2 May 1906.

11 R. McGhee to M. Davitt, 14 Dec. 1885. Murphy was a cabinet maker and Glasier an architectural draftsman.

12 University of Liverpool Library (ULL), J. B. Glasier Papers, Diary GP 2/1/1, 24 Dec. 1879.

13 *Glasgow Star*, 26 Mar. 1904.

14 *Glasgow Observer*, 8 Oct. 1887.

15 *Ibid.*, 13 Oct. 1889.

16 *Ibid.*, 30 Mar. 1889, 3 Sept. 1887. Beatrice Webb was scathing in her judgement of the Kropotkin: '. . . a former Chamberlain to the Czar of all the Russias, now a poverty-striken journalist picking up a living at journalism': N. and J. Mackenzie (eds.), *The Diary of Beatrice Webb* (London, 1982) vol. 1, p. 327. For the background on Irish and Indian nationalist links see, R. Visram, *Ayahs, Lascars and Princes* (London, 1986), pp. 76–8.

17 Thompson, *Enthusiasts*, p. 33.

18 *Glasgow Observer*, 8 Aug. 1885; 21 Jan., 4 Feb 1888.

19 *On the Read to Liberty*, p. 36.

20 *Bridgeton Advertiser and Single Tax Review*, 6 Sept. 1890.

21 *Land and Liberty*, Nov. 1922.

22 In McGhee's case, the revelation of *Progress and Poverty* supplanted his earlier adherence to the SDF. After organising the Knights of Labor, from 1889 he played a major role, along with McHugh, in the development of the National Union of Dock Labourers. He later carried his land taxation struggle

into parliament as an 'advanced nationalist'. McHugh was elected president of the American Longshoreman's Union in 1896, but returned returned to his missionary work in Britain on behalf of the Georgite movement: *Glasgow Herald.*, 21 Mar. 1882. E. Taplin, 'Irish Leaders and Liverpool Dockers: Richard McGhee and Edward McHugh', *Northwest Labour History Society Bulletin*, vol. 9, 1983–4, pp. 36–44. For Glasier's views on George see, GP/2/1/5, Diary 30 Oct. 1897.

23 Mavor, *My Windows*, pp. 174–5.

24 *Land and Liberty*, Nov. 1922.

25 J. B. Glasier, *William Morris and the Earliest Days of the Socialist Movement* (London, 1921).

26 The new 'Lenzie Academy' was inaugurated in September 1886. The public protest he orchestrated over the right of way issue resulted in a new construction which he reported was known locally as 'John Ferguson's Bridge'. For the school campaign see, *Glasgow Herald*, 19–20 Mar. 1885; D. Martin, *The Story of Lenzie* (Strathkelvin, 1989), p. 31. For the Waterside rights of way case: *North British Daily Mail*, 2, 3, 6, 8 Jul. 1885. *Glasgow Echo*, 1 Sept. 1894.; Martin, *Lenzie*, p. 49.

27 Davitt, *Fall of Feudalism*, p. 477; Lyons, *Parnell*, pp. 273–9.

28 *Ibid.*, 16 Apr. 1885.

29 *Ibid.*, 30 May 1885.

30 TCD, Davitt MSS 9328, 180/11, M. Davitt to R. McGhee. He gave his full backing to such a body, 'to be run by Scots, of course'. For useful background see, Fraser, *Popular Politics*, pp. 98–106. Frame, 'America and the Scottish Left', pp. 97–8.

31 McCaffrey, 'Political Reactions', p. 140.

32 *Christian Socialist*, June 1885; *Glasgow Observer*, 8 July 1885. Ironically, one of Maxwell's first recorded public forays in Irish politics had been to defend Biggar who had been

roughly handled on a visit to the Glasgow Stock Exchange: *Glasgow Herald*, 13 Jun. 1881.

33 G. D. H. Cole, *British Working Class Politics 1832–1914* (London, 1941), p. 100.

34 Hutchison, *Political History*, 156–8; McCaffrey, *Scotland*, p. 74.

35 *Glasgow Herald*, 8 Jul., 27 Nov. 1885.

36 See, *Ibid.*, 7 Jul. 1885.

37 *Ibid.* 22 Aug., 24 Oct. 1885.

38 *Glasgow Observer*, 21 Nov. 1885.

39 *Ibid.*, 22 August 1885.

40 Bridgeton had 13.9 per cent Irish born in 1881, Blackfriars had 13.7 per cent : McCaffrey, 'Political Reactions', p. 324.

41 *Glasgow Observer*, 29 Aug. 1885; *Glasgow Herald*, 22 Aug. 1885.

42 *Glasgow Observer*, 27 Jun. 1885; *Glasgow Herald*, 25 Jun. 1885.

43 McCaffrey, *Scotland*, p.78.

44 *Glasgow Observer*, 27 Jun. 1885.

45 *Ibid.*

46 *Ibid.*

47 *Ibid.*

48 *Ibid.*, 22 Aug, 10 Nov. 1885.

49 See for example, *Ibid.*, 25 May 1885; John Redmond's comments, *Ibid.* , 26 Nov. 1885. For the background of Chamberlain's alienation from the Irish party see, *Nation*, 27 Jun. 1885; Galvin, *Chamberlain*, vol. 2, pp. 13–27.

50 University of Birmingham Library, Joseph Chamberlain Papers JC8/63G/2, J. Ferguson to J. Chamberlain, 29, 30 Jun. He had offered to arrange a meeting with Davitt as

Chamberlain wished to talk to an Irish representative in the wake of an attack from Parnell's *United Ireland*.

51 *Ibid.*, 3 Oct. 1885.

52 K. O'Shea, *Charles Stuart Parnell* (London, 1914), vol. 2, p. 25; *North British Daily Mail*, 10 Nov. 1885.

53 *United Ireland*, 28 Nov. 1885. See also, Brady, *O'Connor*, pp. 77–9.

54 *Glasgow Herald*, 26 Nov. 1885; TCD Davitt MSS 9346/470, R. McGhee to M. Davitt, 14 Dec. 1885.

55 *Ibid.*, 28 Nov. 1885.

56 He placed convent inspection at the heart of his election address: *Glasgow News*, 28 Nov. 1885. For Maughan, see, McFarland, *Protestants First*, pp. 230

57 For Henry ('Stitchwell Harry') see, *Clydeside Cameos*, Second Series, 16 Jul. 1886; J. Denvir, *The Irish in Britain* (London, 1894), pp. 269–71.

58 *Glasgow Observer*, 28 Nov. 1885.

59 In Camlachie, the INLGB branch boasted that 1800 Irishmen had turned out for the Tory *Glasgow Herald*, 28 Nov. 1885; *Glasgow Observer*, 5 Dec. 1885.

60 Maxwell polled 1156 votes, one third of the strength of either of the traditional parties.

61 *Irish World*, 5 Nov. 1885; Davitt MSS R. McGhee to M. Davitt 14 Dec. 1885.

62 *Glasgow Observer*, 12 Dec. 1885.

63 TCD, Davitt MSS 9545, Diary 1 Jan. 1886.

64 *Glasgow Observer*, 12 Dec. 1885. Even Davitt who had sent Maxwell an eve of poll telegram of support was not spared.

65 *Ibid.*, 13 Nov. 1886; 11 Dec. for formation of Kinning Park and Plantantion Branch

66 *Ibid.* According to Kiernan's balance sheet, the membership stood at: Anderson 'Sexton' (140), Bridgeton (61), Tradeston 'John Dillon' (230), 'Legislative Independence' (160), 'Glasgow' (200), Northern (140), Parkhead 'Archbishop Walsh' (160), 'William O'Brien' (160). The 'Exile' Branch of Tollcross was only recently established.

67 *Ibid.*, 30 Apr. 1887.

68 *Ibid.*

69 *Ibid.*, 23 Apr. 1887, 14 Jul. 1888.

70 *Exile* , 30 Aug. 1884. It believed a fifth of the City's population were 'of Irish descent'. The Irish born population of the City in the 1881 Census was estimated at 62, 555: Denvir, *Irish in Britian*, p. 384.

71 *Glasgow Observer*, 11 Feb. 1882; see also, *Ibid.*, 17 Mar. for the Shamrock Ladies' Branch.

72 *Glasgow Observer*, 9 Nov. 1889. When they did join, 'gentlemen of the "masher" type', sometimes preferred to set up more exclusive branches, such as the Scottish Metropolitan: *Ibid.*, 10 Apr. 1886.

73 *Ibid.*, 13 Mar. 1886.

74 *Ibid.*, 9 Nov. 1889.

75 *Ibid.*, 19 Oct. 1889.

76 *Ibid.*, 24 Aug. 1889.

77 Kiernan's trade as a tailor gave Murphy the opportunity to dismiss him as 'a knight of the thimble and the goose': *Ibid.*, 11 Dec. 1886. See also, 18 Jul., 1 Aug., 1885 for his expulsion from the HGB, and 6 Jun, 7 Nov. 1885 for copious coverage.

78 *Ibid.,* 13 Mar. 1886.

79 *Ibid.,* 20 Feb. 1886: Father Patrick of Townhead had declined.

80 *Ibid.,* 13 Mar. 1886. From the letter of 21 Mar. 1886, reproduced in Kettle's, *Material for Victory,* pp. 83–4, it would seem that Parnell had not been aware of the executive's decision and found out too late to over-rule it.

81 *Glasgow Herald,* 1 Mar. 1886.

82 *Ibid.,* 13 Mar. 1886.

83 Expansion had required them to seek additional space in the Harmonic Association Rooms in Watson Street, near Trongate. The new hall had a capacity of 700 and included a reading room: *Ibid.*

84 He did not chair the St Patrick's demonstration, but, armed with one of Davitt's telegrams of support, he responded to calls from the floor with 'a brief, but forcible and elegant speech': *Ibid.,* 20 Mar. 1886.

85 *North British Daily Mail,* 9, 19 Apr 1886.

86 *Glasgow Herald,* 21 Apr. 1886.

87 *Ibid.*

88 J. F. McCaffrey, 'The Origins of Liberal Unionism in the West of Scotland', *Scottish Historical Review,* L (1971), pp. 47–71; C. M. M. Macdonald, *The Radical Thread* (E. Linton, 2000). See also G. Walker and D. Officer, 'Scottish Unionism and the Ulster question', in C. M. M.   Macdonald (ed.), *Unionist Scotland* (Edinburgh, 1998), pp. 13–26.

89 *Glasgow Observer,* 31 Jul., 21 Aug., 11 Sept. 1886.

90 *Ibid.,* 17 Apr. 1886.

91 *North British Daily Mail,* 17 Jun. 1886.

92 This was his biographer's estimation: Duncan, *Life,* pp. 81–

96. Note also his criticism of Irish methods to Glasier: ULL, J. B. Glasier Papers, GP1/1/21 [1886].

93 See, for example, *North British Daily Mail*, 15, 21, 23, 28, 29 Jun. 1886.

94 *Glasgow Observer*, 10 Jul. 1886.

95 P. J. O. McCann 'The Protestant Home Rule Movement, 1885–95' (University College Dublin M.A. Thesis, 1972), p.144.

96 *Report from the Select Committee on Municipal Regulation (Constabulary etc.) (Belfast) Bill, August, 1887*, p. 90. For riots see, *Northern Star*, 14–17, 20–24 July.

97 *Glasgow Observer*, 20 Apr. 1887.

98 McCaffrey, *Scotland*, pp. 76–7.

99 *Glasgow Herald*, 21 Apr. 1886.

100 *Glasgow Observer* 2 Nov. 1889; see also Denvir, *Life Story*, p. 231–2.

101 *Ibid.*, 4 Jul. 1886.

102 This was particularly true of the Northern branch which had actually been founded in 1884 to organise the Irish vote at local elections, but boasted that their area had been a stronghold of Irish sentiment for over thirty years: *Ibid.*, 18 Oct. 1887. For other 'historical' accounts see: *ibid.*, 12–19 Oct, 1889.

103 *Ibid.*, 2 Oct. 1886.

104 *United Ireland*, 23 Oct. 1886; see also Lyons, *Parnell*, pp. 356–68; S. Warwick-Haller, *William O'Brien and the Irish Land War* (Dublin, 1990). pp. 81–138.

105 *Glasgow Observer* 2 Oct. 1886; see also his letter in similar terms to *Irish World*, 16 Oct. 1886.

106 *Glasgow Observer,* 2 Oct. 1886.

107 *Ibid.*

108 *Ibid.,* 27 Nov. 1886.

109 *Ibid.,* 4 Dec. 1886.

110 When they heard that HGB members had the temerity to stand with heads uncovered to 'Saxon airs' at this event, the rival Glasgow branches condemned it as a political burlesque: *Ibid.* 11 Dec. 1886.

CHAPTER NINE

Forward with Labour?

The 'yearning eighties', as Home Rulers termed them, were years of open-ended political change on which Ferguson sought impose his own evolving vision. The old obsession of supplanting 'clansman nationalism' with 'humanitarian nationalism' persisted, but, after his own idiosyncratic fashion, he also began to turn a wary gaze towards continental socialism. In its doctrines he found much that, 'the best thinkers in Europe will defend, and . . . much that whose who believe in the teachings of Christ cannot deny'.[1] The 'bourgeoisie' and 'proletariat' now became interwoven with 'the democracy', in his rhetorical tapestry. Yet this a linguistic shift rather than an ideological conversion. Urban and rural poverty remained for him the product of rising land values, rather that an inimical conflict between capital and labour. The Single Tax, by removing the need for further government involvement in the economy, was the true policy which 'went to the root'.[2]

Similarly, in practical politics he remained a vocal, if vacillating, champion of working class representation. Towards the end of the decade, he deepened his engagement with the emerging forces of labour, while remaining personally enmeshed in the organisation and morality of Liberalism. Although his generous vision stood in favourable contrast to the labour movement's exclusive and disputative streak, the relationship was to be a complex one. Labour's democratic value system and political idealism were largely in tune with his own, but the proud proprietor of 'Benburb' found greater difficulty identifying with the symbolic content of a tradition which in Scotland drew on Covenanting history and the Presbyterian ethos. There was also a gap in experience between Ferguson and some of his new colleagues on the left. Whereas he had studied and analysed the industrial system, men like

Keir Hardie and Robert Smillie had experienced its brutality and precariousness at first hand. Born of working class parents in Belfast, Smillie had moved to Lanarkshire and become a mine worker while still in his teens. Here, he recalled:

> ... the spectacle, ever present before my eyes, of certain types of employers of labour grinding their workers to the extreme limit of existence, and feeling no compunction in so doing, whilst they themselves lived in luxury, stirred my compassion for the one and my fierce resentment against the other. Out of such a combination anything may come. It made me a Labour leader.[3]

Ferguson's own radical identity was to prove more subtly layered, if no less passionately expressed.

A plan of campaign

After three visits in the course of 1887, a weary Michael Davitt felt he had to draw the line on addressing Glasgow meetings.[4] His ubiquity was the product of Ferguson's own version of the 'Plan of Campaign' – an intense burst of energy which linked Highland land agitation with opposition to the Unionist government's coercion policy in Ireland. Convinced that the battle for Irish legislative independence must still be waged in Scotland, Ferguson placed the crofting counties in the forefront of the struggle. Here, even the passage of the Crofters Act in June 1886 had not curtailed the pattern of rent strikes, land raids and political protest.[5]

His strategy to capitalise on these developments had two main components. First, he sought to broaden the basis of the Highland struggle by appealing for funds to 'the Irish, Scottish and German reformers of America'. Their contributions, he argued, would transform the Crofter's Aid Committee, which the Glasgow Leaguers had originally formed as a support organisation for land protesters, into an electoral force which could sweep

Scotland clear of Unionist MPs.[6] This was accompanied by a local campaign of public meetings, highlighting the linkage between Scottish and Irish issues. At the first of these in March, Ferguson launched another swashbuckling protege, Robert Bontine Cunninghame Graham MP, whom he anointed as 'the Parnell of Scotland'.[7] Old friends, such as Bradlaugh and Davitt, were also called into action that busy spring and summer.[8] The latter's progress on a major Highland tour during May sent his supporters into transports of pan-Celtic delight, as they contemplated 'the bond between shamrock and heather'.[9] Meanwhile, Ferguson, the businessman, had already his anticipated his success by reissuing his biography as a Cameron & Ferguson edition: 'a marvel of cheapness, with the crisp, racy flavour of your true American booklet'.[10]

Although he had with flirted independent candidatures in his transatlantic fundraising appeal, any doubts over unfolding cooperation with the Liberal Party were initially expressed privately. Leading figures, such as Bailie John Burt, were well represented on INLGB platforms during his campaign, and obediently voiced their contempt for Unionist policy in Ireland.[11] Meanwhile, he remained personally active in the party, representing Glasgow Central and Lenzie and Auchinloch at the Scottish Liberal Association's General Council in 1887 and 1888.[12]

The 'Union of Hearts' faced its first electoral test in Scotland with the Bridgeton by-election in July 1887. Given the impressive base which SLRL had recently laid down in the constituency and the strong presence of Irish electors, a 'Home Rule Radical' candidate seemed a reasonable prospect.[13] In the event, Gladstone selected the distinguished Whig, Sir George Trevelyan, who had recently held the new post of Secretary of State for Scotland in Gladstone's cabinet, but whose pronouncements on Home Rule were so ambivalent that some observers concluded that he remained at heart Liberal Unionist.[14] Determined to make the by-election 'a Scottish protest against coercion', Ferguson had little option but to close ranks and swing the campaigning resources of the HGB behind the Gladstonian candidate.[15]

As he listened in some discomfort to Trevelyan's stumbling, he began to refine and balance his own views on Home Rule and the Liberal Party. He now admitted that a weakness of Gladstone's original Home Rule scheme had been coupling the 1886 Bill with land purchase, a measure which seemed designed to benefit the southern landlord minority, rather than the mass of Irish tenants. Parnell's collusion here was further indication of the subordination of agrarianism to the national question.[16] Its other flaw been the inability to address the 'West Lothian Question' of Ferguson's day – how was a post-devolution Ireland to be represented at Westminster? Isaac Butt's classic exposition of federalism, alongside contemporary European and American examples, provided him with the inspiration to cut this Gordian knot. Meanwhile, the growing agitation around Scottish Rights which had led to establishment of Charles Waddie's Scottish Home Rule Association (SHRA) in 1886 also suggested that a fundamental measure of constitutional change in Britain was not unrealistic.[17] The way ahead was clear:

> Give England, Scotland, Ireland and Wales national Parliaments for purely 'national' purposes. Call into existence an Imperial Parliament for purely 'Imperial' purposes. Let each of the four nations have fifty seats in that Imperial Parliament and thus, as in the United States, you will combine national (or State) independence, with imperial (or Federal) strength and unity. This is the only final settlement of the question.[18]

As party warfare became more embittered, he was to return repeatedly to these simple precepts. His faith in federalism was unshakeable and he remained convinced that if only Gladstone would educate the country in the *principles* implicit in Home Rule, truth would conquer.[19]

If his optimism was rekindled on Bridgeton platforms, the

contest also forced him to question whether close cooperation between Home Rulers and the Liberal Party on the new Parnellite model could realistically achieve his dream. The INLGB's executive were already proclaiming that the Liberals' adoption of a Home Rule policy had ushered in 'an entirely new phase' of work in Britain, where the emphasis would now be on registering Irish voters and educating English ones. Branches were to place themselves in communication with Liberal Associations. Public meetings were held under Liberal auspices, rather than being exclusively composed of Irish nationalists. Even St Patrick's Day was to become a moveable feast to allow MPs to be present at demonstrations.[20]

Much of this was familiar to Ferguson, but he became one of the first of the 'left' of the Irish party to voice public doubts over the new strategy, grasping that without Gladstone's party being itself transformed, unconditional fusion was far from the democratic alliance which he and Davitt had pioneered.[21] Reminding his Irish audience of the maturity of their own organisation in Glasgow, he advised:

> You should act with the Liberal party as loyal allies, but not in any sense as their inferiors. (Cheers.) Your organisation is far better than theirs, your mode of action more prompt and decisive. The Liberal organisation must recognise in you a friendly equal, and concede to you in this and in future contests a position of perfect equality. Not until the Irish Parliament opens in Dublin can we afford to loose our identity in the Liberal organisation. (Cheers.) [22]

It was not only Home Rule demands that he feared trusting to Liberal goodwill. The implication of the INLGB's exclusive concentration on Home Rule implied that social issues might be left in Liberal hands. If the new 'understanding' meant that Scottish seats were to become the refuge of Whiggish carpetbaggers, what would be the fate of progressive social legislation? In August 1887, he made his clearest demand that the Liberal establishment recognise the claims of working class candidates in working class constituencies, arguing that, 'Labour is demanding certain social reforms which none but labour representatives can properly articulate'.[23] Assailed from all sides that Gladstone's nominee in Bridgeton had been a pig in a Unionist poke, Ferguson was blunt in claiming his due:

> Social reformers have displayed their loyalty to Mr Gladstone, and they not unreasonably expect his sympathy in their efforts to return a few men of their ideas to parliament. All effort will be made at the next general election both in the counties. In Glasgow one or two seats can be fairly claimed . . . I hope when a 'Land for the People' or an 'abolition of mining royalties' candidate shall be put forward, Sir George [Trevelyan] will remember how the Home Government Branch of the Irish National League (Michael Davitt's own) and the Scottish Land Restoration Society worked for him . . . We shall ask him to display his liberality by throwing his influence upon the side of the labour candidates who will shortly appear for two or three Scottish constituencies.[24]

He did not have long to wait until he could put the latest 'Benburb Manifesto' into action. In March 1888 the seat of Mid-Lanark fell vacant and almost immediately Keir Hardie, the Ayrshire miner's organiser, pressed his case with the local Liberal Association to stand as a 'Radical of a somewhat advanced type'.[25]

'Fair play' in Mid-Lanark

It is through his participation in the Mid-Lanark by-election that Ferguson generally enters Scottish labour history. The contest itself has, of course, generated a voluminous literature, rather out of proportion to the significance it was accorded by contemporaries. Much of the debate centres on the extent to which the contest marks a 'turning point' in Labour politics, or whether it should be located within the evolving tradition of Scottish Radicalism – or indeed as the outgrowth of Hardie's trade union experiences.[26] In Ferguson's case, the accent is clearly on continuity. From as early as 1872, when he had persuaded Biggar to contest Londonderry, he had used by-elections both to test and 'educate' popular opinion. Mid-Lanark also fitted the thrust of his more recent political activity in Scotland, which had aimed at turning the Liberal flank and replacing caucus dictation with a democratic mandate for social reform. This attention-grabbing strategy seemed all the more promising as the 'Liberal ethos' had itself become fragmented in the wake of the 1886 Home Rule crisis.

Ferguson had already been extending his sphere of operations beyond Glasgow during the late 1880s.[27] However, in the case of Mid-Lanark, the constituency held specific attractions. The area contained not only an estimated 1200 Irish voters, but also a strong mining presence, a combination which had already attracted the attention of the SLRL in 1885.[28] Taxation of mineral royalties was another element in Ferguson's radical platform, encouraging him to bracket the miners along with Highland crofters and lowland farmers as victims of 'loaferage'.[29] Particularly encouraging was the knowledge that a delegation from the Scottish Miners' Federation, led by Hardie, had already lobbied Parnell in early 1887, seeking support in their struggle to limit the working day.[30]

He was determined that Hardie should become the official Liberal representative. Mainstream Liberals, he chided, should recognise that this candidature was necessary for social peace:

Let's have 'fair play' in this effort of Labour in Scotland to obtain representation. No need for bad temper. Capital and labour need friends in these troubled times to bring them together. They are certain to unite if the 'bourgeoisie' do not irritate the 'proletariat' by opposing their reasonable request for representation in the People's House.[31]

Ferguson was, of course, only one of the high-profile enthusiasts drafted into his campaign. C. A. V. Conybeare, the Cornish radical MP; H. H. Champion, editor of the *Labour Elector*, and T. R. Threlfall, Secretary of the Labour Electoral Association, all bustled around the relatively inexperienced candidate offering advice on tactics and campaign finance. His trade union background and advanced reputation also attracted support from the Durham miners, the London branch of the SHRA, and the HLLRA. In 'the father of the Irish movement in Scotland', however, he had acquired a shrewd backer, raised in the hard school of Irish electoral politics. The danger was, however, that the idealistic Hardie might become ensnared by Ferguson's enthusiasm for brokering honourable and workable compromises.

The negative implications of Ferguson's advocacy were far from obvious at the 'great Irish and Radical Demonstration', which he had organised in Glasgow City Hall for 19 March. He had promised that Hardie would have 'names of power' behind him, and invited him to share the platform with Michael Davitt and Cunninghame Graham.[32] His own contribution featured a peculiarly heavy-handed grafting of the nationalist and radical traditions, portraying St Patrick as 'the great Utilitarian of his day'. Hardie himself was permitted a brief address.[33]

The City Hall meeting was one of the few the high points of the Mid-Lanark campaign. Ferguson was convinced that such demonstrations of popular will against 'opulent gentility', when buttressed with his own reasoned arguments, and by Hardie's absolute determination to stand, would secure a labour nomination. His next mollifying tactic was to float the idea of a local postcard ballot from which Liberal constituents could choose from a range of candidates.[34] The local Liberal Association remained unconvinced. After weeks of bickering and brokering, they selected the Welsh barrister, J. Wynford Philipps as their candidate.[35]

Almost at once Ferguson realised that Hardie's decision to battle on as an independent 'Labour and Home Rule' candidate in the face of the Liberal machine was hopeless. Richard McGhee who had also been energetically campaigning for Hardie informed him that even 300 votes would be difficult.[36] His concerns were confirmed by Davitt, who had lobbied in Hardie's favour with Parnell and Francis Schnadhorst, Secretary of the National Liberal Association. 'Party interests' meant neither were enthusiastic. Parnell calculated that while opposing a labour candidate *might* loose him a future general election, supporting one certainly would – by stampeding timid Gladstonians. In the the shorter term, Schnadhorst believed that adopting Hardie as an official Liberal would be enough to let in a pro-coercion Conservative.[37]

Ferguson squirmed. On 11 April, he confided to Cunninghame Graham that he had been seeking 'a way out of the fix with credit'. Whereas Davitt's solution favoured a dramatic *status quo ante,* with the former Mid-Lanark MP being asked to return to the seat, his own escape route involved backstairs intrigue with the new Liberal candidate. He met with Philipps and persuaded him to make 'a friendly speech' which would give Hardie grounds for withdrawing. He would intimate that, if Labour worked through Liberal Association to win backing for Hardie at the next election, he would retire in his favour and support him; till that time he would pledge himself to support both the miners' demands and the principle of labour representation.[38]

Rumours of this scheming were quick to leak out, but Hardie held fast – ironically clinging to Ferguson's 'plebiscite' as the only offer which would induce him to quit the field.[39] As the contest gained increasing national attention during mid-April, the eclectic coalition around him began to look even more fragile.[40] In the Irish camp all was not well. Hardie had been quick to solicit and receive the aid of the HGB, who were attracted by the very fact that their bugbear, Owen Kiernan opposed him.[41] The HGB, however, were campaign workers, not voters. Their incursion into the constituency – complete with brass band – predictably raised the wrath of the local INLGB branch, who had taken direction from the national executive and remained loyal to Philipps.[42] Given Ferguson's sensitivity to public ridicule, the dispatch of a gaggle of Irish MPs to condemn Hardie's supporters as 'Tory bottlewashers' was a particularly cruel blow.[43]

Publicly, he continued to campaign for the Labour cause, where his eloquence was valued, even if thrown away on hostile audiences.[44] Privately, he tried to regain control of the situation by means of further personal diplomacy. On 20 April, Schnadhorst was invited by Sir George Trevelyan, the victor of Bridgeton, to meet Hardie and his colleagues in the privacy of a Glasgow Hotel.[45] An indignant Hardie recalled that Sir George had tempted him with a safe Liberal seat and a salary of £300, if only he would withdraw.[46] In the version which Ferguson offered for public consumption, Hardie had authorised him to make a bargain that he would retire in favour of Philipps, if the Liberal Association would permit a test ballot at the next election. However, as Ferguson could not obtain satisfactory terms, the Labour party in Hamilton had pressed on with their nomination.[47] As usual, Ferguson could see both sides of the question. The Labour party had the right to ask Hardie to stand; the Liberal association had the right to its candidate, as the miners could join it and influence it if they liked – 'the pity was that 'there was not an expedient to make these rights *one*.[48]

As far as he was concerned, his private machinations did not mean he had deserted his principles, for his original goal had to secure Liberal recognition of the claims of labour, rather than to create an independent working-class 'party' for its own sake. On the contrary, he sought to place Hardie's effort on a higher moral plane, while repudiating permanent estrangement from the heritage of Liberalism:

> Upon the side of the *Labour party* it is determined the battle shall be fought upon [the devices] of honest principle by mean too much in earnest to have the time or inclination for personalities, insults or mere scolding . . . these weapons may suit powerful, creed-bound politicians, impatience

of any contradiction. They will not suit a party which has
for its chief, a principle, for its weapon, an idea, and for its
general policy, respect for opposite opinion. The Labour
party will try to remember it fights under the same flag
and is loyal to the great principles of the Liberal party; the
present fight arises from a type of 'discipline' rather than
the great Liberal party.[49]

Even while making a virtue out of compromise, it was to
Ferguson's credit that refused to abandon the beleaguered Hardie,
especially as other radical supporters, such as Conybeare, had
discreetly withdrawn in the wake of the abortive Schnadhorst
negotiations.[50] In the closing days of the campaign, he faced the
worst of both worlds, alienated from the nationalist battalions, yet
facing a torrent of hostility from Orange-tinged working men in
areas like Wishaw, where he was howled down in mid-speech
with cries of, 'You're no' wanted here!'[51] Polling day on 27 April
brought his sufferings to a close. Hardie scored 617 votes, more
than double McGhee's gloomy estimate, but still a disappointing
outcome. As if to sum up the campaign, even Davitt's last-ditch
telegram of support had gone astray.[52]

Verdicts on the result varied. *United Ireland* claimed a 'great
Home Rule victory', interpreting Philipps' return as a knock out
blow for coercion.[53] The *Observer* was more concerned with the
threat which Ferguson had posed to the unity and independence
of the local Irish vote. It judged that had made 'an error of head
rather than heart', which not many nationalists were likely to
repeat. Its position was based on practical logic. With two Home
Rule candidates in the field at Mid-Lanark, 'why select the one
with the most weight to carry? Or are we so mighty that we
can afford to handicap ourselves with all the struggling causes
in the country?'[54] While this 'Home Rule first' perspective has
subsequently been invoked to accord the Irish a major role in
Hardie's defeat, contemporaries came to different conclusions.
'Socialistic doctrines', suggested a gloating *Glasgow Herald*, were
less attractive to the masses than stump orators would like to

believe, but the main lesson for labour was that it was, 'far from being sufficiently well-organised to be regarded as an important factor'.[55]

The editorial had grasped a simple truth: the 'Labour party' of Ferguson's rhetoric was an attitude rather than an organisation. This was a situation which the Mid-Lanark coalition now resolved to address.

The blinded Samson

Keir Hardie's distrust of the Liberal Party had deepened during the Mid-Lanark campaign. His shift towards socialism was often erratic, but he had become increasingly convinced that the working class vote could only be mobilised through a new independent organisation.[56] While this was a conviction shared by many of his trade union allies in Lanarkshire, his vision was of a broader alliance of both industrial and political activists. The outcome was the Scottish Parliamentary Labour Party. After an initial organisational meeting in Glasgow on 19 May 1888, the new body was launched at a conference on 25 August, followed by an open air meeting on Glasgow Green.[57] As one of Hardie's chief campaigners at Mid-Lanark, Ferguson was prominently involved. His absence in Lurgan prevented his attendance at the May meeting, but he took a prominent role at the party's formal inauguration and became one of its two Honorary Vice-Presidents.[58]

His participation was accompanied by serious tactical and ideological reservations. Essentially, the Scottish Labour Party (SLP), as it quickly became, was one of many organisational experiments which took place in labour politics in the period. Ferguson still refused to accept its advent as marking a rupture with radical Liberalism – the creed which he regarded as the voice of 'the democracy' in action.[59] He hoped instead that the party would function as a new force *within* Liberal bloc, shifting the parameters of debate, so that his agenda of land and social reform would become incorporated as a mainstream demand. It was a case of mutual dependency. During the Mid-Lanark contest, he was defiant in his lifelong support of the working man's cause, but he believed with equal conviction that labour representation, freed from the embrace of radical Liberalism, could become a negative and even destructive dynamic. His letter of 17 May, in response to Hardie's proposal for the new party, was eloquent on the contradictions and dilemmas which faced collectivist radicals. Joining the SLP in the hope of preventing class strife, he was conscious that the party's separate existence might actually promote it. He reserved for himself the familiar role of advocate and mediator:

> I am delighted to know the Labour Party is for action. My opinion is it still shd still enter the Liberal Association and work through it. There is certainly an element of danger in two political organisations holding the same principles, coming into collision. In one organisation the labour and trading classes wd have to have a common interest, but divided all the bitterness that Louis Blanc points out as existing between the 'bourgeois' and 'proletaire' in France will arise here. If you cannot induce the Labourers to join the Liberal Association and push their claims through it by all means organise Labour by itself. Better that then nothing. I'll try all I can in the Liberal Association to support Labour claims and if need be I'll stand by the demand of Labour as put forward by you and other Labour leaders against all parties. You must only ask what must be granted if the foundation of our social edifice is not to be destroyed [60]

If it was not enough that radical conscience was troubling him, he also had to contend with Irish views on his latest adventure. The INLGB executive pronounced that they had no objection to Labour candidates – 'where other things are equal' – but they could not swallow the view that it was better to lose with Labour, that win with a middle-class candidate. The success of the Irish cause depended on a more positive commitment to Liberalism as 'the party of progress in their battle against the forces of privilege and reaction'.[61]

A man of less individualistic inclinations might have reconsidered his commitment at this point, but Ferguson could draw some comfort from the basic familiarity of SLP personnel and policies. Hardie became the party's driving force, with other miners' leaders, such as Smillie, also in the vanguard. Yet the socialist parties remained aloof, leaving Ferguson surrounded by a phalanx of fellow radicals. John Murdoch chaired the foundation conference; G. B. Clark was a fellow Vice-President; Cunninghame Graham was Honorary President; Shaw Maxwell chaired the Executive; McGhee was also a notable inaugural member.[62] In querying the wisdom of, 'leading a democratic party by marking it off from the great democratic movement', the Gladstonian *Scottish Leader* could not resist the jibe that not a single office bearer was a 'working man'.[63]

Given the variegated appeal of the party, it is not surprising that in its programme, consensus outweighed coherence. Its lack of 'definite ideas' was a byword from the outset, labour reforms being combined with the conventional radical nostrums of parliamentary reform, temperance and disestablishment.[64] Hardie had resisted the nationalisation of all productive capital in deference to the party's Single Taxers, but land nationalisation became not only a major policy plank, but one of the few unifying imperatives. Equally comforting was the rejection of a class-based identity for Labour – as Hardie had already argued, the Labour party must recognise that the middle classes stood with them, and together they faced 'the idlers' of society.[65]

Ferguson's adherence was also assisted by the SLP's extreme organisational flexibility. Hardie declared his break from the Liberal Party on becoming the new party's organising secretary, but as there were no initial restrictions on members of other parties becoming SLP officials, he was able to combine his vice-presidency with his active involvement in the Liberal Party. The contradictions implicit in this dual allegiance might have become apparent more quickly, if the SLP had pursued an aggressive electoral strategy. However, attempts to mount a Labour challenge at by-elections during 1888–9 came to nothing. Instead, the adoption by the victorious Liberal candidate at Govan of an advanced programme including land nationalisation, seemed to prove the wisdom of Ferguson's strategy of 'permeation'.[66]

In short, his short sojourn in the SLP was an epilogue to his Mid-Lanark adventure rather than a new departure. If anything, his horror of class warfare and fears for the 'social edifice' had sharpened. As he surveyed the prospects for the coming year in January 1889, he was again in apocalyptic mood. When the workers realised how little the 'bourgeoisie' knew of their plight, it could end in one of two ways, reform or revolution: 'There is indeed a blinded Samson in our midst who has his hands upon the pillars of our civilisation, and who in some grim revel may bury us in his ruins'.[67] Yet although Ferguson's relationship to working class politics remained subtle and equivocal, he was becoming increasingly identified in the public's mind with the labour cause.[68] For some nationalists, the implications were deeply disturbing. The 'guide, philosopher and friend' of the Irish movement in Scotland who had led his people through wilderness was now abandoning them within sight of the promised land. As one correspondent plaintively wrote, their old leader was dabbling in 'Socialism and Trade Unionism', when Ireland, 'had the right to the first fruits of his voice and his pen'.[69]

On Trial

There was nothing like an external threat to rally querulous activists and refocus Ferguson's attention on the nationalist agenda. The formal opening of the 'Parnell Crime Commission' in October 1888 amply served the purpose. This tortuous parliamentary enquiry was to hold ten years of Irish agitation up to intense public scrutiny, throwing not only the Liberal alliance into doubt, but testing the very survival of Parnell and his movement.

The question of Parnell's links with agrarian lawlessness and political violence had been nagging away since the spring of the previous year, when *The Times* had published a series of hostile articles entitled, 'Parnellism and Crime', including a facsimile of a letter in which Parnell seemed to apologise for his earlier condemnation of the Phoenix Park murders. Ferguson's response was swift, ensuring that General Council of the Scottish Liberal Association repudiated the allegations and expressed its warmest sympathy for the Irish leader's noble efforts, 'to bring about a real union between the British and Irish peoples'.[70]

Parnell had apparently ridden out the storm, when the issue flared up again in early July 1888, following F. H. O'Donnell's unsuccessful libel action against the newspaper. Convinced that a legal or official enquiry would be necessary to clear his name, Parnell approached the House of Commons for a select committee to be established. It was now that the poisoned atmosphere of late 1880s politics came into its own. Spurred on by Chamberlain, the Unionist government decided not to establish a select committee, but a full-scale Special Commission. Its scope of enquiry would be much wider than the *Times* letters, centering on the range of allegations that had been made against sixty-three Irish MPs and sixty-seven 'other persons' – Ferguson among them – with whom they were accused of associating. The main charges included conspiring to promote Irish independence; the waging of an agrarian campaign by coercion and intimidation; and the assistance and condoning of criminal acts.

This was a mammoth undertaking, featuring the examination of 450 witnesses on some 100,000 questions.[71] Nationalists were in no doubt that the 'Great Inquisition' was really a political trial, with the whole nationalist movement in the dock.[72] As its preliminary meetings got underway in September, Ferguson moved into action. Such was the severity of the crisis, that he was drawn back onto centre stage of the movement. Senior figures in the Irish Parliamentary party had asked him to open an indemnity fund to cover legal costs. His participation was particularly useful to them as the *Times* proceedings had now developed a Scottish dimension. Dissatisfied with the Commission, Parnell had taken out his own libel action. As a London jury would probably hostile, and a Dublin court would be considered partisan, he decided to pursue his case in the Court of Session in Edinburgh as his only route to 'speedy justice'.[73]

Ferguson accepted his task with relish, moulding it to the needs of his own democratic project. Thus he appealed to Irish patriotism of 'the respectable eleventh hour order', but also to, 'British radicals who follow a *principle* and British Liberals who follow a man.' They now shared another common goal:

> No nobler cause was ever fought than that of Parnell against *The Times*.What a triumph it will be for Irish nationalists, British Radicals and Gladstonian Liberals should a Scottish jury give a sweeping verdict for Parnell . . . The grand old nation will rise to the occasion and so will her Scottish allies.[74]

How far this was a genuine rapprochement with the nationalist leadership is highly doubtful. Despite the movement's new-found public unity, the bitterness of the post-Kilmainham years was difficult to dispel. As Davitt explained to McGhee, his support for the Parnell at the Commission was founded in fear of his possible successors: 'Better . . . stick to a sick lion, though he has given you a paw now and then, that to have for masters a crowd of ambitious jackals . . .'[75] He worried too that Ferguson's enthusiasm for bridge-building would end in tears, begging McGhee to restrain him in his renewed relations with the parliamentary leaders.

> For heaven's sake tell Ferguson not to write to *any* of these men. He can expect nothing from the *best* of them, but sneers and ingratitude. I do not like to see a man of his high unselfish and stainless nature seeking recognition or even justice from men who judge him by their own standard and believe him to be activated by some hostile motive when

he is but manifesting his disinterestedness and brotherly feeling.[76]

Ferguson was on firmer ground in judging the potential of the Commission as a campaigning issue. This was not immediately apparent as its wearisome proceedings dragged on into the new year, threatening to exhaust the Parnell Defence Fund.[77] Suddenly on 21 February came the long-expected denouement, as the seedy Dublin journalist, Richard Pigott was revealed as the forger behind the 'Parnell' letters. Although the Commission continued its deliberations on the general charges of conspiracy and criminality, by the time Ferguson himself took the stand on 27 May, its teeth had already been drawn.

He was nevertheless an important witness. It was his initials which had been appended to the 'Tim Horan letter' – a request from a local Land League secretary for central funds to be paid to men injured in a mysterious fray – which was the only proof of even indirect support of the Land League executive for physical violence or intimidation. His initial examination, in which he emphasised his constitutional credentials, took only a couple of minutes, but his cross-examination by the *Times* counsel, Sir Henry James filled most of the day, and was reckoned by one observer to be, 'the most dismally dull and fruitless in the whole course of the trial'.[78] The main point at issue was to discover what he knew of the Horan letter and the missing Land League account books. He was bombarded with questions, but neatly deflected these denying any knowledge of detailed financial transactions surrounding the League's relief function. Instead he turned the exchanges to proclaim himself a British republican and a disciple of Mill and Spencer. He was equally resolute in depicting the Land League as an instrument of moral force – though he cheekily admitted that 'many a thing is moral in Ireland that is not strictly legal'.[79] Elsewhere in testimony, he became even more flippant and evasive. It could not have been comfortable to have some of his more colourful outpourings dredged up after a decade – his remark that Edward McHugh had 'carried the war into Africa', for example, was taken literally to mean that the Land League had financed the Boers.[80] He was on the weakest ground when probed on his correspondence with Patrick Ford's *Irish World*, whose espousal of physical force in the early 1880s had made it an obsession of the *Times* counsel. Ferguson was forced to contradict himself repeatedly on the dates of his subscription to the paper, claiming that he had given it up when its extremist views became 'rubbish'.[81]

Despite these individual lapses, there was no disguising that the Commission was becoming a splendid publicity triumph for the nationalists. The main beneficiary – despite his own poor performance on the stand – was Parnell. Feted by a relieved Gladstone and an ecstatic Liberal press, he now honoured Edinburgh with an official visit. Not only was his libel action in the Court of Session on course for a £5000 settlement, but the normally conservative Corporation had agreed to grant him the freedom of the city.[82] For Ferguson, Saturday 20 July was a special day which seemed to signal the end of his own years in the wilderness. At last, Parnell was poised to assume the mantle of democratic leadership, using his unique authority to reach out to British audiences. The visit all the more remarkable as he had not made a public appearance in Ireland since the Galway election in February 1886. Equally heartening was the spectacle of Scottish 'democracy', who had turned out in their thousands to pay public homage.

A continuous crowd of 30,000, with bands and banners, stretched from the head of Lothian Road to the foot of Calton Hill.[83] Princes Street was thronged and the Irish chief bowed left and right to ceaseless greetings. At the City Chambers he received his Burgess Scroll in an engraved silver casket and was presented with addresses from 160 Liberal Associations.[84] It seemed it was not only the man but the cause which they hailed so eagerly. The encomium from the Liberal workingmen of Edinburgh stated that, 'the mass of the people of Scotland were with the people of Ireland in their struggle, believing that the consummation of their national desire would be the means of more firmly cementing the

true and lasting unity of these islands'.[85] An unusually gracious
and conciliatory Parnell replied in kind, along with some singular
views on the future of the Irish in Scotland:

> . . . justice to Ireland, so far from weakening the greatness
> of the Empire must surely consolidate and increase its
> strength . . . I am thankful to think that the bad old times
> have gone by, and that we shall never again see the return
> of the evil days . . . We ardently long for the development of
> Ireland's material resources, in order to find for our people,
> employment at home so that they may no longer flood the
> labour markets in Scotland and England . . . so that those of
> them who are here may return to Ireland and help us by the
> knowledge they have acquired in your workshops and their
> factories . . .[86]

Ferguson might have disputed his economic analysis, but his
decision to forsake 'Grattan's Parliament' for federalism was
heartily welcome – even if this conversion was assisted by £10,000
from the arch-imperialist, Cecil Rhodes.[87] Indeed, the 'flowing
tide' in national politics at last seemed to have turned in his
favour. Parnell's new standing with the British public suggested
the Liberal alliance could be recast on terms which would prevent
the feared 'absorption' of Irish interests. The Liberals' own policy
platform was similarly evolving. Gladstone might hold out
against federalism – fearful of the consequences for a future
English Liberal majority – but the growing strength of Scottish
Home Rule sentiments within the party suggested greater
leverage for a principle which was 'as old as humanity'.[88] The
prospects for social and economic reform also seemed brighter.
With Chamberlain in exile, the Liberals radical wing had adopted
Henry George as their new mentor. His enthusiastic reception on
constituency platforms during his tour of 1889, suggested that
land-value tax legislation might become a reality if the Liberals
were returned to power.[89]

In Glasgow, Ferguson had clawed his way back to a position
of strength. His concept of 'Home Rule Radicalism' had found

a convincing, if controversial, expression in the activities of the HGB. Although he remained acutely sensitive to personal slights, after almost a decade spent flaunting leadership directives, his standing in the community mitigated official censure. Even those who questioned his judgement on Labour links, tempered their criticisms with tributes to a 'broadmindedness and generosity of feeling worthy of the immortal Davis himself'.[90]

It was precisely these qualities which were soon to be in short supply in nationalist politics. In 1887, when the victory of Home Rule seemed only a matter of time, Ferguson had warned his audience that: 'The chalice had already dropped from the lips of their country when she was about to drink of freedom'.[91] Within months of Parnell's Edinburgh triumph, his prophecy was fulfilled.

Notes

1 *Scottish Leader*, 4 Jan. 1889.

2 See, for example, Grant Allen, *Individualism and Socialism* (Glasgow, 1889).

3 Robert Smillie, *My Life for Labour* (London, 1924), pp. 29–30.

4 TCD, Davitt MSS 9328/180/33, M. Davitt to R. McGhee, Dec. 1887.

5 Following Gladstone's lead, almost all the HLLRA branches had overcome their initial suspicions to offer public support for Irish demands during the Home Rule crisis. Hunter, 'Politics of Highland Land Reform', pp. 54–5. See also Clarke's reminiscences in *Forward*, 13 Aug. 1910.

6 *Irish World*, 30 Apr. 1887.

7 *Glasgow Observer*, 26 Mar. 1887. A rather sceptical *Observer* described him as,' . . . symmetrically-built, with a graceful carriage, a head of flaxen curls almost "woolly" in their crispness and a pointed King Charles beard': *Ibid.*, 8 Dec. 1889. See also, C. Watts and L. Davies, *Cunninghame Graham: A Critical Biography* (Cambridge, 1979).

8 *Ibid.*, 23 Apr. 1889. Ferguson later re-employed the former as a medium of communication with Gladstone to present an address from the HGB, condemning Tory coercion: *Ibid.*, 3 Sept. 1887.

9 *Ibid.*, 30 Apr., 7, 14 May 1889. Davitt later embarked on more private fraternal initiative, quietly sending Ferguson a sum to assist the court case of the Lewis land raiders. The money had come from the Western Isles Fund, but he reasoned, 'Lewis is not a Western *Irish* island, but it is a Western *Celtic* one, I feel sure that subscribers will agree with me . . .': TCD 9545, Diary 14 Jan. 1888.

10 *The Life of Michael Davitt, founder of the National Land League,* by D. B. Cashman: see, *Glasgow Observer,* 2 Apr. 1889.

11 Note cooperation after the arrest of John Dillon: NLS, Acc. 11765/3, Western Council of the Scottish Liberal Association Minutes, 12 Sept. 1888.

12 Ibid., General Council of the Scottish Liberal Association Minutes, 20 Apr. 1887; 5 Nov. 1888.

13 By 1889, the League had established the *Bridgeton Advertiser and Single Tax Review* with a circulation of 8000.

14 *Glasgow Herald,* 12 Aug. 1887. He had originally joined the breakaway group, but had been wooed back by Gladstone.

15 *Ibid.*, 30 Jul. 1887.

16 Bew, *Parnell,* pp. 83–4; Davitt, *Fall of Feudalism,* pp. 504–513.

17 *Forward,* 17 Sept. 1910.

18 *Glasgow Observer,* 30 Jul. 1887.

19 *Scottish Leader,* 4 Jan. 1889; *Glasgow Observer,* 30 Jul. 1887.

20 *Glasgow Observer,* 19 Feb. 1887. The Scottish Liberals reciprocated by tailoring the date of their national conference to fit in with Parnell's projected visit to Glasgow:

NLS, Acc. 11765/3, General Council of Scottish Liberal Association Minutes, 26 Jun. 1889.

21 Davitt's criticisms were launched in a speech in early September: O'Brien, *Parnell*. p.227.

22 *Glasgow Observer*, 30 Jul. 1887.

23 *Glasgow Herald*, 10Aug. 1887.

24 *Ibid*.

25 NLS, MS 176–8, K. Hardie to J. Burt, 15 Mar. 1888.

26 See, for example, W. Stewart, *J. Keir Hardie* (London, 1921), pp. 35–45; J. Kellas, 'The Mid-Lanark By-election (1888) and the Scottish Labour Party', *Parliamentary Affairs*, (1964–5), pp. 318–29; K. O. Morgan, *Keir Hardie. Radical and Socialist* (London, 1975), pp. 23–43; F. Reid, *Keir Hardie. The Making of a Socialist* (London, 1978), pp.110–5. For a useful overview see: D. Howell, *British Workers and the Independent Labour Party 1886–1906* (Manchester, 1984), pp. 144–7.

27 *Glasgow Observer*, 6 Mar. 1886 for address at Whifflet; *Scottish Leader*, 3 Sept 1888 for Dumbarton meeting. These visits also gave him the opportunity to 'recycle' material from some of his earlier speeches to the HGB. His 'flag with trembling hand' was run up more than once.

28 This was Ferguson's claim for the Irish vote: *North British Daily Mail*, 28 Mar. 1888. Hardie estimated that the joint vote of the miners and Irish stood at 3500: NLS, MS 176–8, K. Hardie to H. H. Champion, 15 Mar. 1888.

29 *Irish World*, 12 Jun. 1887.

30 *Glasgow Observer*, 19 Feb. 1887.

31 *North British Daily Mail*, 28 Mar. 1888.

32 *Glasgow Observer* 17 Mar. 1888; Independent Labour Party Archive, Francis Johnson Correspondence, H. Murphy to K.

Hardie, 17 Mar. 1888.

33 *Glasgow Observer* , 24 Mar. 1888.

34 Francis Johnson Corr., T. R. Threlfall to J. Brown, 9 April 1888.

35 *Glasgow Herald,* 9 Apr. 1888.

36 Francis Johnson Corr., J. Ferguson to R. B. Cunninghame Graham, 11 April 1888.

37 TCD. Davitt MSS 9328, M. Davitt to R. McGhee [nd.]. The letter was 'confidential except to Ferguson'.

38 Francis Johnson Corr., J. Ferguson to R. B. Cunninghame Graham, 11 April 1888.

39 *North British Daily Mail,* 11 Apr. 1888.

40 *Ibid.*

41 NLS, MSS. 1809/71–2, K. Hardie to HGB 24 Mar., 24 Apr. 1888; Francis Johnson Corr., T. Rooney to K. Hardie, 16 April 1888. For McGhee's comment's on Kiernan's role, see also, *Glasgow Observer,* 7 Apr. 1888.

42 Francis Johnson Corr., J. Ferguson to K. Hardie, 12 April 1888; *Glasgow Herald,,*2 Apr. 1888.

43 *Glasgow Observer,* 20 Apr. 1888; *Glasgow Herald,* 18 Apr. 1888.

44 Francis Johnson Corr., J. M. Cruikshank to K. Hardie, 30 Mar. 1888; A. L. Runn to K. Hardie, 3 April 1888.

45 Ibid.

46 *Labour Leader,* 12 Mar. 1914.

47 *Glasgow Observer,* 28 Apr. 1888.

48 *Ibid.*

49 *Glasgow Herald,* 20 Apr. 1888.

50 *Ibid.* 28 Apr. 1888.

51 *Ibid.,* 20 Apr. 1888.

52 Francis Johnson Corr., J. Ferguson to Keir Hardie, 17 May.

53 *United Ireland,* 5 May 1888 for cartoon.

54 *Glasgow Observer,* 28 Apr. 1888.

55 *Glasgow Herald,* 24 Apr. 1888. On the negative role of the Irish, see Kellas , 'Mid-Lanark By-election', p. 323; Reid offers an alternative interpretation which stresses the failure of Scottish miners to follow Hardie: *Keir Hardie,* p. 115.

56 Morgan, *Keir Hardie,* pp. 31–2

57 *Scottish Leader,* 27 Aug. 1888; *Glasgow Obsever,* 1 Sept. 1888.

58 D. Lowe, *Souvenirs of Scottish Labour* (Glasgow, 1919), pp. 3–4; Haddow, *Socialism in Scotland,* 16–17.

59 See Smyth, 'Labour and Socialism', pp. 65–6

60 Francis Johnson Corr., J. Ferguson to Keir Hardie, 17 May 1888.

61 *Scottish Leader,* 27 Aug. 1888.

62 Lowe, *Souvenirs ,* pp. 3–4.

63. *Scottish Leader,* 27 Aug. 1888.

64 ULL, J.B. Glasier Papers, GP 1/1/262, J.L. Mahon to J. B. Glasier, 14 Oct. 1887.

65 Reid, *Keir Hardie,* p. 117.

66 Morgan, *Keir Hardie,* p. 35. For Ferguson's views on the Govan contest see, *Glasgow Herald,* 7 Jan. 1889.

67 *Scottish Leader,* 4 Jan. 1889.

68 *Glasgow Observer,* 23 Jun. 1888.

69 *Scottish Leader,* 8 Jan. 1888.

70 NLS, Acc. 11765/3, General Council of Scottish Liberal Association Minutes, 20 Apr. 1887.

71 Davitt, *Fall of Feudalism*, p. 544.

72 *Ibid.* pp. 531–41; Denvir, *Life Story*, pp. 246–7.

73 *Glasgow Observer*, 25 Aug. 1888; *Scottish Leader*, 18 Oct. 1888.

74. *Glasgow Observer*, 8 Sept. 1888.

75 TCD, Davitt MSS 9328, M. Davitt to R. McGhee, 8 Oct. 1888.

76 Ibid.

77 *Glasgow Observer*, 17 Nov. 1888.

78 J. Macdonald, *The Daily News Diary of the Parnell Commission* (London, nd.), p. 254.

79 *Special Commission*, vol.iii, p. 291.

80 *Ibid.*, p. 293.

81 *Ibid.*, p. 292–4. *Irish World*, 29 Sept. 1886. A personal link with the paper was his lieutenant, Martin Clarke, who had emigrated to American and become an *Irish World* correspondent.

82 *Scottish Leader*, 25 May 1889; *Freeman's Journal*, 4 Feb. 1890 for Court of Session judgment.

83 *Glasgow Observer*, 27 Jul. 1889.

84 Ferguson was naturally in the thick of things as a representative of the North West Lanarkshire Liberals: *Scottish Leader*, 22 Jul. 1889.

85 *Glasgow Observer*, 27 Jul. 1889.

86 *Ibid.*

87 G. B. Clark claimed to have acted as initial contact in the deal: *Forward*, 17 Sept. 1910.

88 *Forward*, 17 Sept. 1910; Hutchison, *Political History*, pp. 171–3.

89 Lawrence, *Henry George*, pp. 104–5.

90 *Glasgow Observer,* 17 Mar. 1888.

91 *Ibid.,* 3 Sept. 1887.

CHAPTER TEN

A Patriot of No Party

In the aftermath of the 1885 election, Richard McGhee could not fathom why Parnell had exempted the renegade Captain O'Shea from his November manifesto, while stalwart friends of Ireland were rebuffed.[1] All became on clear on Christmas Eve 1889, when O'Shea filed a petition for divorce from his wife, citing the nationalist leader as co-respondent.

In his heart, John Ferguson must have known that nationalist unity had been as chimerical as the impending triumph of Home Rule. Yet the divorce crisis and subsequent nationalist split tore apart the fabric of his political life. He had grown impatient for Home Rule to be speedily 'settled', so that he could concentrate on issues of social reform. Now, the work of his adult life seemed in ruins. In his anguished response, he gave voice to the despair of a generation of nationalists:

Ireland is off the true path. The pillar of cloud by day and fire by night – emblems of faith and duty – no longer guide her as they did but yesteryear towards the Promised Land. There is a sound of war in the camp, and patriot brothers have their swords in each other's hearts.[2]

His own behaviour during the developing crisis was often inconsistent, but his overriding instinct as an educator and conciliator was to maintain a public detachment from the contending factions. Indeed, in his role as 'a patriot of no party', he sensed the ideological complexities of the split more perceptively than the fervent anti-Parnellite Davitt.[3] In their struggles with Parnell, neither seem to have realised that the real threat to his leadership came from the emerging Catholic right of the party. Both now took the opportunity to air suppressed grievances arising from Parnell's autocratic leadership. Yet, perhaps because of his distance from the death throes of the old nationalist order, it was Ferguson who grasped that continuing disunity would prove fatal not only for the prospects of the Home Rule movement, but also for their own project of welding nationalism and radicalism. While Davitt intervened brutally and early, then faded from the gladiatorial contest, it was Ferguson who quietly concentrated his energies at a local level, protecting the infrastructure of nationalist politics from the worst effects of internecine warfare and lifting his colleagues' eyes to the 'the revolt of labour'. As one observer remembered, 'his gentle character and unvarying inoffensiveness and kept him on good terms of friendship during the whole time with those who most strongly differed from him'.[4] His genuine conception of 'unity' was one which contrasted favourably with *Glasgow Observer's* insistence that those who despised this watchword 'must be swept away'.[5] Amid the competing polemics, Ferguson's strategy may have appeared a self-effacing one, but his restraint was to prove critical in preserving the future capacity of the Glasgow branches to campaign across a range of national and democratic demands.

There remained one legacy of Parnell's fall, which personal discretion could not circumvent. Whatever Ferguson's doubts over Home Rulers surrendering their political autonomy, the Liberal relationship was now more of a necessity than it ever had been. As Irish claims became thoroughly enmeshed in the British party system, the space which had allowed Ferguson to balance his commitment to Irish Home Rule and the claims of labour representation contracted even further.

The fall

The nationalist mood at the beginning of 1890 was summed up by the *Observer* editorial, simply entitled: 'We Don't Believe It'.[6] O'Shea's accusations against a man who was more than a mere leader, but 'soul and centre of a movement' were regarded no more than a reprise of the Pigott forgeries. These were halcyon days for the cause. Between 1883 and 1890, the number of Scottish branches had risen from 52 to 630, with membership increasing from 4000 to 40,000.[7] The branches went about their business in relative tranquility – even the INLGB Convention, which was held in Edinburgh in early October, was less fractious than usual.[8] When the blow fell on 17 November it was all the more devastating for its unexpectedness. The divorce court's decision to grant a decree *nisi* to Captain O'Shea, after two days of unchallenged evidence of Parnell's subterfuge – including hasty exits via a fire-escape – left nationalists stunned and humiliated.

Like many in the party, Ferguson's initial reaction was to close ranks behind Parnell. Speaking in Paisley on 23 November, he explained that he recognised the desirability of retaining him as leader, 'as his connection herewith was essential to the party being maintained in proper unity as the national party.'[9] A dignified and determined Parnell was initially able to capitalise on such sentiments to secure his re-election as party chairman on 25 November, but the intervention of Gladstone almost immediately deprived him of this tactical advantage. Events now moved with devastating speed. With Liberal horror mounting, Gladstone released his memorandum to John Morley, suggesting that Parnell's retention as chairman would render his own leadership of the Liberal Party, 'almost a nullity'.[10] The Irish party, forced to choose between retaining Parnell as leader or risk the Liberal alliance, began to disintegrate. With an adjournment secured until 1 December, Parnell attempted another spectacular stroke by publishing a manifesto to 'the People of Ireland', whose astounding centrepiece was an unprecedented assault on Gladstone's personal morality and presumption in exercising a veto on the Irish leadership.[11]

There followed one of the worst weeks in the movement's history. It was the attack on the lofty eminence of Gladstone which proved one of Parnell's worst errors in the split. Motivated by a combination of personal irritation and the need to present the threat to his leadership as the result of Liberal 'dictation', he misjudged the sentimental regard in which the Irish held

Gladstone. Even nationalists who had been previously loyal or at least uncommitted, found Parnell guilty of personal ingratitude and a cynical betrayal of the rhetoric of the 'Union of Hearts'. At once, Ferguson turned to the defence of his old hero. After the publication of the Morley memorandum, he had supported a motion at the Western Executive of the Scottish Liberal Association, expressing unabashed confidence in Gladstone's leadership. Similarly, at the Govan Liberal and Radical Association on 1 December, he took the lead in forwarding resolutions of approval for his conduct in the crisis.[12] At noon the same day, the Irish Parliamentary Party reconvened the debate on Parnell's leadership. The agony dragged on for almost a week until 6 December, when Justin McCarthy finally withdrew from the meeting accompanied by forty-four MPs, leaving Parnell with a remnant of twenty-six loyalists.[13] The seceding majority proceeded to depose him as leader, but rather than accept the end of his authority, which he believed would also signal the end of nationalism as an effective political force, Parnell was determined to carry the struggle to the people of Ireland.

There seemed little to do but wait on developments. Ferguson's breadth of reading and mastery of scientific authorities had not prepared him for the human frailty so painfully revealed by the split. Yet, after his early interventions at Liberal gatherings, the man who was reckoned to be the most able and eloquent Irish leader in Scotland fell strangely silent. In late February 1891, after being buttonholed by a reporter while on a visit to the House of Commons, he replied tersely that up until that point he had refused to side with either of the Irish parties. Instead he deflected attention onto more practical issues, believing that the organisation of the National League in Britain had completely collapsed and would need reviving if the Irish vote was to be a factor at the next general election.[14]

Ferguson's reticence was untypical in Scotland, where Parnell's fall had unleashed long suppressed views on the record of parliamentary nationalism and its leader. John Torley, the IRB veteran, was only glad that the split had taken place before Home

Rule, so that the constitutionalists could be seen in their true colours.[15] For the *Observer* – ironically an opponent of Ferguson's independent stance during the 1880s – Parnell's centralising tendencies had reduced the Irish in Great Britain to 'docile automatons' and their branches to 'money-making machines'.[16] Meanwhile in Scottish public opinion, the crisis merely served to confirm entrenched views on the 'volatile' nature of the Irish character. The Corporation of Edinburgh hastily ordered Parnell's name to be struck from the Burgess Roll.[17] The radical *Mail* hoped that, 'Ireland's loss might be Scotland's gain', and that Scottish claims which had been postponed for the sake of Ireland could now be brought forward.[18] Most woundingly, for the Unionist press, the Irish cause had become a spectacle served up for Scottish entertainment – 'an Irish melodrama, run under the personal supervision of the ablest of all actor-managers, Mr Parnell'.[19] The *Bailie* naturally had a field-day, wringing the maximum comedy potential from the the plight of a nation which had portrayed itself as 'the purest under the sun'. It offered a pastiche of the border ballad, 'Jock o' Hazeldean', in which the hero sweeps off his rival's bride:

> Her 'hubby' is the 'uncrowned king',
> For whom divorce she bore.
> Wha cleared the casement when O'Shea,
> Was hammering at her door.
> Her love was like a mountain stream,
> Nae obstacle can quell,
> She's broken a' her marriage vows,
> For Charles S. Parnell.[20]

Such hilarity was deeply painful to Ferguson who cherished the progress of the movement, almost as much as he guarded his own dignity. There seemed little to be gained from personally intervening in a dispute which was so clearly exposing its participants to ridicule. Innocuous social occasions now assumed a new political significance. One of his rare appearances on an Irish platform during 1891 was at the reunion of natives of Fermanagh. Here he was required to introduce Jeremiah Jordan, an obscure Irish MP, who had been the first in the party to call for Parnell's political retirement. An unhappy Ferguson cast around desperately for gleams of fellow-feeling between the protagonists. He also struggled to bring some sort of reasoned analysis to bear on the present situation. Inevitably he fell back on the efficacy of 'principles':

> There was discord today in Irish ranks – their enemies laughed them to scorn, and the newspaper press was furbishing weapons it used twenty years ago. It was unable to understand the meaning of Home Rule, but they had taught the newspapers before and they would teach them again. He was pleased to see the kindly allusion in Dr Tanner's telegram to Jack Redmond, and at Clare, Mr Parnell forbade denunciation of Jeremiah Jordan. That was the spirit which should exist among nationalists. What were they fighting for and had the questions, 'Are you Parnellites?' or, 'Are you anti-Parnellites?' to do with the cause? He was a patriot of no party and a soldier of Ireland . . . Had the Irishmen of today been true to principles, if they had followed principles instead of men, and made their leader follow principles, the present crisis would never have arisen.[21]

While anxious to present his aloofness an act of principled neutrality, genuine perplexity and political expediency seem also to have played their part. Neatly-turned epigrams were of little assistance in navigating his way through the new hazards of Irish politics. Nor was much help available from Ferguson's allies who were themselves ranged on opposite sides in the split. His old friends, Davitt and Murphy had rejected Parnell, while his new allies in the Scottish Labour movement, Cunninghame Graham and Keir Hardie were firm supporters.[22]

His private sympathies seem to have rested in the latter

direction, but such was his discretion that this only became widely suspected after the worst of the dispute had passed.[23] Although he refrained from unctuous moralising, the attraction did not lie in an excess of sympathy for 'the only possible leader'.[24] The latest incarnation of 'Parnellism' represented an attitude of mind, not just a man or a policy. Often interpreted as a last desperate aberration, the last ten months of Parnell's career has been reassessed as a purposeful attempt to present a radical agenda which would challenge the developing configuration of conservative social power in Ireland.[25] His campaign contained two vital elements – independent opposition, and a belated attempt to build a coalition of the progressive forces within nationalism – both of which echoed Ferguson's own longstanding concerns.[26] For Parnell, the principle of 'independence' was the alternative to parliamentary subservience, a refusal to surrender the autonomy of nationalist politics before an adequate home rule legislature had been won. In Ferguson's calculation, it meant resistance to the smothering embrace of 'Shopboyism' and 'clansman nationalism'. Parnell's sudden espousal of the cause of labour and equally curious embrace of land nationalisation had clearly opportunistic overtones, raising the wrath of opponents such as Davitt. While well aware that he had used his position as leader in the past to confound progressive initiatives, Ferguson may also, have recognised a challenge to the ethos of proprietorial Catholic nationalism which was gaining ground in the anti-Parnellite camp.[27]

'Parnellism without Parnell' might have been acceptable as a theoretical construct, but not as practical politics in Scotland. The *Observer* had set the tone of the anti-Parnellite onslaught, with an outpouring of repugnance. It singled out Mrs O'Shea for special attention: 'If Mr Parnell had picked up any 'unfortunate' from the streets of London, and endeavoured to foist her on the Irish nation, he would have shown very little more contempt for decency than he has done in the present instance'.[28]

The signals from the INLGB branches were initially more confused, but inexorably the tide began to turn against the

Parnellites.[29] Political considerations generally outweighed piety in their deliberations, but week by week the roll call of branches supporting McCarthy's Irish Parliamentary Party increased. Nationalists in Port Glasgow, Coatbridge and the Johnstone ladies branch held out, but Edinburgh and Dundee were solidly anti-Parnellite.[30] Most of the Glasgow branches also voted to withdraw their earlier motions of support for Parnell, although the issue was hotly contested, with a substantial minority of members dissenting.[31] Although Parnell was to gather many of the more 'advanced' nationalists to his cause, the anti-Parnellite charge in the city was led by Hugh Murphy and the HGB.[32] By spring 1891, the divisions were hardening. At a conference of the West of Scotland branches, organised by the HGB, the sentiment was overwhelmingly against Parnell, with Murphy using the platform to encourage a drive against 'disloyal' branches.[33] A number of Parnell's supporters in the branches gravitated to establish their own 'Glasgow Parnell Committee', under the leadership of John Jackson and F. J. Doran.[34] A Parnellite fight-back in May saw the recapture of the Carluke branch and an abortive invasion of Paisley, but it was a mark of their weakness that plans for Parnell to visit the city, which had received him with adulation in better days, had to be quietly abandoned.[35]

Nor was the wider picture encouraging. Since loyalty to Parnell had been the major test for advancement in its ranks, it was hardly surprising that the INLGB had become badly demoralised. Yet, far from collapsing – as Ferguson had feared – it had begun a witchhunt against any lingering traces of Parnellism. From the outset, the Scottish branches had refused to forward subscriptions until they were satisfied that McCarthy and his party controlled the organisation.[36] At its Newcastle convention in 1891, it was Scottish delegates who pressed successfully for the withdrawal of recognition from branches which did not support the majority parliamentary party.[37] In Ireland, which had become the real cockpit of the crisis, Parnell was also struggling in a changed political climate. Here expectations of land purchase and a speedy Home Rule settlement had mobilised opposition to his cause from a conservative rural bloc. A victim of his past success, three by-election defeats between January and July now testified that his support was contracting to the point of annihilation.[38]

These were hardly the conditions for any nuanced approach – far less for an alignment with any Parnellite grouping. Even Ferguson's expressions of impartiality were interpreted as dangerous equivocation. Since fervent anti-Parnellites remained mesmerised by their former leader's prestige, they believed that nothing less than total loyalty was necessary to conquer this formidable adversary.[39] This was apparent from Ferguson's experience chairing the St Patrick's demonstration in Paisley in 1891. The guest of honour was John Pinkerton MP, the caustic Ulsterman who had been one of his assailants at Mid-Lanark. After listening to Ferguson's reasoned and balanced opening remarks, he taunted that he, 'did not approve of sitting on the fence in the present crisis . . .', preferring clerical dictation to 'a wave of red republicanism sweeping the land'.[40]

It was time for a more assertive initiative for peace. At last in May 1891, as an elder statesman of Irish nationalism, he made his views known through the columns of the precariously Parnellite, *Freeman's Journal*. Introducing a British dimension to the debate, his contribution was an attempt to historicise Parnellism, coupled with impassioned appeal to break out of the paralysing bitterness of the split.[41]According to his dramatic narrative the 'Davitt and his friends' had secured the conquest of British opinion, 'putting mind-conquering principles and prejudice-destroying arguments in the front of the battle'. A year's campaigning on social issues in 1886 would have given Parnell the leadership of British radicalism, but he made a fatal mistake. Like Daniel O'Connell who had surrendered to the Whigs for short-term concessions, Parnell mistook the overtures of 'official Liberalism' for a true alliance with the British democracy, rejecting radical labour candidates like Maxwell and Hardie.[42]

Yet the root of the present crisis, Ferguson believed, went deeper that any one individual's political record. Factionalism had developed its own fatal momentum. With men like Parnell, Davitt, Healy and O'Connor held up to open abuse, the people's faith in public men and public virtue was being eroded. Betraying his own hesitations, he argued that nationalists now faced a grave impasse in trying to mobilise democratic forces:

> Ireland's power is broken in Great Britain. The British radicals . . . do not forget how Parnell helped Gladstone against the Labour party with deadly effect. Official Liberals no longer talk of Home Rule as the question of questions . . . Gladstone will soon retreat further from the Irish idea, now that Ireland is torn by faction, and destroyed, if by the Grace of God and human wisdom do not prevent, years of degrading strife.[43]

For Ferguson, the answer lay in the transfiguring power of sacrifice. Recalling his own self-denial for the sake of nationalist unity in the past, he reached out to patriots on both sides of the suicidal struggle to convene an assembly in Dublin. Here would take place a symbolic gesture which would invest the movement with a new spiritual power:

> The storm of passion is raging. Patriotism and religion are deteriorating into faction and sectarianism. Now is the time for a nobler act of chivalry and devotion that ever the battlefield produced – an act which will live in Irish history for all coming time. Let two or three leaders from each side imitate the noble Roman and retire for a season till their country calls them back to honour. What would be the effect? Sir, from the hearts of twenty million of our race a deep 'God Bless you' would ascend to heaven. The moral power of such an act of self-denial would tell Ireland's foes she was unconquerable.[44]

His scheme was bold and utterly impractical. The split had released the hatreds and suspicions which had quietly matured in the party for over a decade. As the collapse of the negotiations at Boulogne between Parnell, O'Brien and Dillon in the early weeks of 1891 had proved, there was little chance of strategic disengagement on the part of the major participants. Parnell had resisted voluntary withdrawal throughout the crisis, realising this would mean political oblivion. It had become an even more unlikely option in the wake of his latest electoral reversal at North Sligo in April, since he would now appear to be quitting the field in the face of inevitable defeat – an insupportable affront to his personal honour.[45] Prominent anti-Parnellites were equally unlikely to follow Ferguson's path of 'glorious unity'. Jostling for the future leadership of the movement had already begun, with Tim Healy making the running by means of his hysterical and abusive crusade to hound Parnell out of public life. Finally, even if the key leaders on either side had volunteered to stand down, their more enthusiastic followers would probably have condemned any settlement which seemed the product of compromise.

It was fortunate that the *Freeman's Journal* initiative did not exhaust his creative approach. Indeed, after his initial disorientation, it was Ferguson rather than Davitt, who provided a distinctive radical voice during the split. The 'Labour Samson' grinding painfully at Mammon's wheel, was again pressed into service as the dominant motif in a series of open letters from the latter half of 1891. Hoping to shock the 'shop-boys' in the Liberal associations out of their propriety, he summoned up a disturbing portent: the next Liberal Ministry would be 'simply dominated' by Labour; the Labour party would not destroy the official Liberal party if it could use it, but if it could not, it would, 'sweep it at the second general election, out of existence'.[46]

His initiative was timely, as labour issues were increasingly moving to the forefront of public consciousness. Not only had the Royal Commission on Capital and Labour commenced its lengthy deliberations, but a more immediate catalyst came in June with the publication of Pope Leo XIII's encyclical, *Rerum Novarum*, which condemned the 'greed of unrestrained competition' and sanctioned Catholic involvement in movements for social and economic reform.[47] Ferguson was enraptured by, 'a triumph song of Heaven for the Brotherhood of Humanity', which seemed to soar above the degrading strife which had overtaken Ireland.[48]

His response introduced themes which were to be lovingly elaborated in his mature thought and writing, but also revealed how well his omnivorous reading kept him abreast of recent developments in the social sciences. The issue which absorbed late Victorian commentators was the persistence of poverty in a society of plenty. The first volume of Charles Booth's *Life and Labour of the People of London*, for example, had appeared in 1889, with the second volume following in 1891, while Alfred Marshall's *Principles of Economics* was published in 1890. For Ferguson, abstract questions of land economics were now balanced by further study of labour conditions. In his fascination for carefully accumulated data he had found a way of associating himself with working men and simultaneously bearing witness to their sufferings. Yet these were facts, he argued, which were also available to an increasingly literate working class, whose demands society could no longer resist. Acting as their advocate, he set out the standard labour programme of a living wage and shorter working hours, which he trusted would allow the worker to, 'enjoy his domestic life, his evening class or country walking'.[49] This ameliorative prescription was linked to his discovery of the new enemy – 'commercialism'. Using this concept in preference to 'capitalism', he identified an entire social and economic system – 'with all its forces of cupidity, legal and literary, pride and respectability' – which had reached its limits and whose very foundation had deteriorated.[50]

It was his custom to tackle social issues in an evangelical spirit, seeking, in the spirit of the economist and social reformer, Arnold Toynbee, to 'moralise' the practical science of economics.[51] It was his belief that 'unofficial preachers of the Gospel', such as John Ruskin, Thorold Rodgers, and even Gladstone's confidant, John Morley – had already discovered higher laws which modified the discipline's stern individualism.[52] Now, with Papal authority on his side, his critique of 'commercialism' again became suffused with a mystic invocation of the 'eternal verities of God'. Whereas in the past God had winked at the 'wickedness of slavery, chattel or wage', he had now ordained 'intelligent and irresistible forces in order to ensure social justice. Ferguson announced the long-awaited betrothal of the spiritual and the secular: 'Religion has come with her thread of gold and science with her thread of silver. Offspring of the Divine Father, they have united to weave garments of righteousness and truth with which to clothe and comfort the wronged children of industry'.[53]

The encyclical clearly offered a personal salvation from the spirit of Irish factionalism, but it also rejuvenated Ferguson's hopes for mankind's evolution to a higher social order. His latest prophetic mood also drew on Marshall's 'new economics of chivalry', which envisaged the restoration of the intelligence and humanity destroyed by the division of labour and the release of worker's 'higher energies'.[54] Thus his new society would be one in which :

> ... idleness shall not fatten upon industry, and in which leisure and opportunity shall call into existence a refined and cultivated, who whether they carry bricks up a ladder, or rivet a bolt, shall display chivalry and courtesy – shall be in short 'knights of labour'. Let society plead that the natural order is that which exists, and that the survival of the fittest is best worked out by competition. This devil-take-the-hindmost doctrine cannot hold many man in misery much longer.[55]

But if humanity was only a day's journey nearer home, he was determined that the Irish – purged of party warfare – would be in the advance guard. Now that the Pope had reconciled the Roman Catholic church with social progress, Ferguson trusted, that conflict had ended between: 'that glorious and undying instinct of our Irish nature, "Nationality", and that still more glorious and more catholic instinct, "the Brotherhood of Humanity", which the world-transforming words, "Our Father", compels us to accept'.[56]

A parting of the ways

By the early 1890s, Ferguson had taken upon himself an impossible peace mission. He wished not only to soothe the partisan spirit of the Irish, but also to mediate personally between the Labour and the Liberal parties. Yet, for a man who delighted in detail, he was still unwilling to define his terms of engagement with any degree of precision. The near future, he freely predicted, belonged to 'labour' or 'the Labour party': while franchise reform had made, 'Labour, King *in posse,* in under a year or two Labour will be King *in esse'*[57] But was 'Labour' the battering ram of the radical democracy – or was it the party of the working class? In an age when political allegiances were notoriously fluid, Ferguson's lack of precision was a reasonable strategy, but as the orbits of Liberal, Labour and Irish politics refused to glide into perfect alignment, he would at last be forced to prioritise his political allegiances.

In its claims to be labour's political voice, the SLP still shared some of Ferguson's uncertainty: 'its electoral longitude is as uncertain and its social latitude as vague', noted one commentator, 'as the "mythical city of Prague"'.[58] Suffering from the lack of a significant trade union base and frustrated in its attempts to reach electoral accommodations with the Liberal Party, the SLP had not prospered. After three years in existence, Hardie could claim no more than 700 supporters, whereas Liberal reorganisation at the end of the 1880s had a total membership well in excess of 60,000.[59] Yet such setbacks did little to restrict the SLP's ambitions regarding the larger party. At its Annual Conference in January 1892, the relationship with the Liberals was dissected in more unequivocally class-based terms. The lead was taken by Cunninghame Graham.[60] Just as 'the sailor was unable to influence the shark once he had been swallowed', it was

now his opinion that the SLP needed to be 'absolutely separate
and divided from any of the existing parties, as in a party of rich
men they could not expect legislation to benefit those classes
upon which rich men lived'.[61]

Ferguson, who had been unable to attend the conference, was
appalled. In his orotund rhetorical piece, 'The Revolt of Labour
and the Triumph of Home Rule', he had painted a glorious past
for the Irish movement, calling up 'economic and democratic
forces . . . to aid its noble sentiments'. He predicted an equally
glorious future for Labour if it followed the Irish example and
exerted pressure on official Liberalism as part of the democratic
alliance.[62] The SLP now seemed to question the very basis of that
alliance, querying whether 'Labour' *would* remain a formative
strand of Liberalism. In a public riposte, he left his Labour
allies in no doubt where his own true loyalties lay: he was an
honorary official of the SLP and had done his share in spreading
its principles, but he was 'no partisan'. He looked instead to the
Liberal Party, 'as the real instrument to obtain reform, and to
Mr Gladstone as the noblest British statesman in our annals'.
Recovering his composure, he made one of his regular pleas for
generosity in political fighting, calling upon Labour to remember,
'the principles by which a working man nineteen centuries ago
united the earthly to the Divine, established the brotherhood of
man in the Fatherhood of God, and dignified Labour by precept
and example . . .'. Delivering a sermon to Keir Hardie was a
dangerous tactic. He responded with a barbed homily of his own
which absolved Ferguson from 'smart practice', but expressed
his astonishment at how, 'he, and so many other good men lend
their conscience to the trickery practised by Liberal managers on
reformers of all kinds and the working classes generally.[63] The
effect, wrote a delighted Cunninghame Graham, was to dispose
of his opponent '*voila tout*'.[64]

In fact, it took a great deal more to dispose of John Ferguson.
He remained an indefatigable 'friend of Labour', even pushing
the cause in the unlikely setting of the Lenzie Literary

Association.[65] Nevertheless, the episode marked the beginning of an estrangement from organised Labour politics and a general refocusing of his political activity. While the SLP was gaining the reputation for hugging the delusion that, 'their rustic cackle was the murmur of the world', the pulse of Home Rule politics was already quickening in anticipation of the next general election. In February 1892, after almost a year's absence, Ferguson re-surfaced among the Glasgow Irish.[66]

By now, the worst of the heat seemed to have gone out of the battles in the branches. After further 'leakage' following Parnell's death in October 1891, the balance of Parnellite and anti-Parnellite forces had stabilised overwhelmingly in favour of the latter.[67] Ferguson was anxious to encourage a healing momentum by sponsoring causes, such as amnesty for Fenian prisoners, or support for evicted tenants, which would unite nationalists of all persuasions.[68] A visit from Michael Davitt during March 1892 provided the usual symbolic rallying point, but there was no doubt over the ultimate test of unity for the Irish. After six years in power, Lord Salisbury finally called a summer general election.[69]

This contest placed Labour and Irish Home Rule on a collision course. It was to be Labour's first real electoral challenge, with seven candidates at the polls.[70] For the majority of nationalists, who had placed their faith in the Liberal alliance's ability to deliver Home Rule before Parnell's leadership, it was the hour of the last instance – 'the final effort against factionalism and the foes of Irish freedom.'[71] Of course, the tension between the two political forces was not of recent origin. The central political convention of mainstream Irish nationalism had been that class and social conflict should be suppressed until the attainment of Home Rule. For the Irish in Britain, the situation had been complicated to some extent by the recognition that the social profile of the community remained heavily working class. Here the question was less of containing conflicting interests within nationalism, than of agreeing the priority of national and social agendas. While insisting on the primacy of Home Rule, the

Observer had attempted to understand Labour's assertion of
independence, noting that: 'once Home Rule were out of the
way, the Labour cause would be our own. The Catholics of Great
Britain, are, in the mass, mostly workers, so that our interest in
the redress of Labour grievances is substantial and real'.[72] These
subtleties had little place the present emergency. The choices
were brutally expressed. A vote for the Liberals was identified as
a vote for Ireland, while supporting Labour meant, 'sacrificing the
welfare of a nation to the caprice of a class'.[73]

Ferguson was now unwavering in his support of Liberal
candidates, but he felt it necessary to justify his latest position. [74]
He was only fifty-six, but for some years now had assumed the
garb of a weary patriarch, hungry for Zion:

> He hoped the Scots did not think them selfish in pushing
> Home Rule over the movement in favour of Labour. He had
> done all he could for the labour movement, but the years
> were creeping over him, he was growing old in the cause
> and he intended to end his days, as he had begun them, in
> the service of Ireland. He was not going to desert the flag
> now after fighting so long . . . If today there was a parting
> of the ways between themselves and labour, it was with the
> object of getting Home Rule first, and then securing time to
> deal with Labour questions.[75]

Yet this was not a surrender to anti-Parnellite orthodoxy. In
his strengthened commitment to the Liberal-Nationalist alliance,
the ethic of independence was not wholly eclipsed. He remained
profoundly suspicious of the 'white-washed coercionists' of
official Liberalism who would be Gladstone's successors, even
chiding the Grand Old Man himself for his continued refusal to
reveal the principles of the Home Rule scheme upon which he
was known to be ruminating.[76] The lack of 'historic or scientific
knowledge' in the party was reason enough for own continued
cooperation. Also striking was his ability to see the bigger picture
beyond the gaining of Home Rule. Increasingly fascinated by

statistical arguments on taxation, his doubts grew as to whether constitutional change would be enough to secure the future of Ireland. The over-taxation of Ireland, he argued constituted a fatal drain which would threaten national regeneration.[77]

For the moment, the task was to get the Liberals back into power. As he worked assiduously for this goal, he could hardly have been more blatant in disobeying the SLP's directive to abstain from voting Liberal if opposition to their own candidates was not withdrawn.[78] He appeared on many Liberal platforms, but he reserved his most prominent advocacy for Liberal candidates constituencies of Tradeston and Camlachie – precisely those where the SLP were in contention.[79]

The 1892 General Election brought the Liberals success. In Ireland, where the contest had been intense and bitter, the anti-Parnellites triumphed with seventy-one seats.[80] For the SLP, the outcome was a disappointing one, though later claimed as a moral victory.[81] All the Labour candidates were defeated, although in Camlachie and Tradeston they polled well enough to split the vote and allow Unionist victories.[82] The *Observer* thundered at their, 'vanity and self-seeking ambition', but, in defeat, the SLP were even less forgiving.[83] At their fourth annual conference in January 1893, the party's constitution was changed to prevent those who were members of other political bodies from holding office in the party.[84] Driven from a formal association with Labour, a joke was already circulating that Ferguson had retired to a cave in the Campsie Hills.[85] In fact, he was about to enter the most productive phase of his political career. The new battleground was Glasgow. In the politics of that most dynamic, yet problem-ridden of municipalities, Ferguson could at last build a democratic alliance on his own terms.

Notes

1　TCD, Davitt MSS 9346/470, R. McGhee to M. Davitt, 14 Dec. 1885.

2　*Freeman's Journal*, 11 May 1891.

3　Davitt, *Fall of Feudalism*, pp. 642–5.

4　*Glasgow Star*, 28 Apr. 1906.

5　*Glasgow Observer*, 13 Feb. 1891.

6　*Ibid.*, 11 Jan. 1890. For an excellent account of the subsequent crisis see, F. Callanan, *The Parnell Split 1890–1* (Cork, 1981). For Scotland, see, Handley, *Irish in Modern Scotland*, pp. 280–283.

7　D. M. MacRaild, *Irish Immigrants in Modern Britain 1750–1922* (London, 1999), p.146.

8　*Glasgow Observer*, 4 Oct. 1890.

9　*Freeman's Journal*, 24 Nov. 1890.

10　*Glasgow Herald*, 26 Nov. 1890; R. Shannon, *Gladstone. Heroic Minister 1865–1898*, Harmondsworth, 1999, pp 498–9.

11　O'Shea, *Parnell*, vol. 2, pp. 165–174.

12　NLS, Acc. 11765/3, Western Executive of the Scottish Liberal Association Minutes, 28 Sept. 1890; *Glasgow Herald*, 2 Dec. 1890.

13　See, Justin McCarthy, *Reminiscences* (London, 1899), vol. 2, pp. 114–6.

14　*Glasgow Observer*, 28 Feb. 1891.

15　*Ibid.*, 6 Jun. 1891.

16　*Ibid.*, 31 Jan., 7 Feb. 1891.

17　*Glasgow Herald*, 17 Feb. 1890; *Labour World*, 22 Nov., 20 Dec. 1890.

18　*North British Daily Mail*, 3 Dec. 1890.

19 *Glasgow Herald,* 13 Dec. 1890.

20 *The Bailie,* 26 Nov. 1890. See also, 10 Dec. 1890 for 'Ireland's Last Wrong' on the same theme.

21 *Glasgow Observer,* 7 Feb. 1891.

22 *Freeman's Journal,* 13 Dec. 1890, 13 May 1891. One of Parnell's most energetic supporters was Chisholm Robertson, the Stirlingshire miner's leader: *Glasgow Observer,* 8, 15 Dec. 1890.

23 *Glasgow Star,* 28 Oct. 1903; 28 Apr. 1906.

24 He held that there were other Christian Commandments as important as the one Parnell had broken: *Freeman's Journal,* 11 May 1891.

25 Callanan, *Parnell Split,* p. 4.

26 Lyons, *Parnell,* pp. 578–81.

27 *Glasgow Observer,* 14 Mar. 1891.

28 *Ibid.,* 13 Dec. 1890. It followed up with a readers poll, containing the single question: 'Do you think that Charles Stewart Parnell has any longer the right to pose as the Irish leader?'

29 In Hamilton, for example, the 'William O'Brien' supported Parnell, while the 'Michael Davitt' opposed him: *Ibid.,* 20 Feb. 1890.

30 *Ibid.,* 8 Dec. 1890, 31 Jan., 20 Feb., 27 Jun 1891.

31 *Ibid.* In Govan the voting was 31 to 25 against Parnell, in Pollokshaws 40 to 20. In contrast, the result in Edinburgh was 300 to 17 against .

32 *Labour World,* 7 Feb. 1891.

33 *Glasgow Observer,* 21 Mar. 1891.

34 *Ibid.,* 16, 30 May. 1890.

35 The HGB assured him that outside the Orange Lodges he had no more than a hundred supporters in the city: *Ibid.*, 18 April. 1890.

36 NLI, J. F. X. O'Brien Papers, MS 13467, J. Denvir Report 4 Dec. 1890; Denvir, *Irish in Britain*, pp. 377–8.

37 *Ibid.*, 22 May. 1891; Brady, *O'Connor*, p. 123.

38 Callanan, *Parnell Split*, pp. 60–80, 110–39.

39 Lyons, *The Irish Parliamentary Party 1890–1910* (London, 1951), p. 17.

40 *Glasgow Herald*, 17 Mar. 1891.

41 *Freeman's Journal*, 11 May 1891.

42 His reference was to O'Connell's Lichfield House Compact, by which the Whigs got office and O'Connell was offered a more liberal Irish adminstration: see, F. O'Ferrall, *Daniel O'Connell* (Dublin, 1998), pp. 89–90. For an elabortion of these arguments see Ferguson's contribution in *Glasgow Observer*, 24 Oct. 1891.

43 *Ibid.*

44 *Ibid.*

45 Bew, *Parnell*, p. 121.

46 *Glasgow Observer*, 24 Oct. 1891.

47 *Ibid.*, 17 Mar. , 6, 13 Jun. 1891.

48 *Ibid.*, 27 Jun. 1891.

49 *Ibid.*, 6 Jun. 1891.

50 *Ibid.*, 27 Jun. 1891.

51 See, G. Himmelfarb, *Poverty and Compassion*, pp. 272–3.

52 *Glasgow Observer*, 27 Jun. 1891. Rodgers was a champion of

trade unionism. His *Eight Chapters in the History of Work and Wages* had been published in 1884.

53 *Ibid.*, 9 Jan. 1892.

54 For Marshall see, D. Reisman, *Alfred Marshall. Progress and Politics* (New York, 1997).

55 *Glasgow Observer,* 6 Jun. 1891.

56 *Ibid.*, 27 Jun. 1891.

57 *Ibid.*, 19 Mar. 1892.

58 *Glasgow Herald,* 4 Jan. 1892.

59. J. Smyth, 'The ILP in Glasgow, 1888–1906: the struggle for identity', in A. McKinley and R. J. Morris (eds.), *The ILP on Clydeside* (Manchester, 1991), pp. 20–2; Howell, *British Workers*, p. 152.

60 *North British Daily Mail,* 6 Mar. 1890.

61 *Glasgow Herald,* 4 Jan. 1892. Only 30–40 delegates were present – a turnout which Cunninghame Graham attributed to members sleeping off the effects of Hogmanay: *Glasgow Observer,* 9 Jan. 1892.

62 *Ibid.*, 9 Jan. 1892.

63 *Ibid.*, 8, Jan. 1892.

64 Francis Johnson Corr., R. Cunninghame Graham to K. Hardie, 8 Jan. 1881.

65 *Glasgow Observer,* 30 Jan. 1892: 'John Ferguson', it reported, 'has conquered Villadom at last'.

66 *Glasgow Herald,* 17 Jun. 1892, *Glasgow Observer,* 9, Jan. 1892.

67 Even the Parnellite organiser, Johnstone had defected: *Ibid.*, 2, Jan. 1892.

68 *Ibid.*, 16 April, 5 Mar., 7 May, 1 Oct., 19 Nov. 1892.

69 In the course of a busy schedule, he addressed the St Patrick's day rally, had lunch with Ferguson at the Liberal club, and laid a turf of Donegal shamrock to inaugurate the new Celtic Park: *Ibid.*, 26 Mar. 1892.

70 Three were from the SLP and four from Chisholm Robertson's breakaway Scottish Trades Councils Labour Party: Smyth, 'ILP in Glasgow', pp. 186–9.

71 *Glasgow Observer*, 2 Jul. 1892

72 *Ibid.*, 11 Jun. 1892.

73 *Ibid.*, 18 Jun. 1892.

74 His earlier identification with Labour had already come back to haunt him in April, when the *Mail*, which had a horror of Liberal-Labour compacts, attempted to smear him with reference to the 'Tory funding' of previous independent candidatures: *North British Daily Mail*, 19 Apr. 1892.

75 *Glasgow Observer*, 7 May. 1892

76 *Ibid.*, 21 May 1892.

77 *Ibid.*, 31 Dec. 1892. His views anticipated the appointment of a Royal Commission to consider the whole question of Anglo-Irish financial relations in May 1894.

78 *Glasgow Herald*, 17 Jun. 1892.

79 *Glasgow Observer*, 7 May, 4, 11 Jun. ; *Glasgow Herald*, 12 May, 4, 9, 10 Jun. 1892. The candidate in Camlachie was Cunninghame Graham. He had remained a loyal friend of Parnell, appealing successfully to his supporters in Glasgow to assist the Labour campaign, while expressing nothing but contempt for the 'vivisectionist Irish', who had betrayed their leader: *Glasgow Herald*, 6 Jun. 1892; *Glasgow Observer.*, 10 Oct. 1892.

80 Lyons, *Parliamentary Party*, p. 37.

81 Haddow, *Socialism*, p. 19.

82 They polled 11.9 per cent in Camlachie and 10.7 per cent in Tradeston: Smyth, 'Labour and Socialism', p. 169.

83*Glasgow Observer*, 9 Jul. 1892.

84*Glasgow Herald*, 4 Jan. 1893.

85*North British Daily Mail*, 19 Apr. 1892.

CHAPTER ELEVEN

Bravo Benburb!

With the passing of Parnell, the passion seemed to ebb from Home Rule. Ferguson sensed the forces falling back and blamed the new generation's lack of enthusiasm on their distance from the early struggles of the movement.[1] With a more jaundiced eye, the radical *Echo* believed that it was the nature of the Irish question itself which had changed. It had been a great social issue, involving the very existence of landlordism in Ireland, but now it had, 'fallen from the economic region to the barren wastes of political theorising'.[2] Either way, for all the bluster of standing by 'the old flag', Home Rule could no longer frame the boundaries of political debate for the Irish in Britain as it had in the 1880s. A growing number of activists had come to sympathise with Ferguson's struggle to align ethnic consciousness with a broader democratic spirit.

Again, he was to cut through the complexities of the situation with a supremely practical solution. The synchronicity of local and national politics had been a striking feature of early career, but now separation was vital. In parliamentary contests the Irish would doggedly support Liberal candidates as representatives of the only party which could grant Home Rule, but in the supposedly 'non-political' climate of municipal politics they were free to explore more creative alliances. Orthodox nationalists were naturally sceptical of this electoral *apartheid*, but utility outweighed ideological purity. Not only did this flexible approach allow the Glasgow Irish to claim a distinctive place within labour politics, but it established John Ferguson as a truly popular figure in his city of adoption and introduced him to a new British audience.

Ferguson's reincarnation as a municipal politician was more than an escape from political paralysis. The condition of Glasgow, he pronounced in 1893, 'was so frightful that in fifty or a hundred years men would wonder if they had been a civilised people at all'.[3] The city's population had increased by over a quarter of a million since he had first arrived as a young man in the early 1860s.[4] While the epidemics of these years had subsided, the insidious problems of disease, poverty, and overcrowding remained, confirming Glasgow as the unhealthiest city in Scotland. As Dr James Russell revealed in his 1888 lecture 'Life in One Room', 126,000 citizens lived in single apartments. These small flats accounted for 32 per cent of all the children who died in Glasgow, before their fifth year.[5] These revelations of children's whose lives were, 'short parts in a continuous tragedy', had a dramatic impact on Ferguson who had lost his own daughter as an infant. However, if this was the 'arithmetic of woe', he had the solution. Glasgow's peculiar historical position, with its relatively small area of fiscal jurisdiction, high urban values and scarce and expensive building land provided the perfect laboratory for the land taxation theories which he had nurtured for two decades. He may have regretted that earlier in his career that circumstances had not permitted him to be returned to parliament, but the task of governing Glasgow conferred a practical authority which most Westminster MPs – and Irish members above all – could only dream of.[6]

The 'Fighting Fourth'

The first task was to get elected. The pressure from INLGB branches for a voice in local affairs had grown during the late nineteenth century. In Liverpool, an impressive ethnic electoral machine had delivered an Irish nationalist councillor in 1875, the first of forty-eight to sit on the Council between 1875 and 1922.[7] Nor was Ferguson was the first Irish nationalist in Scotland to gain a seat. The redoubtable John Torley had become county councillor for Duntocher, Dunbartonshire in April 1890.[8] In Glasgow, the urgency of Irish claims could have no better testament than the *Observer's* willingness to fall into line with Hugh Murphy and the HGB. Comparing the city to 'Orange

Belfast' in its denial of political rights, it believed that bigotry lay at the core of the problem, with the Irish excluded on the basis of faith and nationality. The familiar geography of Irish settlement, it admitted, also played its part, for in no ward were the Irish strong enough to wrest representation for themselves. In addition, the ostensibly non-partisan nature of municipal contests denied them the chance to broker the balance of power, as Rule 14 of the INLGB constitution excluded branches from formal campaigning unless candidates were official Liberal nominees.[9] If these obstacles were not enough, a final challenge lay in the social composition of the Irish community. For the duration of Ferguson's political career and beyond, the Irish remained concentrated in unskilled or semi-skilled manual occupations. By 1911, as Smyth suggests, just under twenty per cent of the Irish-born male workforce were engaged in occupations explicitly described as 'labouring'.[10] Municipal elections, however, favoured the more prosperous skilled worker, as the ratepayers' franchise meant not only that rates had to be paid in full before each November, but that occupants of the cheapest property whose rates were compounded were automatically excluded. In this way, more that a quarter of households were without a municipal vote in the 1890s.[11]

There were two conclusions to be drawn. First, the branches' basic work of voter registration was as vital ever; second, as the *Observer* recognised, the only hope lay, 'in cooperation with the other progressive forces in the different localities'.[12] In Manchester, which, like Glasgow, lacked Liverpool's demographic advantages, collaboration with the Liberals had already proved fruitful, but this option had receded locally after broken promises to allow a clear field to an Irish candidate during the 1891 election.[13] The alternative for the Glasgow Irish was a re-evaluation of their relationship with the labour movement – itself adopting a more assertive posture on political representation in response to the weakness of local trade unionism.[14] Balancing their disappointment with the Liberals, the *Observer* now argued that since more than nine-tenths of Glasgow Catholics were wage earners, the labour cause is, 'ours and our battle theirs'.[15] Yet the candidates who emerged could never be wholly 'Irish' or 'Catholic' as some nationalists hoped. The issue of how the INLGB was to receive its political 'reward' thus injected an element of instability into what was viewed as an expedient arrangement between separate 'parties' or 'interests'.

Ferguson's assault on Glasgow Town Council in November 1893 was a milestone in the search for a workable democratic coalition. For one who had spent a lifetime electioneering, he was at last to become a candidate for public office in his own right. The battleground was to be the Forth Ward. This comprised of the Calton district, once famous for its radical weaving tradition, but now displaying the city's social problems in a nutshell.[16] Despite the impact of the 1866 City Improvement Act, the sanitary sub-district of 'Calton proper' had a death rate of 31.1 per 1000, compared with 23.3 for the city as a whole. With a density of 217 persons per acre it was also one of the most overcrowded in the city.[17] The ward stretched west from Bridgeton Cross to the Saltmarket, bounded by the Gallowgate in the north and Glasgow Green in the south, containing a largely working class electorate, with a significant Irish component. The HGB's headquarters in Watson Street was only a stone's throw away, and the inclusion of Glasgow Green – where Ferguson had addressed many a meeting – allowed him to claim he was the true 'local' candidate. In a period when many municipal wards were uncontested, Calton was already known as the 'Fighting Forth'.[18]

The genesis of the campaign was rather shadowy, but there was no mistaking the enthusiasm which it generated. It was to be one of the most memorable elections in the city, 'more like a parliamentary than a municipal contest'.[19] Ferguson believed that the initial impetus had come from the local INLGB branches, but the Irish had also been quick to secure allies.[20] The Trades Council were approached in August, and as soon as Ferguson's name began to be mentioned in public as a candidate, it became clear that the 'Labour party' would not oppose him.[21] Another powerful boost came from the adherence of the Scottish Land Restoration Union (SLRU). Formed three years before from an amalgamation of the SLRL and other local land reform societies, the organisation boasted a strong presence in the Bridgeton and Calton areas.[22] Even the Parnellites were swept along, endorsing Ferguson as 'a good Irishman and Protestant', though reserving their warmest support for their own Glasgow candidate, Chisholm Roberston.[23] Ominously, Ferguson's official Liberal nomination proved the most controversial element of his popular ticket, secured by only the narrowest of majorities from the executive of the local association.[24]

As the contest progressed, it illustrated with some force the complexities of electioneering in the absence of conventional party labels. Ferguson originally stood as the candidate of 'Labour and Social Reform', but after dissident Liberals brought forward the businessman William Bow as the 'Temperance, Social Reform and Liberal Candidate', he decided to become the 'Liberal, Labour and Temperance Candidate' – or as the *Herald* wryly observed, since Mr Bow claimed to be 'the friend of the people', Mr Ferguson decided to become 'everybody's friend'.[25] The prominence of the temperance issue, in fact, concealed the deeper undercurrents of opposition ranged against him. There is no doubting the moral fervour of local temperance activists, but support for 'temperance principles' could also signify coded antipathy against the Irish, who were particularly prominent in the drink trade, as one of the few commercial avenues open to them.[26] His opponents happily admitted that Bow had been brought forward not only because he was more 'forward' on temperance, but to block Ferguson who was, 'first and foremost the candidate of the National League'.[27]

Ferguson must have been the only 'temperance crusader' to receive an endorsement from the *National Guardian*, the official newspaper of the Scottish licensed trade.[28] He approached the issue as a reformer rather than an ideologue, backing the local veto and the municipalisation of public houses, but rejecting other temperance shibboleths such as 'one man, one license'.[29]

He was much happier on his home ground as an evangelist for radical social change. Among the myriad of pledges expected from municipal candidates, he campaigned on commanding social issues, such as the taxation of ground rents, and the eight-hour day and union rates for Council employees.[30] The Orange clergyman, J. U. Mitchell dismissed his platform as, 'thoroughly visionary and utopian', but it was precisely this quality which caught the electorate's imagination, viewing the contest as struggle against bigotry and privilege.[31]

When the votes were finally counted on 7 November, it became clear that Ferguson had overcome the combined hostility of the temperance party, the Orangemen and the Glasgow press, to win a solid majority over his rival.[32]

A Daniel come to judgment?

Expectations were running high, with Ferguson's supporters convinced he would be a 'power in the council against all evils'.[33] At first sight, he appeared as a firebrand tossed in among his douce municipal colleagues. He was openly contemptuous of their 'non-political' pretensions, apparently taking little trouble to learn the ropes of Council procedure.[34] A glimpse of the new councillor in action at the beginning of 1895, suggested that his voluble presence was almost too big for a municipal stage:

Members of the Town Council seem to regard a speech by Mr John Ferguson very much as a trembling schoolboy does the flourish of his master's tawse. When John is about to get up to give one of his sledgehammer speeches , all sorts of expedients to avoid the ordeal. 'Must this question really be debated at length?' 'Has Mr Ferguson not gone over this ground before? 'Is the motion Mr Ferguson opposes not about to be withdrawn?' But once John is on his feet, nothing deters him. 'By all means let the debate by shortened', he said last week, '. . . if you like, when I am finished'.[35]

While they continued to be in awe of him, the distance between Ferguson and his fellow councillors was actually less than it appeared. Indeed, there was a tolerance of his brand of individualism – even eccentricity – in the City Chambers if this was felt to be in the interests of public service.[36] As he gradually became socialised into the working practices of his new political environment, he was to master the mechanics of committee system and turn it to his advantage.[37]

Ideological contestation among the councillors may have been muted, but there were other aspects of Glasgow's civic identity with which Ferguson could identify. He was no stranger to the business ideals of drive and efficiency which motivated his colleagues. While he was one of the few non-Scots on the Town Council, its widely shared vision of a lost agrarian society harmonised with his own rising fury at the evils of city life. His social reform crusade could also draw on a remarkable tradition of purposeful civic activity. The concept of 'municipal socialism', for example, had already been popularised by Robert Crawford as a sensible electoral strategy in 1890. Drawing on Ruskin and Chamberlain – two of Ferguson's own influences – it originally echoed his distaste for 'class' politics, seeking cohesion and progress in an era of instability.[38] Indeed, even radical land taxation schemes had found a municipal audience: John Burt's proposal on land values taxation had discussed by the Council for eighteen months during 1890–1, but was eventually abandoned after a narrow defeat.[39]

Similarly, Ferguson's views on the rights and responsibilities of municipal government drew on the prevailing spirit of civic pride. Those who mocked his championship of a civic flag, to be hoisted when the Council was in session, failed to realise that behind such crusades lay a serious purpose.[40] He believed that the duties of a councillor were legislative as well as administrative:

> For there were matters of importance which the governors of
> the City of Glasgow should . . . have the power to regulate for

themselves apart from the Imperial Parliament. His Home Rule propensities went much further than the concession of local government to Ireland or Scotland: he wanted to see a municipal parliament for Glasgow, with powers sufficient to manage Glasgow affairs . . .[41]

This was local democracy in action. But just as he valued an Irish parliament for what it could accomplish on behalf of the Irish people, he was also determined that the municipality must serve the needs of its citizens. While he professed admiration for the efficiency and sense of public duty displayed by the Town Council, he believed that it needed 'educating', as in its principles and mode of thought it was simply, '"bourgeois": it knows nothing of the social problems of our age upon which the highest minds of our age have delivered themselves upon . . .'[42] He was anxious to undertake this task personally, translating diffuse reforming sentiment into action guided by 'scientific principles'. Therefore, during his first few months on the Council, he displayed both a furious energy and a remarkable tenacity of purpose, even when his most sacred causes were swamped in post-prandial debate.

Foremost among these causes were the taxation of land values and the 'living wage'. The two were intimately related, as Ferguson's 1894 essay on 'The Philosophy of the Living Wage' explained. The argument was a familiar one. The laws of economics, as described by Spencer, Mill and economists from Smith to Marshall, revealed that taxation based on the wages of labour and the profits of capital retarded production. Tax, following Mill, should be on unearned income not on individual prudence and industry. However, 'unearned increment' – ground rents and mining royalties – amounting to £200,000,000 per annum in Great Britain and Ireland, should be appropriated back to the whole community. Unless these natural agents were taken into community ownership then 'God and Nature's plan for bettering workers' would be frustrated. It was true that profits alone could not support the living wage, as labour and capital had to support a section of 'economic loafers' who consumed one sixth of total profit. Capitalists must instead take the side of workers against loafers: 'lest workers forget what science and religion teach them, that capital and labour are natural friends and allies'.[43]

Ferguson moved onto the attack within a few weeks of his election, signalling his intention to introduce a motion to appropriate land values, 'for the service of the whole community', through the granting of parliamentary permission for the city to tax ground landlords to the tune of one and a half million pounds.[44] He orchestrated a vigorous campaign, but despite nineteen resolutions in support of the measure from the city's various progressive organisations, the Council repeatedly delayed consideration of the motion until it was finally voted out in March 1894.[45] Undeterred, he pressed on. A 'betterment' motion, in June which sought to empower the Corporation to impose a special rate of tax on property values increased as a result of public expenditure was more fortunate. A new committee to consider the issue was not created, as he had requested, but it was remitted to the Special Committee on Council Work.[46] Issues which drained the municipal purse proved less popular, with his attempts later in the year to win an eight-hour day and a 'living wage' of 21/- for Council employees being deferred or defeated by large majorities. He was well aware of the source of his colleagues' apprehension, believing that they were on the eve of an expenditure so large, 'to make the working classes comfortable', that sensible men shrunk from its contemplation.[47] He appeared to have won a real breakthrough in July, when he won the vote to establish a committee to investigate the 'unearned increment' of the city and how to tap it for municipal purposes.[48] 'Bravo Benburb!' was Michael's Davitt's reaction to a step which, he believed, showed the enormous strides which Single Tax doctrines had made since 'Philosopher John' entered the Council.[49] Observers more familiar with the methods of Glasgow Town Council, hinted that by remitting the measure to a committee they had successfully killed it.[50] The work of education would continue.

Mid-Lanark revisited

The sight of a councillor actually attempting to fulfil his election mandate was a novelty for Glasgow's democratically-minded citizens. Meanwhile, for the Irish, Ferguson's hero status was confirmed. The INLGB branches rushed to shower him with honours, as his supporters declared that, 'he had done more for democracy in his first three months in office than the whole pack of the Town Council'.[51] To the *Observer* it seemed that he had claimed the place in the hearts of Glasgow's Irish labourers which, 'Mr Parnell in his zenith occupied in the hearts of his countrymen the world over'.[52]

In the national arena, there was also a sense of triumph by default. Home Rule politics were becoming increasingly dominated by a squalid power struggle between John Dillon and Tim Healy. The key issue was whether, as Dillon insisted, the strong leadership and discipline of the old Parnellite party should be reimposed over the sovereign rights of constituencies. Even though Ferguson had suffered from the centralised system in the past, he had little love for Healy's posturing as a champion of constituency rights. His response was to protest against the spirit of faction, using amnesty platforms to bring together a remarkable assembly of, 'McCarthyites, Redmondites, Dillonites and Healyites', together with Young Irelanders and even a young Maud Gonne.[53] However, he was ultimately forced to throw his weight behind Dillon's conception of unity, arguing that: 'One man must be the voice of the people of Ireland in the Irish parliament'.[54]

The difficulty was that the gilded link between discipline and unity which had given the party its unique power had been broken for ever. In a fragmented political landscape, a politician of Ferguson's stature was bound to loom large. Nor could he resist dabbling in the Irish constituencies which were becoming the new sites of party warfare.[55] Back in Glasgow, his help as a fundraiser was also sorely needed. After 1894, the party began to suffer a severe financial crisis as overseas donations dwindled. He responded with alacrity, convening a committee of local Irish businessmen to make maximum use of Davitt's moral authority during one of his periodic visits.[56] For these services he attempted to extract his own price from Dillon, revealing a quietly manipulative streak. Not only was he free with his advice and exhortations, but he also sought to advance the careers of generous Glasgow 'friends' of the party.[57]

As the Liberal alliance began to falter, this capacity for personal intrigue continued to flourish. The failure of the second Home Rule Bill in September 1893 had come as an expected blow. The Bill itself had been a disappointment, retaining considerable powers to the Imperial Parliament, but failing to address Ferguson's concerns over the burden of Irish taxation. Its rejection by the House of Lords, in Davitt's view, merely confirmed 'the evils of landlordism'.[58] More distressing for nationalists, was Gladstone's replacement in March 1894 by the Scottish aristocrat, Lord Rosebery. The new premier immediately attempted to stamp his authority on his party by a Salisbury-like declaration in the House of Lords that Home Rule would have to wait until England had been convinced of its 'justice and equality'. A further mollifying speech in Edinburgh might have been enough to convince Dillon that the Liberal commitment to Home Rule was safe, but for Ferguson it was 'brimful of rubbish'.[59] He now faced his old demons. Since the 1880s, he had warned against dangers of setting alliance above independence – indeed the recent crisis of the crofters movement after submerging its identity in Liberalism seemed to confirm his fears.[60] Like Davitt, he was forced to cling even more tightly to his faith in the inevitability of Home Rule .[61] He would work on the Liberals from the inside using his unique gifts. Perhaps Lord Rosebery – like most mortals in Ferguson's opinion – merely needed 'education'.

It was his determination on these points which explained his conduct at the second Mid-Lanark by-election in April 1894, an episode which bewildered admirers of his municipal record. In a repeat of the 1888 contest, the local Liberal Association had refused either a plebiscite or a free run to Bob Smillie, the Miners' Association candidate.[62] Instead, they selected James Caldwell, a land reformer, whom Ferguson had been carefully nursing in INLGB circles since his defeat in Tradeston in 1892.[63] Hardie approached Davitt for support for Smillie, but Ferguson had already persuaded his friend that an SLP victory was impossible, even with Irish votes. His intrusive presence in the constituency was soon to make this prediction a reality. The campaign was short and bad-tempered. Not only did Ferguson publish Davitt's letter to him denouncing Labour's 'grave political blindness', but he also prevailed on him to come to Caldwell's assistance in person.[64] The exchange was satirised in the *Labour Leader's* poetry corner:

> Writes Johnnie av Benburb to Mick of Ballybrack,
> 'Yez might send us down a line to keep the bhoys on track;
> And if yez can cam o'er yourself, it may be just as well,
> For Hardie, Small and Smillie's like to damage dear
> Caldwell.[65]

As Ferguson and Davitt tore around the factory gates in their election brake, relations between the nationalists and Labour's political wing unravelled. After a series of rousing meetings, Caldwell was narrowly returned. Although Smillie's failure to capture Mid-Lanark was also due to the lack of a strong trade union base in the area, an infuriated Hardie blamed the follies of 'official Irishism', while the SLP Chairman, Adam Adamson declared that the real battle in the future would between 'the Irish workingman and the Scotch workingman'.[66] For his part, Smillie never forgave Ferguson. He claimed the Irish leader had encouraged the SLP to contest the seat, then moved heaven and earth to secure Caldwell's return: in the future, he would become 'doubly shy of Glasgow's adroit wire-puller'.[67]

The bitterness of the contest was also a revelation for Ferguson and deepened his distrust of socialism. Once, he had declared himself 'passive' on the doctrine, but now he claimed that socialist tactics such as street-lamp breaking would mean, 'the people being bayonetted in the streets and every force of law being turned against the legitimate demands of labour.[68] The threats made by the SLP during the campaign that they would launch an anti-Irish crusade against the Liberals had also reawakened his defensive mentality. He responded in June 1894 by reviving the tradition of public parades, mounting a show of strength which was as much for the benefit of their comrades in arms as for their common enemy.[69] They would, 'show the Liberals what a powerful ally they had in the Irish democracy, and show Keir Hardie and those socialists who talk of a war against races how significant are the Irish forces they threaten'.[70]

Towards a 'Progressive Party'

Liberals and Irish nationalists drifted towards the General Election campaign of July 1895 united in their disarray. Ferguson set to the work with a vengeance. Rushing back from Ireland on Thursday 4 July, his activities at Liberal meetings during the next week give an extraordinary snapshot of him on the election stump. On Friday, he spoke at Tradeston and at Cranstounhill; on Saturday, he gave socialist youths a severe dressing down for interrupting him at Parkhead; on Monday, he went to Holytown; on Tuesday, he spoke at Renton; on Wednesday, at Coatbridge; on Thursday, at Ballieston; on Friday, he was back supporting the Liberals in Central Division. His only regret was that he had been unable to get back to Ireland to campaign among the Protestant farmers of South Tyrone.[71] Yet for all his efforts, the Liberal campaign was doomed. The party struggled to retain two seats in Glasgow, while a solid Unionist majority was returned nationwide. It was little consolation that Labour fared even worse, with Ferguson winning the price of a new hat by betting on the miserable size of Shaw Maxwell's vote in Blackfriars.[72]

As Home Rule was cast into the political wilderness, his

first response was to indulge himself in some rhetorical brinksmanship, threatening extreme confrontational methods to 'tear the hypocritical mask from the face of English government'.[73] Parliamentary opposition would become more difficult after changes to parliamentary procedure, but this was not the time for Ferguson forsake moral force. While he proclaimed that 'the fight must go on', the struggle would be conducted in the public halls and not on the barricades. Approaching sixty, he had lost none of restlessness – nor his appetite for a telling speech. To the INLGB branches he boasted that he spend twelve nights in every month expounding on 'the good old cause', but had also plunged himself into SLRU activities, carrying the Single Tax gospel across Scotland and Ulster.[74] Clearly, his life continued to be one defined outside the domestic realm. The Ferguson family was now grown up. The youngest son William had graduated in medicine from Glasgow University in 1891, moving south to build up a substantial practice in Newcastle-upon-Tyne.[75] His brother John's progress seemed less impressive, but in 1896 he obtained post of inspector in the Corporation Sanitary Department – an arrangement which in time was to prove embarrassing for Ferguson *père*.[76] Anna, his only surviving daughter, remained unmarried, and alongside Mary Ferguson, continued to give him prominent support in his public work. By 1891, the household at Benburb had also been joined by Mary's spinster sister, Anna.[77]

Municipal affairs continued to absorb him.[78] He hammered away at Land Values taxation, beating the path for John Burt's successful motion on 17 June, 1895 which was hailed as 'a beacon light to Single Taxers'.[79] The outcome was a survey of Scotland's sixty-two assessing authorities, which intimated their willingness to join with Glasgow in petitioning parliament to permit local land values taxation.[80] His civic agenda was also broadening. The Scottish economy had been slowly recovering from the pressures of the 1880s, but Glasgow, as a capital goods producer, continued to reel from cyclical crises during the winter of 1894.[81] In response, Ferguson advocated emergency poor relief and farm colonisation schemes as efficient ways of giving employment to the deserving poor of the city, 'in the interests of the ratepayers'.[82] When a further attempt to introduce a minimum wage for Council employees failed in April, he moved on to attack both the management practices and salaries of Council officials. [83] He kept up the pressure with his motion to forward the principle of 'betterment', arguing that the costs of new projects should be met by a levy on the improved property values, rather than by increasing the city's taxation burden.[84]

Ferguson was beginning to learn some important lessons. His advent on the Council had been hailed as the beginning of a new era, dividing the members into two groups – 'those in favour of progressive action and those in favour of what might be called the status quo in municipal affairs'.[85] In fact, the disposition of forces was more complex. As he admitted, he had received better support from Tories than 'burning Liberals' and others 'pledged up to the eyes' for progressive legislation.[86] While individual councillors might be prepared to consider financial redress from private interests who were directly profiteering from public investments, convincing them of the case for more radical and wide-ranging land taxation measures was proving more difficult. In these circumstances, Ferguson was prepared to follow policies which might meet Glasgow's social problems in the short term. For all that he was popularly identified as a 'Single Taxer', this incremental strategy earned the contempt of Georgite purists on the SLRU, who held that taxation of land values was the only just solution.[87] Not only did they opposed his minimum wage motion on the grounds that it would increase taxes, but Councillors Burt and McLardy were also sceptical over Ferguson's betterment initiative, prompting him to comment that, 'he could teach a parrot to talk about land values, but it took a mind to apply them . . .'[88]

The conduct of his well-intentioned, but fractious, allies suggested that Ferguson's dream of building 'a progressive party' on the Town Council would be difficult to realise.[89] Some INLGB branches still wavered, as witnessed in their attempts in October

1895 to form an independent Central Municipal Election Council to broker the Irish vote.[90] Yet all minds were concentrated as the decisive municipal elections of November 1896 drew closer. Every Glasgow ward would be up for contestation, following a comprehensive redistribution which promised to rectify the imbalance against working class electors. When the Trades Council launched its new joint electoral initiative in June, Irish delegates gingerly joined with those from the ILP, the SDF and the Cooperative movement to draw up an initial programme and establish and a Workers' Municipal Electoral Committee (WMEC).[91]

Ferguson became the dominating personality in the new organisation. Placing his distinctive stamp on its public programme, he also relished his private influence in candidate selection. Old associates like Hugh Murphy and Shaw Maxwell appeared in the lists alongside new acolytes, such as Boyd S. Brown, who regarded Ferguson's endorsement as a ticket to campaign success.[92] He was never to forget the principles which had propelled him into a public career, but after decades of patient campaigning, the exercise of political power had become something of a fascination in itself.

Notes

1 *Glasgow Observer,* 12 Dec. 1896.

2 *Glasgow Echo,* 5 Apr. 1894.

3 *North British Daily Mail,* 27 Oct. 1893.

4 *Municipal Glasgow: Its Evolution and Enterprises* (Glasgow, 1914).

5 Robertson, *Glasgow's Doctor,* pp. 205–6.

6 I. Sweeney [Maver], 'The Municipal Adminstration of Glasgow, 1833–1912: Public Service and Scottish Civic Identity', University of Strathclyde Ph.D. Thesis, 1990.

7 J. Belchem, 'The Irish middle class in Victorian Liverpool' in, R. Swift and S. Gilley (eds.), *The Irish in Victorian Britain: the Local Dimension* (Dublin, 2000), p. 209.

8 Councillor M. Flannigan was also returned for St Giles Ward, Edinburgh the same year: *Glasgow Observer*, 19 Apr., 11 Nov. 1890.

9 *Ibid.*, 21 Nov. 1891; 24 Sept. 1892.

10 Smyth, 'Labour and Socialism', p. 157–8.

11 W. H. Fraser, 'From civic gospel to muncipal socialism', in D. Fraser (ed.), *Cities, Class and Communications: Essays in Honour of Asa Briggs'* (Hemel Hempstead, 1990), p. 185. Note also Denvir's observations on the lack of Irish voting power: *Irish in Britain*, p. 449.

12 *Glasgow Observer*, 24 Aug. 1895.

13 S. Fielding, *Class and Ethnicity: Irish Catholics in England, 1880–1939*, (Buckingham, 1993), p. 61

14 McCaffrey, 'Political issues ', in Fraser and Maver, *Glasgow*, p. 219.

15 *Glasgow Observer*, 7 Nov. 1891. Hugh Murphy was also able to play a personal mediating role through his membership of Glasgow Trades Council as the cabinetmakers' delegate: *Glasgow Trades Council Annual Report 1892–3*.

16 J. Macfarlane, *The Old Calton, Glasgow Green and the River Clyde* (Glasgow, 1921); J. Ord, *The Story of the Burgh of Calton* (Glasgow nd.).

17 *Twenty-Forth Annual Report on the Operations of the Sanitary Department of the City of Glasgow, 1893*.

18 *Glasgow Herald*, 8 Nov. 1893.

19 *Glasgow Echo*, 1 Sept. 1894.

20 *Glasgow Observer*, 15 Jun. 1895.

21 *Ibid..*, 26 Aug. 1893. In turn Ferguson was extravagant in his praise for the work of the Trades Union Congress, meeting in his native Belfast: *Ibid.* 12 Sept. 1893.

22 *Bridgeton Advertiser and Single Tax Review,* 2 Aug. 1890;*North British Daily Mail,* 26 Oct. 1893.

23 *North British Daily Mail,* 6 Nov. 1893.

24 *Glasgow Echo,* 27 Oct. 1893.

25 *Glasgow Herald,* 8 Nov. 1893.

26 Smyth, 'Labour and Socialism', p. 159: Irish-born males formed 15.12 per cent of publicans and wine and spirit merchants in the 1911 Census. See also, I Maver, 'Local party politics and the temperance crusade 1890–1902', *Scottish Labour History Society Journal,* 27 (1992), pp. 44–63.

27 *Glasgow Echo,* 27 Oct. 1893.

28 *National Guardian,* 15 Nov. 1893.

29 *North British Daily Mail,* 31 Oct. 1893.

30 *Ibid.,* 27 Oct., 2 Nov. 1893.

31 *Ibid.,* 27 Oct. 1893.

32 *North British Daily Mail,* 8 Nov. 1893.

33 *Ibid.,* 12 Oct. 1893.

34 *Ibid.,* 31 Oct. 1893; *Glasgow Echo,* 1 Sept. 1894.

35 *Glasgow Observer,* 9 Feb. 1895.

36 Maver, 'Municipal Adminstration', vol. 2, p. 726.

37 He was appointed to the committees dealing with churches and churchyards and municipal libraries.: Glasgow City Archives (GCA), Minutes of the Town Council of Glasgow, 16 Nov. 1893.

38 Ibid., vol. 1, p. 428–9.

39 *Single Tax,* Jul. 1895–see Nov. for Burt's profile.

40 GCA, Town Council Minutes, 3 Dec. 1896; *Bailie,* 22 Nov. 1899.

41 *Glasgow Observer,* 15 Jun. 1895.

42 *Single Tax*, Aug. 1894.

43 *Ibid.*, 4 Aug. 1894.

44 *Ibid.*, 25 Nov. 1893; GCA, Town Council Minutes, 7 Dec. 1893.

45 Ibid., 1 Mar. 1893, p. 102.

46 Ibid., 7 Jun. 1894, p. 291.

47 *Glasgow Observer*, 4 Aug. 1894.

48 *Single Tax*, Aug. 1894.

49 TCD, Davitt MSS 9556, Diary 1 Aug. 1894.

50 *Labour Leader*, 4 Aug. 1894

51 He became Honorary President of the Springburn; the Kinning Park 'Bernard Kelly'; and the Dillon Branches, *Ibid.*, 16 Dec. 1893; 10 Feb., 27 Nov. 1894; *Glasgow Echo*, 16 Mar. 1894. He later achieved the ultimate accolade of an INLGB branch – Clydebank and Yoker – named in his honour, while the Glasgow Irish National Foresters Branch No. 370 also became the 'John Ferguson'.

52 *Glasgow Observer*, 9 Jun. 1894.

53 *Ibid.*, 26 Oct. 1895.

54 *Ibid.*, 19 Dec. 1896.

55 He was active, for example, in North and South Tyrone and in Louth: TCD, Dillon MSS 6788/40–1, J. Ferguson to J. Dillon, 10, 12 Mar. 1896. See also *Irish News*, 22 Jul. 1895.

56 A Celtic jubilee match in August, with Davitt as guest of honour, disappointingly raised only £60 for the new Parliamentary Fund, but Ferguson's drive for business subscriptions resulted in almost £200 pledged in a week: TCD, Davitt MSS 9556, Diary 3 Aug. 1894; *Glasgow Observer*, 11 Aug. 1894. Another figure whom Ferguson hoped would take a greater public share in the INL's work was the grocery magnate, Sir Thomas Lipton. He was an Ulster

Protestant who generally preferred more subtle expressions of his abiding nationalist and populist sympathies. He gifted Michael Davitt 1000 Lipton shares, a fact which was only discovered on Davitt's death: TCD, Dillon MSS 6788, J. Ferguson to J. Dillon, 5 Jul. 1896; Thomas Lipton, *Leaves from the Lipton Logs* (London, 1931).

57 Ibid., J. Ferguson to J. Dillon, 9 Jan. 1898. Mr William McKillop, the successful restauranteur and Celtic FC director, was a typical protégé. This 'good Irishman' was willing to pay his own way if sent to parliament, and was willing to hold a 'Celtic Sports Day' to add another £200 to the hundreds he had already raised for the party. For his subsequent political career see, *Glasgow Observer*, 15 May 1904.

58 *Glasgow Observer*, 16 Sept. 1893.

59 Lyons, *Dillon*, p.162; *Glasgow Observer*, 31 Mar. 1894.

60 Hunter, 'Politics of highland land reform', p. 61.

61 *Ibid.*, 10 Mar. 1894.

62 *Glasgow Echo*, 24 Apr. 1894.

63 Howell, *British Workers*, pp. 154–6; *Glasgow Observer*, 1 Apr., 23 Sept. 1893

64 *Glasgow Echo*, 30 Mar. 1894; TCD, Davitt MSS 9555, Diary 31 Mar., 2–5 Apr. 1894. His opposition to Smillie was despite his personal liking for the man, and he assured him he would get the Liberals not to oppose him next time.

65 *Labour Leader*, 14 Apr. 1894.

66 *Ibid.*, 7 Apr. 1894; *Glasgow Echo*, 2 Apr. 1894.

67 Smillie, *My Life for Labour*, pp. 105–6.

68 *North British Daily Mail*, 27 Oct. 1893.

69 *Ibid.*, 9 Jun. 1894. The occasion was a Trades Council demonstration against the House of Lords in which the

Irish agreed to participate. Besides rejecting Home Rule, the Lords had also rejected the Employers' Liability Bill.

70 *Ibid.,* 15 May 1894.

71 *Glasgow Observer,* 13, 27 Jul. 1895; *North British Daily Mail,* 6–8 Jul. 1895.

72 *Glasgow Observer,* 20 Jul. 1895.

73 *Ibid.,* 17 Aug. 1895.

74 *Ibid.,* 23 Mar. 1895; *Single Tax,* Dec. 1894, Jan.–Feb. 1895.

75 W. Innes Addison, *Roll of Graduates of the University of Glasgow, 1727–1897* (Glasgow, 1898), p. 189.

76 *Corporation of Glasgow, Annual Report of Officials and Salaries as at 31 March 1906,* (Glasgow, 1906), p. 30.

77 1891 Census, Cadder Parish (West District), Lanarkshire.

78 After two years service on the Council, he was elected to the Diseases of Animals Act Committee, the Special Committee on Corporation Work and the Committee of Management: GCA, Town Council Minutes, 7 Nov. 1895.

79 *Single Tax,* Jul. 1895.

80 *Ibid.,* Nov. 1898

81 I. Maver, 'Civic Government', in Fraser and Maver, *Glasgow 1830–1912,* p. 381; McCaffrey, *Scotland,* p. 89.

82 *North British Daily Mail,* 15 Feb. 1895; GCA, Town Council Minutes, 20 May 1895.

83 Ibid., 6 Jun., 3 Oct., 2 Apr. 1895; *Glasgow Observer,* 6 Jul. 1895.

84 *Ibid.,* 28 Sept. 1895.

85 *Glasgow Echo,* 1 Sept. 1894.

86 *Glasgow Observer,* 22 Aug. 1896.

87 *Single Tax,* Jan. 1897.

88 *Glasgow Observer*, 26 Oct. 1895, 9 May 1896; *Single Tax*, Nov. 1896. David McLardy, Vice-President of the SLRU had been returned for Fourth Ward in December 1896.

89 *Glasgow Observer*, 9 Jun. 1894.

90 *Ibid.*, 26 Oct. 1895; see also Smyth, 'Labour and Socialism', p. 177–8.

91 *Ibid.*, 20 Jun. 1896.

92 Brown liked to claim that he was 'a colleague of John Ferguson' – a privilege which the *Herald* sardonically noted was enjoyed by 75 members of the Council: 3 Nov. 1897.

CHAPTER TWELVE

City of Progress

'The Lion of Benburb' was a relieved man on polling night. Not only had November 1896, five were returned. When allied to existing 'Labour' and Liberal-inclined 'Progressive' councillors, the arrival of the Stalwarts meant the development of a radical bloc in municipal politics, which embraced social reform with a new urgency.[1]

The Stalwarts' days of triumph were brief, but, as their opponents feared, they were to propel Glasgow into the vanguard of a national campaign for land values taxation under Ferguson's leadership.[2] After the Parnell split, Irish politics may have settled back into the traditional postures of localism, but here was a 'local' politician who took a seemingly limited stage and expanded it to suit his ambitions.[3] Across Britain, there had been a boom in domestic investment, drawing on private and public finance. The private sector had been encouraged by low interest rates and restricted overseas alternatives, but the wave of urban expansion fed by this required municipal investment in collective capital. Even more galling than these social costs were the huge private gains in land values that followed from the development of vacant sites. Despite the tortuous mass of fiscal detail, the question underpinning the local taxation debate was a simple one: 'Who pays'?[4]

But if Ferguson's profile grew in these years so did his personal pride. He had once made a revealing boast to John Dillon that he could beat his opponents with contempt.'[5] As his enemies began to regroup, he was to need every element of this self-belief.

The Sunward Bound

The Stalwarts' electoral platform in 1896 had been built on Ferguson's efforts to puncture the non-partisan pretensions of city

councillors. His own manifesto seemed uncharacteristically terse when set beside his colleagues' nine-point programme, but the two issues on which he focused – the taxation of land values and the 'living minimum' – were to be the props of the new campaign.
[6] The Stalwarts' detailed demands also included municipalisation of the drinks trade and support for the unemployed. While these issues could be dealt with directly by the new 'Glasgow Corporation', land values taxation – the means by which a self-sufficient municipality could finance social reforms – would require the granting of parliamentary powers.

Still parading his intellectual dominance over the 'economic babes' in the Council chamber, Ferguson was delighted to launch the campaign.[7] Unlike many radicals of his day, he had a keen awareness of the international context for urban policy, drawing on a range of examples from Basle to Toronto. As a personal link between single tax faddism and municipalism, he also displayed in generous measure both the utopian and pragmatic currents which now drove the land reform movement. In practice, this meant that the dry bones of local taxation became infused with a prophetic spirit that alternated between hope and despair. It is a quality best captured in his 1900 pamphlet, *Glasgow, the City of Progress* – part electioneering device, part emotional outpouring.

Opponents may have wearied of his 'long studies on dreich subjects', but the pungent *City of Progress* was of a different order. '*Zeit Geist*' had entered his conceptual armoury and the work embodied both the man and his age.[8] Much of it was classic Ferguson. 'Loafers' and other feudal remnants remained the enemy. The 'Municipal Parliament' was dominated by the 'governing class bourgeois', but the remedy was still the natural alliance between capital and labour, divided into hostile camps by an unnatural system. Yet his vision had grown darker over the years. The urban environment promised only further human degeneration:

The cities, Saturn-like, devour their offspring . . . The rural population is decreasing rapidly. Soon the supply of healthy

parents from the country will be exhausted, and then the
intellectual and physical decay of our noble nation must be
very rapid . . . The child whose playground was the dark
close or the filthy quadrangle, is the adult of wild enjoyment,
rowdy life, and early death.

   . . . At present the vast majority are simply human manure
out of which here and there some forms of highly cultivated
and beautiful flowers of mankind appear.[9]

Fin de siècle pessimism was prominent both as a literary idiom
and a philosophical undercurrent, but Ferguson's fears were
tempered by his faith in ultimate human destiny.[10] While holding
fast to Mill's environmentalist tradition, he was now even more
ready to repudiate the 'Pagan' aspects of the utilitarian heritage.

   Adam Smith, Malthus, Mill, Ricardo and Herbert Spencer,
   formulated great and true principles by which industry has
   been organised, wealth produced, and the Social Evolution
   immensely advanced; but Society has hardened these
   principles into creeds admitting of neither new articles
   nor modification by new principles. There is no finality in
   nature. New conditions of life have been developed, and
   larger and wider systems of economics spring from these by
   natural development.[11]

If Glasgow was to take the 'gallant sunward bound' to a
higher social stage, it must abandon the principle of survival of
the fittest. Marx, Manning, Marshall and Ruskin had revealed
a deeper truth. A collective effort was necessary to secure
'economic rent' in order to pay the costs of both municipal and
imperial government – £100,000 per annum was waiting to be
plucked from the speculators. Political freedom had been won,
the weapon was now at hand to win economic freedom:

God give us men! A time like this demands

Great hearts, strong minds, true faith and willing hands . . . [12]

Stand by the Stalwarts

For two invigorating years it looked as if the men in the Stalwart camp might just succeed. Ferguson had opened the 1896 campaign with his ritual attack on officials' salary rises.[13] Municipal housing, fire insurance and even a clothing factory, now regularly peppered the Council agenda. His factory proposal failed, but the fire insurance issue was addressed by the Parliamentary Bills Committee in September 1897.[14] The following year, the Stalwarts succeeded in measures to promote slum clearance and provide for further Corporation housing. Even more striking was the progress made on the minimum wage for municipal employees. The proposal, which had secured only twelve votes when Ferguson had originally introduced it, was finally adopted in October 1898, setting a wage of not less than 21/- per week of six days for every able-bodied man.[15] Confident that Glasgow Corporation would thus spread a higher tone of duty to the capitalistic class, it seemed to him as much a moral as a material victory. [16]

The real prize remained land values taxation. Here the struggle would be more fraught, illustrating the Stalwarts' need for allies on the Council.[17] Ferguson launched a new motion in February 1897, asking his colleagues to seek the cooperation of Scotland's principal towns in an attempt to present a bill to parliament to secure local taxation based on land values. The result, in the view of *Single Tax*, was 'confusion and disaster'.[18] Of the forty-nine councillors who had been returned in 1896 pledged for land values taxation, only twenty-seven supported the motion. This falling off was widely blamed on Ferguson's earlier tactical wriggling which had seen the Stalwarts favour a known conservative for the post of City Magistrate over a member of the 'forward' party.[19]

Duly chastised, he began to rebuild the municipal coalition. A second attempt the following month was more successful, winning agreement to petition parliament, and establishing a small sub-committee of the Parliamentary Bills Committee to consider Valuation and Taxation of Land Values. Ferguson became as its chairman, with the Progressives, Chisholm and Bilsland serving as members.[20] It was now the real work began. Over the next six months, the group hammered out the details of a bill, framed as an amendment to the existing Valuation (Scotland) Act of 1854, and designed to permit the shifting of the burden of local rates onto land values throughout the Scottish Burghs. The result fell short of blood and thunder expropriation. Every proprietor would be required to submit a yearly written assessment of the annual value of the ground they owned to the Burgh Assessor. The resulting 'land value assessment' would not exceed 2/- in the pound, with the proceeds of the new tax becoming part of the Burgh's revenues.[21] For Ferguson, this was only the beginning: the tax would gradually increase to a Georgite 20/- in the pound, with the ultimate object of obtaining the entire land value for the service of the community.[22]

The draft bill had a stormy passage, with the City Treasurer, James Colquhoun and other opponents on the Parliamentary Bills Committee arguing that it was merely an proposed an additional local tax rather than an overhaul of existing taxation. Despite the unequivocal rejection of his Bill by Colquhoun's Committee in December 1897, Ferguson refused to accept defeat and reconvened his own sub-committee.[23] In April 1898, he proposed to increase its powers to bring forward a further bill that was explicit in proposing a Land Values as an assessment in addition to existing assessments. Once permission for this neat stroke had been secured, the way ahead was clear. On 20 October 1898, his taxation initiative at last won approval by a narrow margin.[24] The next month, Ferguson, Bilsland and Chisholm were empowered to take all the necessary steps to introduce it to parliament as a 'public bill'.

The 'Glasgow Bill', as it was to become known, was destined for a long and unhappy life in parliament, but contemporaries at once recognised Ferguson's achievement in bringing the taxation of land values within the sphere of practical politics.[25] Glasgow's prominence as a land tax bastion was signalled in October 1899, when the city acted as host to the 'National Conference to Promote Land Values', drawing almost 600 delegates from throughout Britain and the Empire.[26] Ferguson cut a heroic figure in their midst. He announced that the Glasgow Bill was just the beginning. Sensing that some in his audience wanted to go further, he urged a judicious programme:

> In God's name let them carry this first, and then see what could be done afterwards. They must agree to fundamental principles before they settled down to the details. He proposed that the city of Glasgow should be a city rate-free within the next ten years, and if he lived ten years, and the people supported him as they had done for the last half-dozen years, he would make the city rate free.[27]

At the very hour of their triumph, however, the Stalwarts' fortunes were already on the wane. It had began almost imperceptibly the previous year with the formation of the Citizen's Union – 'a sleepy conservative-looking business', according to the *Single Tax* – but an organisation which signalled that the ratepayers' reaction to civic expansionism and the labour interest in local politics was already setting in.[28] By the municipal elections of 1899, the battle had been taken to Ferguson's own ward, where a campaign against excessive taxation reduced his majority by 1000 and 'gave Benburb a shake'.[29]

The Stalwarts were ill-prepared for adversity. A underlying problem was that they constituted a ginger group rather than a cohesive political party. By 1900, according to Ferguson's estimate, the Stalwarts still numbered only twelve – or 16 per cent of the total Council. [30] Shaped in his own image and held together by his magnetic personality, they also shared his peculiar mixture of conviction and compromise. Some of the most prominent Stalwarts were ILP and Trades Union men like Shaw Maxwell,

George Mitchell, P. G. Stewart and John Cronin, but others like John Battersby were drawn from the radical Liberal tradition.[31] In 1897, their ranks were joined by another old colleague of Ferguson's – the publican Patrick O'Hare, a convinced Single Taxer, who had been involved in Irish politics from the early 1870s.[32] Ferguson found O'Hare's lack of factionalism reassuring, but others were to prove less obliging fellow travellers.[33]

The challenge for this amorphous grouping was to maintain their dynamism once the great battles of municipalisation had been won. Extending provision into areas like foodstuffs, pawnshops or the drinks trade merely threatened to antagonise other WMEC partners, such as the co-operators or the Irish.[34] Ferguson, as an instinctive free trader, was quite definite on this point. Reacting to a proposal to impose Corporation tolls on private trading outside Corporation-owned markets, he propounded his 'true principals of municipalism'. In no case, he argued, should the municipality undertake any commercial enterprise except where it was justified on the grounds that private enterprise could not so well discharge its duty to the public. No muncipal monopolies could be tolerated unless other than commercial considerations, such as public health, intervened.[35] Pressure to improve wages and condition for Corporation employees would continue, but even incremental reform measures threatened the delicate balance of the reforming alliance of councillors. Ferguson's latest pet project to tackle unfair rents on public houses, for example, raised the wrath of orthodox Georgites who denounced its 'serious economic weaknesses'.[36] Relationships with the temperance-minded Chisholm and the Progressives had also grown tense due to the candidacy of 'trade' figures, such as O'Hare.[37] It was little wonder that by the end of the century his pleas to 'stand by the Stalwarts' were rather shrill:

> For while the parties with their thumb-worn creeds,
> Their large professions and their little deeds,
> Wrangle in selfish strife, lo! freedom weeps,
> Wrong rules the land, and waiting justice sleeps.[38]

Disunited Irishmen

It was one thing to send radical land bills to parliament, it was quite another to win a hearing for them. The 1895 General Election had laid the basis of a solid Unionist hegemony. For the rest of his life Ferguson would have to face the consequences of this simple political fact. The tempo of nationalist politics had also slackened. The immediate consequence for Home Rule was not the coercion he had feared, but a more skilful and emollient approach from the new ministry. Resolute government was to be combined with positive initiatives like the 1898 Local Government Act. Even Ferguson had to admit that this measure, which set up elective district councils to replace the old grand jury system, promised to 'storm the strongest stronghold of the invaders of Ireland'.[39] It seemed that the drive for constitutional change must compete with the search for more tangible social and economic reforms. With measures to revive Irish agriculture and obtain financial redress from Britain drawing support from nationalists and moderate unionists alike, it had never been more important for the Home Rule movement to restate its moral force and its distinctive historical mission. Yet, with Parnell's youthful party grown into embittered career politicians, the old cause had seldom seemed more tarnished.

For the Irish in Scotland, the Unionist victory merely emphasised the reality of their dependence on the Liberal Party. Liberalism, however, was changing its colours. Its traditional Gladstonian creed continued to yield ground to Rosebery's fascination with the economic opportunities of Empire and efficient government. This was an agenda which left little time for Irish Home Rule, which was conveniently subsumed in a generalised commitment to constitutional change.[40] Despite the advancing cooperation in local politics, the poor performance of the ILP in the parliamentary field in 1895 remained discouraging for hopes of an alternative alliance.

With backsliding Liberals in his sights, Ferguson believed it had become imperative to keep Irish claims separate from what he described as the 'drivel' of Home Rule all Round.[41] Trevelyan's resignation in February 1897 gave him a useful opportunity to test this strategy in his home ground of Bridgeton.[42] When Sir Charles Cameron, proprietor of the *North British Daily Mail* was selected by the Liberals to contest the seat against the Solicitor General, Scott Dickson, Ferguson was determined to use the contest as a showcase of personal and communal power. The candidate was a Georgite radical on the land question, but his paper had been consistently scathing on the pretensions of Ferguson and the Glasgow Home Rulers.[43] The price for INLGB support was a private interview in which Cameron was grilled on Irish issues.[44] With Liberals tormenting him hourly to declare for their man, and expectations rising that he might back a last minute Labour candidate, Ferguson urged John Dillon to extricate him from an awkward situation. Dillon's public endorsement of Cameron would enable him to present the matter as one of 'party discipline', thus safeguarding relations with his municipal ILP supporters.

> We will make Home Rule echo all over the Empire this election. Cameron knows I sat upon 'Official Liberals', 'Single Taxers', 'Scotch allies' and 'Progressive Unionists' and the whole newspapers of Glasgow last November. My word is half the constituency and I polled 2900 which Sir George [Trevelyan] only had 3200 at the General Election. The Irish can poll 1000 votes in the whole constituency, the labour party could poll 3000 and would I were with them, as it is I have to keep their vote under 1000, perhaps 800 . . . It is well, as in Butt's and Parnell's days, it should be known that Ireland has men who can turn elections in British cities.[45]

Fortunately, Ferguson's blushes were saved. No candidate was nominated, and the contest could be presented simply as one of 'progress' against 'reaction'. Yet the much-touted Irish vote was far from solid. Cameron scraped home to victory, but an unholy alliance of Bridgeton Orangemen and Irish Roman Catholics favourable to the Unionist educational policy was reckoned to have swelled Scott Dickson's support.[46]

As Irish Home Rule shrunk from the status of a campaign for national and democratic rights to become a rather squalid electoral variable, the Irish political machine in Scotland fell into an equally sorry state. Healy's blanket expulsion from the Irish political organisation in November 1895, had achieved little beyond adding to the number of nationalist factions. 'Tim the Terrible' had few friends in Glasgow, but typically mustered enough support to form a local branch of his People's Rights Defence Association.[47] His public appearance in the city in June 1897 saw ladies in the front row scuttle for cover as Healyites and Dillonites struggled violently on the platform.[48] From scenes like these could spring only disenchantment. Individual INLGB branches, including the 'John Ferguson', struggled to stay in existence, while their enemies gloated on the 'cataleptic body of Home Rule'.[49]

This was a painful time for Ferguson whose municipal achievements failed protect to him from the bilious state of community politics. As usual, the flashpoint was the feud between the HGB and *Glasgow Observer*. His own relationship with the paper had also been deteriorating for some years. Along with a group of local Irish business and professional men, he had provided it with financial assistance during a troubled period in the early 1890s; in return the paper proved more than willing to publish his lengthy speeches and essays.[50] When the entrepreneur and journalist Charles Diamond took over outright control in 1894 a fresh set of editorial priorities became apparent.[51] A former collaborator of Davitt on *Labour World*, Diamond was now an ambitious, Dillonite, devoutly Catholic and hysterically pro-temperance. He initially provided generous support for Ferguson in his Town Council work, but had grown suspicious of his links with the ILP and his failure to condemn the drinks trade. The circumstances of his election in 1896 particularly rankled, as Diamond interpreted his failure to publish his expenses as tacit admission that the campaign had been financed by the publicans.[52]

The latest breach came in early 1898 when Hugh Murphy intervened in an election in Owen Kierwan's new bailiwick of Yorkshire. When Ferguson backed Murphy, the *Observer* sneered at the hypocrisy implicit in his role the friend *and* the employer of labour.[53] The well-meaning Murphy only made things worse by defending his colleague as someone who in the past had kept the *Observer* alive. [54] Diamond pounced and refused to let go of his quarry. He demanded that Ferguson disassociate himself from these remarks, when he remained silent, readers were informed of Cameron, Ferguson & Co.'s own financial difficulties.[55] Henceforth, Ferguson could do no right in the *Observer's* eyes. His vanity, his tendency to misquote verse, his dismissal of a Catholic University for Ireland as a 'red herring' were dutifully recorded.[56] Opening the wounds of a decade, the ultimate heresy was his 'Parnellism':

> Mr Ferguson has been a Parnellite all along, so praise of the tormentors and denouncers of the Liberals is rather in his line. It is quite true he has never openly professed his Parnellism because Parnellism in Glasgow was and is a small quantity. Mr Ferguson likes to be of the majority.[57]

A hunger for history

The centenary of the United Irishmen's 1798 rebellion provided not only an ironic counterpoint to these squabbles, but also the inspiration for ending them. The drive for unity originally came from Ireland itself, where William O'Brien had emerged from semi-retirement to launch a new agrarian movement in 16 January 1898.[58] The United Irish League (UIL) was clearly inspired by the Land League's tactics and organisation, but the differences between the two movements underlined the changing balance of forces in the Irish countryside after two decades of legislation. The new League would keep strictly within the law to avoid government suppression, launching attacks the traditional enemy of 'landlordism', but focusing on land purchase rather than on rent reduction as a permanent solution to the land crisis. Above all, O'Brien intended the UIL to retain its local dynamic and remain aloof from national politics. Given the reputation of parliamentary nationalism, he was convinced that the people and not the party should be the basis for a new mobilisation of national strength.[59]

By 1898, Ferguson too had decided that local initiatives were the path to salvation. He admired the overwrought O'Brien – he had once dubbed him 'the dashing Murat of Irish chivalry' – but John Dillon remained for him the 'centre of unity'.[60] In Glasgow, the immediate goal of grassroots pressure was to gather the shattered remnants of parliamentarianism by blending the Dillonite watchword of 'unity' with the old Parnellite cry of 'independence'.[61] Under the auspices of the HGB, proposals for reunion, starting from a joint conference of parliamentary representatives, were sent in March to the Glasgow INLGB branches, and to the local Healyite and Parnellite organisations.[62] The Healyites and a number of the League branches immediately repudiated these overtures, but Ferguson was determined to try again with another delegate meeting.[63] By April, a 'Committee for Irish Unity' had been established, calling for a reunion of the two nationalist sections in the House of Commons on the condition of 'absolute independence from all British parties'.[64] Inevitably, the *Observer* remained sceptical of the 'unity dodge', but Ferguson's persistence was rewarded by Dillon's decision to use a Glasgow platform in October to issue his own invitation, phrased in general terms, to the Parnellites to take part in a representative conference. Although rejected by the minority group, this intervention marked an important step along the circuitous path to reunion.[65]

Perhaps it was already too late. The political space created by the fragmentation of the Home Rule movement had allowed Ferguson to experiment with labour links, but it had also encouraged a new ethnic and separatist strain in nationalism, which in time would destroy the politics of his generation. Some already sensed the danger, concerned that the growth of Amnesty Associations and '98 Clubs would wean the faithful from constitutional agitation.[66] In fact, a subtler warning note was the quickening of interest in Irish Gaelic. Cameron, Ferguson & Co's prodigious output had helped to build national identity in the years when the language seemed in terminal decline, but for a growing number of nationalists, parlour songbooks and popular histories were no longer enough. The William O'Brien Branch in Glasgow had established its Gaelic class in 1895.[67] Study of the language flourished in the city during the late 1890s, when an increasing number of classes affiliated to the central Gaelic League of Dublin.[68] In sentimental mood, Ferguson once claimed that he too would have given a great deal, 'to have the sweet language that Dathi's warriors whispered around the camp fire from his mother'.[69] However, when pressed on his real priorities, the Belfast utilitarian shone through. He might have paid his subscriptions dutifully to the Irish Language Fund, but he was heard to comment that the money and organisational power expended on the language revival, 'could have been spent to the greater advantage in assisting the Home Rule, the Land agitation, and other practical objects'.[70]

If the quest for linguistic purity did not have his unconditional support, Ferguson could at least identify with a broader desire to anchor Ireland's claims for nationhood in a unique historical birthright. Elsewhere the language of politics may have been shifting away from a historical frame of reference, but for the Irish, historical certainties were vital in the face of recent political disappointments. It was after the failure of the Second Home Rule Bill, that Ferguson began to rediscover his love of Irish history.[71] Ireland's ancient Celtic and Christian heritage fascinated him and he tried to convey its magic to Scottish and Irish audiences, aided often by limelight slides and musical accompaniment.[72]

The celebration of the United Irishmen's centenary also gave a welcome boost to his publishing business, stimulating the market for cheap reprints of Irish classics. Alongside the *American Fourpenny Library* and the *'Merry Bells' Series of Twopenny Songbooks*, nestled his own contribution to the spirit of '98: *Three Centuries of Irish History. From the Reign of Mary, the Catholic to that of Victoria, the Protestant. An Unbroken Record of Confiscation and Persecution, Mixed with Massacre, and Terminating in Extermination by Unjust and Ruinous Taxation*. The body of the work was standard nationalist fare, drawing heavily on John Mitchell's, *Conquest of Ireland* which had influenced him as a young man. The denouement as the magisterial title suggests, remained his own, capping the account of usurpation and bloodshed, not with a stirring call to arms, but an analysis of Ireland's unjust taxation burden. Here the inspiration was eminently practical. Using detailed statistical evidence from the 1894 Financial Relations Commission, it drew on a favourite obsession, and was one of the few issues to lend any spark to the Irish parliamentary activity in recent years.[73]

The real novelty of *Three Centuries* lay in Ferguson's eagerness to insert himself into the heroic narrative. Drawing the benefits of political longevity, he had become a historical figure in his own right – the 'Nestor of Irish politics'. At the ill-fated Irish Race Conference, held in Dublin in 1896, he had represented a symbolic link between the genesis of the Home Rule movement and its later development, with a speech which recalled 'men of the old time with us no more'.[74] Now, his writing was suffused by a sense of faith found in disappointment, as he realised that he might not live to see the Dublin parliament that had been his life's work:

I have lived through and taken part for a generation in the fight for the restoration of that Parliament. Once or twice I thought it certain I'd see the opening of it. It was my intention to avail myself of an honour more than once offered me by my warm-hearted countrymen, and when

that National Assembly would crown our triumph I hoped,
if but for a Session or two, to spare me from an active
business life, the time that would enable me to enjoy the
pride and satisfaction of sitting and working in that 'old
house at home' . . . That hope is now rapidly dying, but faith
in 'Home Rule' or 'National Self-Government' becoming an
accomplished fact is as strong in my mind as it was forty
years ago.[75]

He was also forced to admit that it was his fellow Protestant
Irishmen who had risen to destroy his dreams, betraying the
patriotic vision of their forbears of '82 and '98. In the heat of battle,
he had directed a Biblical rage against his native Belfast, but now
he had grown more philosophical:

When Irish Protestantism stands forth for the right
of Ireland in all purely Irish affairs to make her own
laws, provided such are not in conflict with the rights
of minorities and other established principles of social
compacts, nor calculated to interfere with the strength and
integrity of the Empire; when it becomes as patriotic as
Belgian Protestantism or Dutch Catholicism; in short, when
it become Irish instead of West British Protestantism, then it
will have a fair chance in our Irish isle.[76]

Amid these well-intentioned exhortations, his emphasis on
'Empire' was revealing. Despite declaring himself to be 'an extreme
nationalist' who believed that 'absolute separation' would stop the
ruin of Ireland, the federalist vision of the 1870s lived on. Indeed,
his position on future of Anglo-Irish relations illustrates the
ambiguities of 'Imperialism' and 'anti-Imperialism' among radicals
and Home Rulers at the end of the nineteenth century. Ferguson
was clearly an 'anti-imperialist' in the sense that he opposed
further territorial expansion – the British conquest of Ireland
he compared to the government's recent campaign in Mashona
land – but he remained ultimately enmeshed in the British and

Imperial model of national development which younger, cultural nationalists so eagerly repudiated. Like his hero Gladstone, his vision of Empire was of a community of nations held together by the uniquely British blessings of political freedom and free trade:

> ... I think the majority of educated Irishmen see today that from geographical position, mixture of peoples, historical relation, identity of interest in relation to other nations, adaptation to produce commodities for each other and various economic causes, Ireland could enjoy within Empire, under 'Home Rule', a higher social condition that that of 'absolute separation' with its warring tariffs, armed watchfulness, foreign intrigues, contentious questions arising out of past relations ...[77]

In the new world order, which he believed was inherently unstable and inimical to British interests, the thrust of his position was to strengthen not weaken the Empire. If only atonement could be made to Ireland for past wrongs, England would gain a true and powerful friend. His prophecy was of partnership in adversity:

> Let the despots of Europe combine if they will ... reduced though our nation is, I doubt not that 200,000 recruits will muster rapidly under the green flag to sustain the honour of their nation and ratify its compact, and, if the despots of Europe will have it, Irish bayonets will redden in the front of another decisive battle of the world, by which baptism of blood ancient wrongs shall be forgotten, and a future of unity and peace between England and Ireland shall date from that day of common triumph.[78]

He was growing old. Observers noted the resemblance to the Salvation Army's General Booth, not only in appearance, but in terms of his all-pervading earnestness.[79] Some even said that John Ferguson had become 'respectable' with his advancing years. For years, the Stalwarts had sought a bailieship for their leader, but each time they had been shut out by a Council caucus.[80] At last in 1899, after some frantic horse-trading with the Progressives to ensure that Samuel Chisholm became Lord Provost, they succeeded.[81] With his leading municipal adversary James Colquhoun despatched to Duke Street Jail on charges of embezzlement, Ferguson was elevated to the Glasgow magistracy.[82] The *Bailie* was gleeful, noting that the shillelagh-wielding hothead of yesteryear had become the 'King of the Causey'.[83] More graciously, the *Herald* hoped that on accepting the gilded chain of office, 'Samson would not be shorn of all his locks'.[84] The challenges of the new century would test whether civic dignity had indeed quenched his fighting spirit.

Notes

1 Maver, 'Municipal Administration of Glasgow', p. 440.

2 *Select Committee on the Land Values Taxation etc. (Scotland) Bill, 1906,* Arthur Kay Memorandum. See also, Sir James Bell and James Paton, *Glasgow. Its Municipal Organisation and Administration* (Glasgow, 1896).

3 Hoppen, *Elections, Politics and Society,* p. 482.

4 Offer, *Property and Politics,* pp. 231, 252. Ferguson estimated that £35,000 per annum was added to the ground values of Glasgow by the efforts of her citizens: *Glasgow: The City of Progress* (Glasgow, 1900), p. 8.

5 'With 336,000 working men ... behind me, as you well know!': TCD, Dillon MSS 6788, J. Ferguson to J. Dillon, 12 March 1896. He was also outraged that the Post Office dared to file a letter addressed to 'John Ferguson T. C., Glasgow' as undeliverable mail: *Glasgow Observer,* 30 Jul. 1898.

6 See, *ibid.,* 31 Oct. 1896.

7 *Ibid.,* 18 Oct. 1899.

8 *Ibid.*, 30 Jul. 1898.

9 *City of Progress,* (Glasgow 1900), pp. 6–7.

10 Michael Davitt was also a exponent, holding that 'alien rule' threatened a fatal weakening of the vital energies of the Irish race: *Fall of Feudalism,* p. 721.

11 *Ibid.,* p. 9.

12 *Ibid.,* p. 12.

13 GCA, Corporation Minutes, 19 Nov. 3 Dec. 1896.

14 Ibid., 3 Mar. 1898.

15 For Ferguson's role see, ibid., 7 Jul. 1 Sept. 6 Oct. 1898.

16 *City of Progress,* p. 4.

17 See, James Colquhoun, *Reminiscences of Glasgow Town Council* (Glasgow, 1904).

18 *Single Tax,* Mar. 1897.

19 *Glasgow Observer,* 27 Feb. 1897.

20 *Single Tax,* Apr. 1897; Corporation Minutes, Taxation of Land Values Sub-Committee, 26 Apr. 1897.

21 *Single Tax,* 17 Nov. 1897.

22 *Select Committee on the Land Values Taxation, etc (Scotland) Bill, 1906,* p. 3.

23 Corporation Minutes, Parliamentary Bills Committee 23 Dec. 1897; Taxation of Land Values Sub-Committee, 31 Mar. 1898.

24 Ibid., 20 Oct. 1898.

25 *Single Tax,* Nov. 1897. Charles Cameron who had been returned in Bridgeton introduced the original 'Glasgow Bill' to parliament, but it failed at its first reading in March 1899.

26 Corporation Minutes, 5 Oct. 1899 for debates over the Corporation's role in the conference.

27 *Ibid.*

28 *Single Tax*, Nov. 1898. See also, GCA, TD 488/9, Citizen's Union Minute Book, 12 May 1898.

29 *Glagow Herald*, 4 Nov. 1899. The Citizen's Union believed it was only the foul weather on polling day which had saved Ferguson's seat by a margin of 29 votes: Secretary's Report, 15 Nov. 1899.

30 *City of Progress*, p. 11.

31 For Stewart see, *The Councillor*, Jan. 8 1898; *Glasgow Herald*, 23 Oct. 1918. Battersby: *Members of the Glasgow Corporation 1907–1910: A Poetical Sketch* (Glasgow, 1910). Cronin: *Glasgow Observer*, 28 Apr. 1900; Mitchell: Maver, 'Municipal Administration of Glasgow', p. 938.

32 *Glasgow Observer*, 6 Nov. 1897, 24 Jun. 1899.

33 His admiration for O'Hare's 'life of honour and integrity' continued. In 1905, he lobbied for him to become Nationalist MP for North Monaghan, assuring John Redmond that there was no difficulty with him, 'as regards the Party Pledge or loyalty. Any difficulty *as I have often known* during 30 years of political labour will arrive in *private* meetings, but once the vote is taken he is loyalty and obedience personified': NLI, J. Ferguson to J. Redmond, 20 May, 1905, Redmond Papers, 15245(5). In contrast, Mitchell, publicly rejected his proposals to press for a further increase of the minimum wage, while Shaw Maxwell used the platform of the HGB to denounce Ferguson's failure to support his preferred candidate in the November 1898 municipal elections: *Labour Leader*, 17 Sept. 1898.

34 Smyth, 'Labour and Socialism', p. 124.

35 *Glasgow Observer*, 31 Dec. 1904.

36 *Single Tax*, July 1897. For further rounds in his campaign see, GCA, Corporation Minutes, 1 Dec. 1898, 20 Feb., 2 Mar., 14 Jun. 1899.

37 Maver, 'Local party politics', p. 52.

38 *City of Progress,* p. 12.

39 *Glasgow Observer,* 17 Dec. 1899.

40 Hutchison, *Scottish Politics,* pp. 170–1.

41 TCD, Dillon MSS 6788, J. Ferguson to J. Dillon, 7 Feb. 1897.

42 *North British Daily Mail,* 8 Feb. 1897.

43 See, *The Bailie,* 10 Feb. 1897.

44 *North British Daily Mail,* 9 Feb. 1897. It was scene which was to be repeated in North West Lanarkshire two years later, where Ferguson supported Dr C. M. Douglas, the Liberal candidate, over the ILP's Chisholm Robertson, one of the staunchest Scottish supporters of Irish Home Rule. On this occasion he was credited with 'leaning' on Douglas to make him more publicly amenable to the uniqueness of Irish claims, in the process reducing the candidate's 'principles to pulp': *Glasgow Herald,* 21 Feb. 1899.

45 TCD, Dillon MSS 6788, J. Ferguson to J. Dillon, 7 Feb. 1897.

46 *North British Daily Mail,* 16 Feb. 1897. Ramsay Macdonald had been a prospective ILP candidate, but had 'funked' the challenge: J. B. Glasier Papers, GP2/1/5, Diary 6 Feb. 1897.

47 *Glasgow Observer,* 5 Mar. 1898.

48 *Ibid.,* 5 Jun. 1897.

49 *Glasgow Observer,* 20 May 1899; *Glasgow Herald,* 10 Oct. 1898.

50 Thomas Lipton had also assisted by taking out advertising space – his reward was generous coverage of his yachting exploits.

51 Handley, *Irish in Modern Scotland,* p. 284.

52 *Glasgow Observer,* 22 Jan. 1898.

53 *Ibid.,* 15 Jan. 1898.

54 *Ibid.,* 22 Jan. 1898.

55 *Ibid.,* 12 Feb. 1898. He claimed that Ferguson had used the *Observer* as an intermediary to find an individual in London to act as surety for his composition bill.

56 *Ibid.,* 5 Mar., 2, 30 Jul. 1898.

57 *Ibid.,* 22 Jan. 1898.

58 Warwick-Haller, *William O'Brien,* pp. 168–71.

59 Hoppen, *Elections, Politics and Society,* p. 481.

60 *Glasgow Star,* 21 Nov. 1903 for his claim to have predicted the UIL 's success. *Glasgow Observer,* 12 Dec. 1896.

61 *Ibid.,* 15 Aug. 1898.

62 *Ibid.,* 5 Mar. 1898.

63 *Ibid.,* 18 Mar. 1898.

64 *Ibid.,* 9 Apr., 9 Jun. 1898.

65 Davitt, *Fall of Feudalism,* p. 692; Lyons, *Irish Parliamentary Party,* p. 79.

66 *Glasgow Observer,* 12 Mar. 1898.

67 *Ibid.,* 23 Mar. 1895.

68 *Ibid.,* 15 Aug. 1896. The *Observer* began its own Gaelic column on 10 October 1896. For developments in Liverpool: Denvir, *Life Story,* p. 256. For a recent reassessment of the metropolitan movement: J. Hutchinson and A. O'Day, 'The Gaelic revival in London, 1900–22: limits of ethnic identity', pp. 264–276, in Swift and Gilley (eds.), *Irish in Victorian Britain;* see also, J. Hutchinson, 'Irish Nationalism', in *Revisionist Controversy ,* pp. 100–17.

69 *Ibid.,* 20 Apr. 1895.

70 For an exchange of views on Ferguson's attitude to the revival see, *Glasgow Observer.* 28 Apr., 5 May 1906. The Cameron & Ferguson edition of Henry George's, *The Irish*

Land Question was translated into Gaelic in 1901: *Single Tax,* Aug. 1901.

71 *Ibid.,* 6 Apr. 1895.

72 See, for example, *Ibid.,* 10 Oct. 1895; 4 Apr. 1896; 18 Mar. 1898. Other topics included 'Billy and the Boyne' and 'Ireland and her Illustrious Dead'.

73 See, Lyons, *Dillon,* pp. 177–8.

74 *Glasgow Observer,* 22 Aug. 1896.

75 *Three Centuries,* p. 77.

76 *Ibid.,* p. 78.

77 *Ibid.,* pp. 125–6.

78 *Ibid.,* p. 126.

79 *Glasgow News,* 26 Apr. 1906.

80 *Glasgow Observer,* 6 Nov. 1897; *North British Daily Mail,* 4 Nov. 1898. Their action in backing Chisholm was despite protests from the ILP.

81 *Glasgow Observer,* 11 Nov. 1899.

82 *Glasgow Herald,* 29 Jul., 31 Jul., 2 Aug. 1899; *North British Daily Mail,* 4 Aug. 1899.

83 *The Bailie,* 22 Nov. 1899.

84 *Glasgow Herald,* 9 Nov. 1899.

CHAPTER THIRTEEN

Monument Building

God's fruit of justice ripens slow;
Mens' minds are narrow, let them grow;
My brothers we must wait.[1]

Rejecting his own counsels of caution, Ferguson was in no mood
to wait. He was at the peak of his oratorical powers and political
influence. Again parliament had become a tantalising prospect as
a 'progressive coalition' candidate for a Glasgow constituency.[2]
But there was a taskmaster more demanding than mere ambition.
He had begun to be gripped by the fear that time was running
out. The plight of the 'dying Ireland' –a nation killed by the
flight of her people – was now a recurring figure in his speech
and writing. Still more insistent were the intimations of his own
mortality. The constants that had guided his politics for over
three decades seemed to be in peril. For the sake of his country
and the onward march of humankind, he needed quick victories.
The achievement of Irish Home Rule and the taxation of land
values would build him what he craved – a monument worthy of
a life's labour.

Burghers of the Queen

In 1904, the silver casket containing Parnell's Edinburgh burgess
scroll was discovered for sale in a South London pawnshop.[3]
By the time this remnant of better days was salvaged, the Irish
movement had at last managed to build unity of a sort. John
Dillon's Glasgow speech had been an early catalyst, followed
by his resignation as chair of the party in February 1899.[4] Over
the next twelve months, a measure of agreement was tortuously
achieved. The election of John Redmond of the Parnellite body
as chairman of the parliamentary party in early February 1900

settled the leadership question, although a new challenge quickly emerged in the shape of the relationship between the party and the populist UIL.

As usual, the answer was a national convention to seal the bond of unity. Meanwhile, British-based Home Rulers felt abandoned in a netherworld until the INLGB could be absorbed into a new national organisation. Typically in the west of Scotland, grassroots reunion had been quick enough to get underway among surviving outposts, but the general picture was of a collapsed branch structure – a situation desperate enough to force Hugh Murphy and Owen Kiernan into co-operation.[5]

Ferguson's seniority allowed him to brush aside political and personal rivalries when it suited his purpose. Glasgow admirers hailed his letters campaign following Parnell's fall as contributing substantially towards reunification – he was not about to loose momentum now.[6] He had been a friend and colleague of John Redmond's father and had introduced John and his brother Willie to a Glasgow audience when they were boys. He could thus temper his proprietorial pride in the new leader with some candid advice. On Redmond's visit to the city in May 1900, he was in the mood to knock heads together. He acknowledged Redmond as leader of the parliamentary party, but warned him that he would only become leader of the Irish nation if he showed the courage and dedication of a Butt or Parnell. This would not be done by abandoning O'Brien and the UIL to face the Unionist government.[7]

When the Great Irish Convention was finally convened at Whitsuntide, he was gratified to hear the UIL receive accreditation as *the* national organisation and Redmond accept its chairmanship.[8] Yet the fragility of this hard-won reconciliation was amply illustrated in his own machinations backstage as he tried to persuade O'Brien to support a 'once and for all' purge of Healyites.[9] Nevertheless, the awakening of nationalist forces in Ireland and Britain continued during the summer. He toured indefatigably in Ulster and the west of Ireland on behalf of the

League and was rewarded by co-option onto the thirty-man UIL
Directory inaugurated at the Rotunda in December, 1900.[10]

The revived movement faced its most serious test with the
outbreak of the Boer War in the autumn of 1899. It responded
with spirit and determination. Dillon, Healy, O'Brien and
Davitt led the charge inside and outside parliament against an
expansionist conflict for which they found it difficult to discover
any just cause.[11] As sons of a small nation, they identified with
the plight of the Boers, a people whom ironically the *Glasgow
Observer* had once described as possessing, 'all the vices of the
North of Ireland Orangemen'.[12] Ferguson played his part as best
he knew, by chairing a rally in Glasgow City Hall in March 1900,
bringing together Gladstonian radicals, Irish nationalists and the
ILP. On the platform were the South African anti-war activist,
S. C. Cronwright – Schreiner, Keir Hardie, and the new star in the
Liberal firmament, David Lloyd George MP.[13] Ferguson's speech
was carefully crafted to pay tribute to the fighting qualities of
Scottish and Irish regiments, while condemning the deaths of,
'the gallant farmers who were defending their country'.[14] The
industrial west of Scotland, however, had generally rallied behind
the British cause, and a crowd of Union Jack-waving students
besieged Ferguson's meeting.[15] His temper was set ablaze at the
threat they posed to the right of public meeting. Forgetting the
Boers for a moment, he strode from one end of the platform to the
other, warning that anyone interrupting would be removed 'with
whatever violence, I as chairman, may think to be necessary: just
that and no more'.[16]

Just as his reputation appeared unassailable, opposition
resurfaced. It was a pattern wearily repeated throughout his
political career. As one of his supporters remarked, it seemed as
if some Irishmen, despite their talk of unity, were 'ever on the
alert to find a weak spot in their comrades in arms' convictions'.[17]
An early warning came with the end of the amiable silence
surrounding Cameron, Ferguson & Co's publication of Orange
songbooks. Once regarded as, 'a mere harmless foible, derived

from early associations', nationalist tolerance snapped once the anti-catholic detail of the ballads had been scrutinised by a Donegal newspaper.[18]

Two other incidents prompted his fall from grace. In December 1900 he offered public support for the creation of a local corps of volunteer irregulars – the 'Burghers of the Queen', or, more soberly, 'Citizens Reserve' – for the purpose of home defence. The motivations for the new initiative were explained as, 'deep, real, earnest, resolute patriotism' combined with the more orthodox Liberal aim of obviating conscription.[19] Sharing a platform with Samuel Chisholm and Andrew Bonar Law, the recently elected Unionist MP for Blackfriars, his role seemed to sit strangely with his 'Stop the War' activities.[20] This was followed by his attendance at the memorial service for Queen Victoria at Glasgow Cathedral in February 1901, to which the Town Council marched in proud procession behind a detachment of bluejackets.[21] Ferguson viewed official mourning as part of his civic responsibilities, but by his very presence he had set himself against nationalists who, like Richard McGhee, felt there were scant grounds for condolence for a reign that had diminished Ireland.[22]

In 1886, Home Rule purists had condemned him for importing dangerously radical social doctrines, now he stood accused by another generation of nationalists of undermining the national dignity by 'flunkeyism' and 'West Britonism'. An extraordinary portion of vitriol was poured upon him. At best he was a good man gone wrong, at worst the 'erratic Bailie' had degenerated as a consistent nationalist, and his involvement in displays like the royal funeral was likened to a dog walking on its hind legs.[23]

Scottish onlookers found such wrangling highly amusing. In the *Evening Times* 'Finn McCool' column, which documented the proceedings of an imaginary UILGB branch, a character who was unmistakably Ferguson held forth on whether Irish children should attend the Coronation celebrations:

Would they allow it to go down from the mountain top of time, throughout the rolling vistas of the centuries which were coming with their centrifugal forces – (Cheers) – thought the days of stress and storm through which they had passed and would yet pass; would they allow it to be told at the old homesteads of the old green land, say in the twenty-fifth century; would they allow it to be told with hushed and bated breath – (Cheers) – that members of the Finn McCool branch had allowed their children to be debauched with Corporation buns and water (No No!).[24]

In fact, there were serious issues of communal identity at work. By 1901, the Irish community in Glasgow was undergoing a structural shift. The Irish-born population in the city as a whole had fallen to 8.68 per cent.[25] The pattern was repeated elsewhere in Great Britain, where it has been estimated that the ratio of British to Irish-born stood at 3:1 by the early twentieth century, few with any real intention to return 'home'.[26] Intermarriage and upward mobility threatened further to erode the potential for ethnic mobilisation. If the Irish in Ireland felt swamped by British values, how much greater were the fears of the exiles in 'the land of the mountain and the flood'. It was a situation of which Ferguson was keenly aware. In his new year's address to the Young Irishmen of Scotland in 1904, he observed that decades of peaceful progress had meant that Irish Catholics and Scottish Protestants were rapidly becoming, 'a political and social homogeneity'. While this was a lesson in community relations to the inhabitants of Belfast and Portadown, he feared that, as the connection with Ireland became less direct and the Scottish press drove out Irish newspapers from Irish homes, it was becoming more difficult for his younger countrymen to hold, 'a burning sense of Ireland's wrongs, required to induce him to continue the sacrifices of time, money and social advantages needed for an early victory'.[27]

Federalist Home Rule remained the solution, a scheme which Ferguson invested with the British radical norms of local freedom, common humanity and social progress. Federalism would forge a new relationship between the British nations, Ireland and the Empire: 'an up to date system of government that [would] combine National or State independence with Imperial or Federal strength and unity, to lead the van of the world's progress for ages to come'.[28] It was perfectly possible, he believed, for Irishmen to do their duty to their own country and the country in which they lived, especially in Scotland's case where they were privileged to live in, 'the best governed country in the world'.[29]

Some in his intended audience were already seeking an alternative moral framework for the national community. For them, salvation lay in a quasi-mystical demarcation from the society and culture surrounding them. Significantly, the Gaelic language had continued to prosper in Glasgow. By 1902, the city contained twelve Gaelic League branches, leading the visiting Patrick Pearse to comment that in no other centre outside London had the language movement made such progress.[30] Fascination had also grown with Celtic music, literature, pastimes and even the prospect of a reversion to traditional Irish dress.[31] As Denis Brogan, the President of the Glasgow Gaelic League, explained, the culture of Ireland's ancient Celtic civilisation was not only aesthetically pleasing and distinctive, but was precisely the 'Irish possession that Britain had done much to destroy'.[32] Realising that their own movement was open to accusations of acclimatisation, it was a tide which more perceptive members of the UILGB were willing to harness in order to re-energise their own brand of political nationalism.[33] Attempts at the 1903 Liverpool convention to limit membership to the Irish-born flew in the fact of demographic realities, but the League's new secretary Joseph Devlin – one of the few younger recruits to the Parliamentary Party – remained anxious for 'the cultivation of Irish ideals' in the League. It was to become more than a mere electoral machine, and instead 'a truly *national* organisation'. A higher cultural tone was to prevail in the branches. While Gaelic classes, choirs and Irish dancing were to be welcomed as incentives to a younger Irish element, 'the stage Irishman' definitely was not: 'Songs should be thoroughly Irish in tone and sentiment and the platform should not be used for vulgar performances ... which are gross caricatures our race'.[34]

In this atmosphere it is easy to understand why Ferguson's 'loyalist' transgressions raised such acute sensitivities. But, despite the howls of his critics, his alternative vision of Ireland and Britain's partnership for progress had been an enduring thread in his public professions from the 1870's. It was not Ferguson who had changed but Irish nationalism, allowing less space for his complex brand of patriotism. His immediate penance was to draw a distinction between the Empire and the policies of aggressive imperialism being currently waged in its name, calling down the Curse of God on the latter's 'burning of homes and its crushing of liberty.'[35] In more positive vein, he attempted to engage with the new cultural forces on his own behalf. Again history was his chosen medium. His limelight lectures on the *Three Centuries* theme remained popular with audiences desirous of a 'true version' of their history.[36] He also remained wary of the sectarian spirit which haunted the recent rediscovery of 'true' Irish identity. So insistent had been his championship of non-sectarian nationalism in Glasgow throughout his career, that not even his fiercest opponents dared to drag his religion into 'Queen's Burghers' furore.[37] He was now defiant in declaring himself to be, 'a Celtic Protestant of the Irish nation'.[38]

Pygmies and Titans

Ferguson had become one of the busiest councillors in Glasgow. His remit extended from City Improvements to telephones, tramways and parks. In 1900, he had been appointed to no less than eight standing committees – the maximum number for any councillor – and to four special committees.[39] In two of these, the Proposed Fire Insurance Committee and the Committee on the Value of Licensed Premises, he was the convenor. His work rate did not slacken when he completed his term as a Bailie in November 1902. He was appointed to the Commission of the Peace for the County of the City of Glasgow, an honour giving great satisfaction to the local Irish population. From the bench of the Eastern Police Court, the new magistrate dispensed justice to illegal whisky hawkers with a firm hand.[40]

For a man nearing seventy, the circumstances were hardly ideal for running a complex business enterprise like Cameron, Ferguson & Co. As the *Observer* had revealed, all was not well with the firm – it was rumoured that the speculations of his late partner Duncan Cameron had left it reeling from a debt of £15,000.[41] Despite these financial worries, he refused to limit either the range of his political causes, or his dogged pursuit of them. He continued to press for 'betterment' measures, chairing another sub-committee on the scheme, but this was 'a salve to a sore' compared to the root principle of taxation of land.[42] He managed to get a sympathetic land values taxation sub-committee established in March 1901, followed by a successful motion convening, a Special Conference of representatives from Rating Authorities.[43] The conference met at the Hotel Metropole, London on 21 October 1902, under the chairmanship of Samuel Chisholm, attracted 160 delegates from England, Ireland and Scotland.[44] At the meeting Ferguson was appointed convenor of a nationwide Muncipal Conference Committee, charged with drafting two bills promoting rating reform in England and Scotland to be presented to Parliament. The English bill which emerged, was later described by Ferguson as 'less drastic', but the Scottish measure was essentially his own Glasgow Bill – the 2/- in the pound municipal land tax – for which he had won Corporation support in 1898.[45]

The signal had been given for a new wave of nationwide campaigning, but Ferguson remained the antithesis of a single-issue politician. He was eager to bring other imperial questions like free trade onto the municipal agenda, arguing that Chamberlain's proposals to tax food in 1903 were very much the concern for 'the assembly of a great manufacturing city.[46] Indeed no cause was too great or small for his advocacy if it would advance the onward journey of mankind. Hospices for consumptives, agricultural rating and the teaching of modern languages, joined Corporation pensions and working conditions as battles worth fighting.[47] Animal welfare also stirred him in his later years, with campaigns waged on behalf of the caged eagle in Maxwell Park and against the cruelties of the Irish cattle trade.[48] Typically, he grasped the bigger issues among the details of suffering, arguing that, 'a nation which blunts the instincts of humanity by permitting cruelty rapidly deteriorates and a judicial blindness prepares it for destruction.' [49]

His inexhaustible energy could not conceal that the Stalwarts were in difficulties. Some of these were personal and immediate. Ex-Bailie Ferguson J.P., ally of Lord Provost Chisholm, became an obvious target for the latest *enfant terrible* of Glasgow Corporation, Andrew Scott Gibson.[50] Victorious in Springburn ward in 1901–after plagiarising Ferguson's *City of Progress* in his election address – this diminutive twenty-three year old lost no time in launching a populist crusade against jobbery, temperance and general self-righteousness in municipal affairs. He had already earned his spurs by attacking nepotism, a delicate subject for Ferguson whose son was a Corporation employee.[51] Gibson, the gadfly, returned to the attack in June 1902 with an indictment of costly magistrates' lunches and councillors' expenses. Previously one of the sternest critics of such claims, it transpired that Ferguson himself had claimed generous expenses for his trips to London on land taxation business. At least one Calton ratepayer was gravely disappointed by, 'a noticeable change from advanced radicalism to time-serving toadyism', observing that Ferguson's elevation to the magistrate's bench had, 'sapped and undermined his democratic principles'.[52]

His personal record of service and public probity meant that would ultimately rise above these barbs, but his discomfiture at the hands of an opportunist like Gibson suggested a deeper shift in public attitudes against the Stalwarts. The group had once prided themselves on their fearless and consistent conduct, but now seemed much like any other set of quarrelsome and venial local politicians. Loose at the best of times, the democratic coalition was now pulling apart. Relationships with Chisholm and the Progressives continued to be cautious, but the Labour camp was also divided among itself. By 1900, the nationalists were left wondering whether their financial and organisational contribution was worth the effort, when Hugh Murphy failed to attract the support of Shaw Maxwell and the Camlachie Labour Party for his bid to win Mile End as the Stalwart candidate.[53] A feud erupted in which Maxwell's supporters threatened to oust John Ferguson from Calton, as Murphy, once a pioneer of closer Labour cooperation, led the charge for an independent 'Irish ticket'.[54] The *Observer* joined in declaring open season on the Labour presence on the Council, which it declared had proved worthless. The calibre of representation, it believed, had put Ferguson under increasing pressure, as other wards provided him with pygmies and then expected from him 'the work of Titans'.[55]

As the Stalwart project faltered, the Citizen's Union launched its own offensive.[56] The Union's guiding spirit was Arthur Kay, a Glasgow fine art dealer and collector. In education and lifestyle he was the antithesis of the earnest Ferguson – in his youth he had enjoyed big game shooting north of the Limpopo – but they shared a fascination with the detail of local taxation and a desire to conduct the debate in a national arena.[57] Accordingly, Kay was happy to supply ammunition to a series of articles on the curse of municipal socialism published by *The Times* during 1902.[58]

The adversaries were also well matched in their talent for grassroots organisation. The Citizen's Union had rapidly developed as a rallying point for frustrated ratepayers, with convenors in each of the city's wards, and was pursuing a determined electoral strategy of targeting the strongholds of the most prominent Stalwarts and Progressives. Indeed, by November 1901, it could boast that only one out of seven Stalwart candidates had been returned.[59]

As the next year's elections approached, both sides craved a decisive victory. Provost Chisholm had proposed to petition parliament for leave to borrow £750,000 in order to extend housing provision to the poorest and labouring classes. In the opinion of the Citizen's Union, this was an extravagant gesture which would drive up the price of land, curb private enterprise and increase taxation.[60] In contrast, Ferguson's position was one of nuanced support for Chisholm's scheme as, 'a philanthropic effort in the right direction', while admitting that it would take his own Glasgow Bill to end the private monopoly in land and solve the housing problem.[61] Whatever the finer points of doctrine, he realised that housing was a vote-winner that might counter the difficulties of the Stalwart alliance. As he shifted into campaigning gear, he published a four-page pamphlet, *The Dark Shadow upon the Bright Record of Glasgow,* which circulated in large numbers throughout the city to coincide with the deliberations of the Glasgow Municipal Housing Commission in the summer of 1902.[62]

It was clear that Calton would be one of the most hotly contested seats in Glasgow. The Citizen's Union had backed a strong candidate, and fears for Ferguson's return were real enough to make some of the Irish reconsider their cooler relationship with Labour.[63] Although the housing issue had helped the Stalwarts rally elsewhere in the city, he scraped home by a mere fifty votes.[64] Chisholm was less fortunate, loosing his Woodside seat to the ubiquitous Scott Gibson, despite Ferguson's attempts to secure Stalwart support for his embattled ally.

The Citizen's Union were disappointed with the overall result, sniffing that their own propaganda had been too subtle for an electorate beguiled by socialist promises.[65] Yet Chisholm's defeat was to mark a turning point in civic affairs. From 1903 onwards, 'economy' became a watchword which even Ferguson and the Stalwarts could not afford to ignore.[66] If Glasgow wished to maintain its municipal commitment, the restructuring of local taxation became even more of an imperative.

A purer patriotism

For Ferguson, 1903 was also a personal watershed. His rhetoric, once dominated by learned authorities, now assumed the tone of personal pleading as he realised the end of career was in sight. He had shared hopes with electors of Calton when fighting to retain his seat:

> Three years would probably be as much as his age would permit him to work in the service of the people. He intended to die as he had lived and try to make the world better than he had found it, and having done that his duty to society would be done, and he should when his time came, feel conscious of having lived according to his light, an honest life in the service of the people.[67]

In recent years, death had harvested heroes and colleagues alike: Gladstone, John Torley, Pope Leo, John Murdoch, Herbert Spencer, had all passed in succession. Indeed, when Ferguson addressed the Dublin Convention on the Irish Land Bill in April 1903, he was the only speaker present who had also addressed the landmark Home Rule Conference, convened by Butt thirty years before.[68] His mind often went back to the giants of those days, when he thought of what might have been for Ireland.[69]

For a time that year it had looked as if he too would be lost to the movement – in Enniskillen they had already begun to compose his obituary.[70] During the early summer he had fallen seriously ill and was ordered to take a complete rest from business and politics. His convalescence was slow and he was forced to remove to the banks of Loch Katrine in an attempt to regain his health.[71] He had only begun to get back in harness when he suffered another grievous blow. After nine o'clock mass on 23 August, Hugh Murphy was rushing to a political meeting in Airdrie when he collapsed with a brain haemorrhage. He died a few days later, aged forty-seven.[72] Ferguson was devastated. For the rest of his life, he would falter at the memory of, 'the pale-browed, black-haired Fermanagh youth, full of Fenian fire, but well-controlled by reason and democratic sympathies'. [73] On the morning of the funeral, the old man presented a poignant figure as his grief overcame him. Characteristically, he struggled on through the day, attending an Emmet commemoration at Glasgow Green, but his strength was spent and he suffered a further collapse.[74]

His unceasing fight for land values taxation was perhaps both the cause and the consequence of his physical decline. Even after his collapse, he was determined to press on, determined to see this one great project come to fruition. From his Irish experience he knew the value of national conventions in establishing a critical mass for reform and in concentrating and directing the campaigning process. Following Chisholm's defeat, it was Ferguson who increasingly assumed the mantle of leadership, chairing a second conference, again under the auspices of Glasgow Corporation, at the Westminster Palace Hotel, London on 9 December 1903. Here the work of his Muncipal Conference Committee gained the approval of delegates from over a hundred municipal bodies.[75] This was followed by a further conference, chaired by Ferguson, on 3 March 1904, and another on 7 October 1904, at which his Committee was reconstituted with himself as Convenor.[76] The conferences were a personal triumph, their successful termination being attributed to his urbanity and despatch in the chair.[77] Indeed, the movement seemed to be sweeping all before it. In the spring of 1904, Charles Trevelyan, who had presented an unsuccessful Urban Site Values Bill in 1902, at last saw the bill for rating reform in England which had emerged from Ferguson's Committee pass its second reading by sixty-seven votes.[78] Well might Henry George's disciples rejoice that, 'the dreams of one generation are the realities of the next'.[79]

Of course, Ireland claimed her place in the struggle. From the outset, Ferguson had been keen to involve the Irish municipalities, soliciting Davitt's help to this end.[80] He was equally convinced that taxation of land values should enter into the mainstream of the Irish parliamentary programme, taking advantage of the UIL conference at Dublin Mansion House in January 1902 to raise the case of the 'tenants in towns'. The rates of Dublin, he suggested, could be wiped out by taxing landlords' increased increment in a civilised way by taking every penny back to the nation to which it belonged.[81] He was on fertile ground, as the previous year Dublin Corporation had declared its desire to borrow £500,000 to re-house the poorest citizens and encourage suburban building to relieve its housing crisis.[82] A UIL committee was established and Redmond and Dillon were sufficiently impressed to pledge their best attention to its deliberations. By 1904, a new national organisation, the Town Tenants League, was actively campaigning to win the same legal protection against urban landlords as enjoyed by rural labourers.

Land was already back in the heart of the nationalist agenda, but Ferguson's desire to enlarge the framework of reference to include urban issues had its own motivations. At the most basic level, he realised that he would need the help of Irish MPs to sponsor and promote private members bills in favour of land values taxation. Indeed, it was support to which he felt entitled as recompense for his selfless work in Ireland's cause.[83] His radicalism on urban land issues was also some compensation for the compromising stance he was forced to adopt on George Wyndham's Land Bill which had been unveiled in March 1903. The bill promised a generous measure of land purchase, creating thousands of peasant proprietors as a lasting settlement to the Irish land question. Like many of his colleagues, Ferguson was initially sceptical of such schemes, but he came to recognise that – as in the case of Chisholm's housing proposals – ameliorative action was urgently necessary given the scale of rural distress.[84] Yet he felt his retreat from Georgite ideals keenly, especially when taken to task by no less an expert on Irish land reform than Scott Gibson.[85] He took comfort from his belief that taxation of land values would provide the ultimate solution in the city and the countryside alike, compelling reluctant landlords to sell under Wyndham's initiative.[86]

Not for the first time, national fame had failed to dissipate his immediate worries. The Corporation's generous sponsorship of the land conferences – to the tune of £2000 to £3000 – was to give Arthur Kay and his allies fresh grounds for complaint.[87] This was of great concern as it seemed that, due to the resignation of a fellow Calton councillor, he might have to seek re-election before the expiry of his three-year term in 1905.[88] Trouble had also resurfaced among Irish ranks with William O'Brien's resignation from parliament in November 1903, over his party's attitude to the Land Act. Ferguson was forced to embark on another mission of reconciliation, touring local halls to insist, 'they were all one in principle, but differed merely on a question of policy'.[89] He was already showing the strain during the build up to Trevelyan's bill, when he quarrelled with John Burns, MP in the lobby of the House of Commons.[90] The final straw came with the fundraising drive which he had spearheaded to raise a fitting monument to Hugh Murphy. At the unveiling of the fine granite obelisk at Dalbeath Cemetery in April 1904, he shared with the audience his vision of the purer patriotism of the exile:

> The man who serves his country in a foreign land, headless of danger, loss and shame is a higher order of patriot than he who strives for his country at home. For the patriot at home has national opinion to sustain him and the hope of rising with the fortunes of his country.[91]

It was almost his own epitaph, for his health had broken down again. He was forced back to Loch Katrine, contenting himself with lengthy epistles on early Irish missionaries.

Checking the 'fat boy'

After a stormy decade in power the Unionists resembled, 'a woebegone flock of timid sheep in want of a drover'.[92] Yet as long as they clung on to power, Ferguson knew his dreams would never be realised. He had received a salutary reminder of this in February 1904, when he led a deputation to meet Walter Long, the President of the Local Government Board and Graham Murray, the Scottish Secretary. These gentlemen politely but firmly informed him that the present government that were unlikely to undertake the taxation of land values at any time.[93] Compared with the prospects of Irish Home Rule under a Balfour administration, this was a warm endorsement. In pursuing the Unionists downfall, Ferguson was willing to risk all. The challenge would not only be to marshal the Irish vote, but to win back a Liberal Party worth voting for.

The one thing upon which Liberals had agreed upon in the aftermath of the previous 1900 General Election was the scale of their defeat. Attempts to blame it the loss of 'the Catholic vote' on the education question, neglected the their own deficiencies in organisation and party unity.[94] With Liberal Imperialists and Gladstonians at each other's throats over the South African War, many Irish activists longed for the old straight fight between 'liberty and reaction' and had doubted the Liberals' basic ability to win.[95]

The situation deteriorated further with Rosebery's attempt to wrest back the leadership from the loyal but lacklustre Gladstonian, Henry Campbell-Bannerman. As a full-frontal assault began on the party establishment in Scotland, the concordat permitting individual candidates to form their own positions on Home Rule was blown apart.[96] For Rosebery, the party's Irish policy was a liability which should be jettisoned. For the Irish, the ex-premier was 'the fat boy of the renegade Liberals' and they took delight in humbling his allies when they dared to contest Scottish by-elections.[97] Ferguson's own struggle for the soul of the party was coloured by a similar personal detestation of Rosebery – 'the disgraced and disregarded howler of Israel' – who had stolen the prophetic mantle of Gladstone and threatened to lead the faithful tribe off the true path to federal reform.[98]

Indeed, it seemed that his patience with Liberalism had finally run its course. In 1903, he wrote that the party seemed to have survived its capacity for utility:

> It is little better than a worn-out old reformer talking over and over again his old campaigns and expecting an advanced world to be interested. The forces of Labour, under many names, are making it more manifest daily that Tory and Liberal are dead issues.[99]

With sentiments like these, it was hardly surprising that Rosebery's friends in the press began to wonder why Irish activists were still on Liberal committees.[100]

Like his regular threats to retire from public life, this latest breach with Liberalism contained an element of posturing. In fact, his fascination with the party's internecine warfare continued. He identified strongly with progressive forces within the party, becoming an honorary vice-president of the Glasgow Branch of the Young Scots Society. With their motto, 'For Scotland and Gladstone', the Young Scots had been formed in October 1900 for 'the purpose of educating young men in the fundamental principles of Liberalism, and of encouraging them and stimulating them in the study of social science and economics'.[101] Embracing Home Rule and land values taxation, this was an organisation dear to his heart.

Ferguson also helped Liberalism retain its reputation for radicalism through his own efforts as a reform campaigner. A crisis of unemployment in Glasgow during the winter of 1904, reckoned to be the worst for twenty years, presented an ideal opportunity. It was his belief that real solution was to approach parliament for powers to deal 'scientifically' with the problem which he defined as the product of migration from the land.[102] However, his immediate attempts to alleviate the worst of the suffering by the judicious use of public funds allowed him to restate the ethical tradition of Glasgow Liberalism. As the Chairman of the Corporation's Unemployed Committee, he had his colleagues sift though 2000 applications for relief. Discounting the 'loafers', 1500 were put to work on put to work at a maximum wage on 15/- a week.[103] His strength rallying, he even found the energy to reprise his role as a rights of way campaigner in Lenzie. Returning from his Sunday walk, he found a crowd gathered at the padlocked entrance to the 'Lady's Mile'. On discovering that a railway company had attempted to block this popular footpath, he called for a crowbar, but his wife and daughter hurried him homewards. He soon returned to the fray armed with a chisel. Having worked loose the chain, he sent it to the company manager, threatening legal action and a mass trespass.[104]

With another general election in prospect, Ferguson's strategy seemed at first sight straightforward. The formula he delivered in October 1904 was economically expressed: the Irish vote should go with Labour in all constituencies where such a course would secure victory, but where Irish and Labour votes could not return a candidate the Irish vote should go to the Liberal.[105] In practice, this stance was highly disingenuous, given that the number ILP candidates in Scotland was likely to be small, and the cases in which they were opposed by a diehard Roseberyite even smaller. Addressing the national conference on the Irish vote in Scotland at the end of 1904, he was more frank on the priorities at stake. With Ireland on her knees, he proclaimed, 'Scotland and the Labour question would have to wait'.[106]

This policy had already been given a practical outing the North-East Lanark by-election of August 1904, where Ferguson's support ensured that the Liberal, Provost Findlay received the official UILGB endorsement over the ILP's John Robertson. Not everyone appreciated the complexities of his position. Some of his Labour friends approached him after the contest to tell him that they would never support him again, while the Irish were far from united behind him[107] As Keir Hardie observed to Davitt: 'The advice was most strongly resented by hundreds of active, intelligent Irishmen who, with every desire to be loyal to the INL, felt they could not be so and follow the advice tendered, without being disloyal to their interests as working men'.[108]

The trumpeting of 'Ireland supreme', however, was not intended to isolate him from the broader democratic agenda. His lack of an official position on the UIL Executive – queried by a concerned *Observer* during 1904–was itself revealing. Assuming such a post would probably have entailed severing his connections with the Liberal Party, an action which might in turn have compromised his campaigning of behalf of land values taxation.[109] His views on the Labour vote were also underpinned by his enduring belief that Labour – 'drawn from the class which numbers seven-tenths of the population' – should work in harness with Liberalism and not supplant it. The true value of strong parliamentary Labour representation would be revealed if the Liberal Party was returned at the next election on 'mere general principles' – in other words, led by a Campbell-Bannerman cabinet consisting of 'a coalition of earnest reformers and mere opportunists'. In that event, Labour members would stiffen the backbone of the Premier and the House of Commons on the key issues of Irish Home Rule and land values taxation. The ideal solution remained one which would avoid the unpleasantness of North-East Lanark and harmonise the goals of national self-determination and social reform. A precedent was provided by the cooperative compact negotiated the previous year by Chief Whip Herbert Gladstone with the Labour Representation Committee in England. Quite simply, preached Ferguson, the Liberals should meet Labour's demands to run candidates half way. This would be: 'True Liberalism . . . *Fiat justitia, ruat caelum'*.[110]

Findlay's victory at North-East Lanark was one of a number of by-election successes during the course of 1904 which convinced Liberals of various shades that the tide was turning at last. The messy end to the Boer War had blunted the challenge of Liberal Imperialism, while the old rallying call of free trade helped reconcile competing wings of the party. Meanwhile, the Home Rule camp was alive again with enthusiasm and a sense of purpose, as the coming general election was reckoned to be, 'the most vital in Ireland for a generation'.[111]

Back in Calton, the prospect of a ratepayers challenge in November was swept aside by 'an avalanche of opinion'.[112] After thirteen years and representing the ward five times, it was the first occasion Ferguson had been returned unopposed. Freed from this burden, he turned to rally the troops. At the T.P. O'Connor demonstration the next month, the visionary had returned:

> They were met today for a sacred duty, sanctified by the blood and tears of a dying nation – dying of oppression influenced by ignorance and factionalism, but not yet dead. No thank God, the eyes of friends and foes alike are being opened as were the eyes of the servant and prophet of Israel. They see the dry bones clothed in flesh and alive. They see the whole valley filled with horsemen and chariots of the Almighty upon the side of a wronged and suffering people . . . the stars in their courses fight upon our side, and that by natural law, certain as gravitation, Home Rule is rapidly approaching its consummation. Our Irish trumpet must give no uncertain sound, we must harness ourselves for the day of battle.[113]

Notes

1 *Glasgow Herald*, 16 Dec. 1902. Ferguson was responding to Single Tax critics who accused him of compromise on the housing question.

2 *Glasgow Star*, 2 May 1903.

3 *Ibid.*, 2 Jul. 1904.

4 Davitt, *Fall of Feudalism*, pp. 692–4.

5 *Glasgow Observer*, 7 Apr. 1900. Kiernan was back in the driving seat as organiser for Scotland and the North of England.

6 *Glasgow Observer*, 14 Dec. 1901.

7 *Ibid.,* 12 May 1900. The British organisation adopted the title United Irish League of Great Britain (UILGB) at the same convention.

8 *Freeman's Journal,* 20, 21 Jun. 1900.

9 *Glasgow Observer,* 29 Dec. 1900 for Ferguson's 'secret history' of the convention. Healy had launched a series of bitter attacks on O'Brien in his *Daily Nation* newspaper. He had ignored the convention and refused to dissolve the People's Rights Association.

10 *Ibid.,* 11, 18 Aug. 1900; *Freeman's Journal,* 21 Dec. 1900.

11 Lyons, *Dillon,* pp. 216–9; Moody, 'Michael Davitt', pp. 73–4. Davitt resigned his parliamentary seat and went to South Africa as a journalist. For his pro-Boer dispatches, 'For Land and People': *Glasgow Observer,* 9 Feb. 1901.

12 *Ibid.,* 7 Jan. 1900.

13 They were embarking on a tour of the country under the auspices of the Stop the War Committee: S. C. Cronwright-Shreiner, *The Land of Free Speech: Record of a Campaign on Behalf of Peace in England and Scotland in 1900* (London, 1906), pp. 63–76. (My thanks to Ewen Cameron for this reference).

14 *Glasgow Herald,* 7 Mar. 1900.

15 S. J. Brown, '"Echoes of Midlothian": Scottish Liberalism and the South African War, 1899–1902', *Scottish Historical Review,* vol. LXXI, (1992) p. 163.

16 *Glasgow Observer,* 10 Mar. 1900.

17 *Ibid.,* 2 Mar. 1901.

18 *Ibid.,* 25 Aug. 1900.

19 *Evening Times,* 19 Dec. 1900.

20 *Glasgow Observer,* 9 Feb. 1901. It was feared that his association with this 'Falstaffian band' would lead to enlistment being pressed on unwilling Corporation employees.

21 *Glasgow Herald*, 4 Feb. 1901.

22 *Glasgow Observer*, 2 Feb. 1901.

23 See, for example, *Ibid.*, 23 Feb. 1901. The Davis Branch of the UILGB of which he was honorary president now refused to pass a vote of renewed confidence. He sent a letter of resignation which he was later persuaded to withdraw.

24 *Evening Times*, 3 Jun. 1902.

25 The inner city stood at 9.71: Smyth, 'Labour and Socialism', p. 289. See also, MacRaild, *Irish Migrants*, p.43 for wider Scottish and British perspectives.

26 Hutchison and O'Day, 'Gaelic Revival', p. 256.

27 *Glasgow Observer*, 2 Jan. 1904.

28 *Ibid.*, 7 May 1904.

29 *Ibid.*, 2 Jan., 7 May 1904.

30 *Glasgow Star*, 14 Jun. 1902.

31 *Ibid.*, 5 Oct. 1901.

32 *Glasgow Observer*, 7 Sept. 1901.

33 *Ibid.*, 3 Oct. 1903. The League by this point had 91 adult branches and 2 juvenile branches in Scotland.

34 *Glasgow Observer*, 17 Nov. 1903.

35 *Glasgow Herald*, 23 Dec. 1901 for the full speech which was hailed as 'one of the most dazzling oratorical lighting flashes that ever issued from the lips of John Ferguson'. He was required to perform his balancing act in miniature at the visit of Colonial Troops to Glasgow in August 1902 in connection with the Coronation celebrations. He attended their military display – ironically held at Celtic Park – but covered his tracks by seeking out the Boer General de Wet's nephew and ask him what he thought of his uncle. He followed this up by denouncing the 'affront' to the Corporation when the British Empire League wrote to thank

them for their hospitality to the soldiers: *Evening Times,* 2, 5, 8 Aug. 1902.

36 *Irish Weekly News and Ulster Examiner,* 16 Dec. 1905.

37 *Glasgow Observer,* 23 Feb. 1901.

38 *Ibid,* 28 May 1904

39 The standing committees were: Churches and Churchyards; Libraries; Diseases of Animal Acts; Parks; Tramways; Markets; City Improvements; Telephones. The special committees were: Proposed Fire Insurance; Utilisation of Corporation Land; Value of Licensed Premises; Grading the Salaries of Clerical Staff; Representative Committee for Telephone Wire Attachments to Corporation Property. In 1900, he also served on the Finance Sub-committee of the Telephone Committee; the Extensions Sub-committee of the Tramways Committee; the Music in Parks Sub-committee of the Parks Committee. As a member of the City Improvements Committee, he was involved in a further three sub-committees on lodging houses and district improvements. From, GCA, Glasgow Corporation Minutes 1900–1.

40 *Glasgow Observer,* 1 Nov. 1902; *Evening Times,* 16 Dec. 1902.

41 *Glasgow Star,* 18 Aug. 1906. During 1890–1, Cameron & Ferguson had expanded briefly to become Cameron, Ferguson & Gullick. By 1893, the trading name Cameron, Ferguson and Co. had been adopted. The firm also moved from West Nile St. to North Fredrick St.

42 *Glasgow Herald,* 16 Dec 1902; GCA, Glasgow Corporation Minutes, 21 Nov., 18 Dec. 1901.

43 *Ibid.,* 4 Apr. 1901; *Land Values,* May 1902.

44 *Ibid.,* Nov. 1902.

45 Ferguson, *Taxation of Land Values,* p. 3.

46 GCA, Glasgow Corporation Minutes, 1 Oct. 1903; 15 Sept. 1904.

47 See, for example, *Ibid.*, 6 Dec. 1900; 1 May, 4 Jul. 1901; 19 Jun, 4 Sept. 1902.

48 *Glasgow Herald*, 22 Mar. 1901. The Corporation had been gifted the eagle by a former councillor. It had become a popular attraction, but Ferguson demanded that it be more suitably accommodated elsewhere, or preferably be set free.

49 *Evening Times*, 24 Oct. 1902.

50 He was destined for a bizarre career, resigning from the Council in 1920 after an attempt to cut his throat : Maver 'Local party politics', p. 54.

51 *Evening Times*, 19, 25 Dec. 1900.

52 GCA, Glasgow Corporation Minutes, 3 Jan. 1901; *Evening Times*, 18 Jun. 1902.

53 *Ibid.*, 19 Aug., 24 Nov. 1900. For a full account see, Smyth, 'Labour and Socialism', pp. 181–2.

54 *Glasgow Observer*, 9 Nov. 1901. Ferguson and Maxwell's relationship was to sour considerably. The pair had once been described as 'henchman and pontiff', but 1905 Maxwell was publicly attacking his mentor's use of the black arts of political patronage. The charge was that he had secured the Glasgow Police clothing contract for a Limerick firm: *Evening Times*, 10 Mar. 1905, and *Bailie*, 15 Mar. 1905 for 'The "Boss" Deputationist' cartoon. For Murphy's involvement with the Irish Municipal Election Committee, which had strong HGB links: *Glasgow Observer*, 2, 23 Nov. 1901. The branch was also drawn to Gibson's populism for a time.

55 *Ibid.*, 23 Aug., 26 Oct. 1901.

56 GCA, Records of Citizen's Union, TD488/9: Secretary's Report 4 Mar. 1902. It claimed that in thirteen years the city

debt had risen from 5 to 12 million, and taxation from 2/-5 to 3/-3 in the pound

57 *The Bailie*, 20 Mar. 1901.

58 *The Times*, 6 Oct. 1902.

59 GCA, Citizen's Union: Secretary's Report 15 Nov. 1899; 26 Feb. 1901; 14 Mar. 1902.

60 Ibid., 14 Mar. 1902.

61 *Evening Times*, 1 Sept. 1902.

62 *Land Values*, Aug. 1902. It was such an effective propaganda piece that it was suggested it should be presented in postcard form. Housing also featured prominently in his election address: *Address to the Citizens of the Twenty-Five Wards in General, and Particularly to the Electors of Calton Ward.*

63 GCA, Citizen's Union Minutes, 10 Sept. 1902. Their candidate was James Macfarlane, once a muncipal reformer. For the Irish see, *Glasgow Observer*, 22 Aug., 1902. Hugh Murphy resigned as chairman of the new Irish Municipal Election Committee when it refused to re-enter into a formal connection with Labour .

64 *Glasgow Herald*, 5 Nov. 1902.

65 GCA, Citizen's Union, Secretary's Report, 3 Feb. 1902.

66 GCA, Corporation Minutes, 19 Feb. 1903.

67 *Glasgow Observer*, 18 Oct. 1902.

68 *Freeman's Journal.* 18 Apr. 1903.

69 *Glasgow Observer*, 5 Dec. 1903. See also, *Irish Packet*, 14 Nov. 1903.

70 *Ibid.* 12 Dec. 1903.

71 *Glasgow Star*, 13, 20 Jun., 4. Jul. 1903. He was given the use of the Corporation-owned, Royal Cottage.

72 *Ibid.*, 29 Aug. 1903.

73 *Ibid.*, 9 Apr. 1904.

74 *Ibi.d.*, 5 Sept. 1903.

75 *Land Values*, Dec. 1903. Chisholm had originally proposed the Progressive councillor, W.F. Anderson as chair, but he declined on account of 'ridiculous remarks' made regarding Chisholm by the Single Taxers: *Glasgow Herald*, 5 Dec. 1902.

76 *Land Values*, Apr., Nov. 1905.

77 *Glasgow Star*, 19 Dec. 1904.

78 *Land Values*, Apr. 1904, Ferguson, *Taxation of Land Values*, p. 6.

79 *Ibid.*, Mar. 1902.

80 TCD, Davitt MSS 9447/3571, J. Ferguson to M. Davitt, 10 Oct. 1904.

81 *Land Values*, Feb. 1902. See also *Freeman's Journal*, 1 Sept. 1903.

82 M. Fraser, *John Bull's Other Homes. State Housing and British Policy in Ireland, 1883–1922* (Liverpool, 1996), pp. 83–4.

83 *Glasgow Star*, 10 Dec. 1904.

84 *Ibid.*, 23 Aug. 1903.

85 *Daily Mail*, 1 Apr. 1903. In Gibson's opinion, 'any proposal which would leave a single Irish child disinherited is unworthy of the support of a true land reformer'.

86 *Freeman's Journal*, 13 May 1903.

87 Select Committee on the Land Values Taxation etc. (Scotland) Bill, 1906. A. Kay Memorandum, p.2.

88 *Glasgow Star*, 21 Nov. 1903.

89 *Ibid.*, 21 Nov. 1903.

90 *Evening Times*, 27 Feb. 1904.

91 *Glasgow Star,* 30 Apr. 1904. For the campaign see, *Irish Weekly,* 2 Apr. 1904.

92 *Glasgow Star,* 27 Feb. 1904.

93 *The County and Municipal Record,* 6 Feb. 1904. In the event, despite an open vote on Trevelyan's bill, it was killed quietly by the government preventing it going into Committee: Ferguson, *Taxation of Land Values,* p.6. Caldwell had also introduced the Scottish version of the Bill later in the year, but it failed to pass its first reading.

94 Wood, 'Irish immigrants', p. 80; Brown, 'Echoes of Midlothian', p. 172.

95 *Glasgow Observer,* 8 Sept. 1900.

96 Brown, 'Echoes of Midlothian', p. 156.

97 For the North West Lanarkshire contest in 1901 see, *Glasgow Observer,* 10 Dec. 1904; *Glasgow Herald,* 25 Sept. 1901; Smillie, *My Life,* pp. 107–11; ULL, J. B. Glasier Papers, J. B. Glasier to K Glasier GP/1/1/496–8, 11, 12, 13 Sept. 1901.

98 *Glasgow Star,* 16 Jul. 1904.

99 *Ibid.,* 21 Mar. 1903.

100 *Daily Record,* 1 Feb. 1901. See, NLS 11765/8, Minutes of the Western Committee 21 Jan. 1900; 25 Oct. 1901.

101 *Scottish Patriot,* November, 1903; Hutchison, *Political History,* pp. 232.

102 *Glasgow Star,* 11 Feb. 1905.

103 *Glasgow Herald,* 12, 18, 25 Nov. 1904; *Evening Times,* 30 Dec. 1904.

104 *Glasgow Observer,* 3 Sept. 1904.

105 *Ibid.,* 22 Oct. 1904.

106 *Glasgow Star,* 24 Dec. 1904.

107　*Ibid.*, 24 Dec. 1904.

108　TCD, Davitt MSS 9330, K. Hardie to M. Davitt 4 May 1905.

109　*Glasgow Observer*, 24 Nov. 1904.

110　*Ibid*, 22 Oct. 1904.

111　*Ibid.*

112　*Ibid.*, Nov. 1904.

113　*Ibid.*, 18 Dec. 1904.

CHAPTER FOURTEEN

A Prince and a Great Man has Fallen this Day in Israel

Longing for the day of battle, Ferguson found great resonance in a couplet of Robert Browning:

> I was ever a fighter, so one fight more,
> The best and the last. [1]

While he realised that the Irish vote must be kept united and independent in the struggle, he was determined to mould UILGB policy rather than passively accept it. [2] His approach remained businesslike: he would back strong Labour and Liberal candidates who were sound on Irish Home Rule, but 'pawky Liberals giving Home Rule a wide berth' would be punished. [3]

Blessings and thunderbolts accordingly rained down upon the constituencies of Glasgow and the West of Scotland early in 1905. In a typical week he averaged three to four speaking engagements, boasting that there was no constituency where a Liberal candidate could be returned against the Irish vote. [4] His efforts also extended to the Labour hopefuls, George Barnes in Blackfriars and Hutchestown and Joe Burgess in Camlachie, who had entered the lists before any Liberal opposition. [5]

By springtime, the campaign for land values taxation had also picked up momentum. The fifth municipal conference was held in London in April. Since their last meeting, Ferguson noted that 205 rating authorities had been added to the campaign. [6] Work in parliament resumed with the re-introduction of the Glasgow Bill in May. Following vocal support from Ferguson's Lanarkshire protégés, Caldwell and Findlay, the measure prevailed by twenty votes, although the Government again used procedural niceties to prevent it reaching the committee stage. [7] It was the fate of many a Scottish bill which had cost thousands of pounds to promote.

Left with another moral victory, Ferguson reflected that taxation of land values was, 'the Scotch argument for Home Rule'.[8] In response, he continued his connection with the Young Scots and Scottish National League, organisations which sought to make constitutional change a reality.[9]

His regular forays to London had not escaped the attention of the press who pictured 'The Weary Glasgow Deputationist', puffing contentedly on his cigar amid a haze of champagne bottles and dancing girls.[10] In fact, his efforts in the land campaign, coupled with his continuing political exertions had begun to take their toll. Colleagues noticed that the effects of physical and mental strain were showing, and his doctor advised him, 'in the interests of his health and life', to desist from strenuous platform work.[11] He spend the summer in Ireland, but, far from resting, promptly launched into a speaking tour.[12]

The general election was finally declared in December. With it all hope of respite was gone. Balfour's resignation and refusal to dissolve parliament had forced Campbell-Bannerman to take office with a cabinet drawing from both wings of Liberalism.[13] Ferguson had already become profoundly suspicious of the party's equivocation on Ireland, following experiences like the General Council meeting in October where Home Rule was relegated to a lowly place on the agenda.[14] During the next month, Redmond also took a firm line while on a Scottish tour, declaring his 'natural sympathy' with Labour and echoing Ferguson's call for Liberal party managers to facilitate the return of Labour candidates.[15] Any serious breach was headed off by Campbell-Bannerman's speech at Stirling in November in which he promised a substantial instalment of self-government to ensure Ireland's place as 'a strong, harmonious and contented portion of the Empire'.[16] Although this 'step by step' approach was mainly aimed at healing divisions in the party, it was enough for Ferguson who proclaimed that ageing Liberal leader had, 'at last won his chance to write his name in golden letters upon the records of time.'[17] With Rosebery standing out against the compromise, he explained that it was even more imperative to return Bannerman in a position strong enough to resist the foes of Home Rule.

The result of the contest was generally expected to be a close one, with the Irish bargaining position correspondingly strong. Ferguson found himself in great demand with Liberal agents and appeared on some twenty platforms over the next few weeks, claiming an anti-Rosebery pledge as his price.[18] Although it seemed that the Irish were slipping back into the smooth grooves of the Liberal alliance, the relationship with Labour was also warmer than for many years past. As Hardie explained to Davitt, the Irish would have some hard fighting to do in the next parliament and, 'would have nothing to lose by supporting our men and in so doing and securing their return they will have some reliable supporters in them'.[19] Ferguson, of course, needed little persuading. In North-West Lanarkshire, he supported the ILP's Joseph Sullivan against Dr Douglas, the Liberal Imperialist, but proceeded warily for fear of antagonising the Scottish miners and disrupting the UILGB branches.[20] Blackfriars and Camlachie were also important contests, but here marshalling the Irish behind Labour was far from easy, given the party's support for secular education.[21]

Behind the scenes, there were frantic machinations to secure Labour opposition against Liberal Imperialist candidates in the Leith Burghs and Midlothian. Cunninghame Graham was touted for the Leith seat, held by the arch-Roseberyite Munro Ferguson, but his financial embarrassment was already common knowledge.[22] Despairing that the Labour seats were being 'bunged', Ferguson tried to persuade Davitt to make funds available for Alderman West of London to run, having personally checked his suitability and discussed the situation with Redmond. Again this challenge came to nothing and in the absence of a Labour alternative, the UILGB Executive was to back the Unionist.[23] The situation seemed brighter in Midlothian where Rosebery's son, Lord Dalmeny, was standing.[24] Davitt himself had been sounded out for this seat in November, but even the prospect of 'the triumph of a gaol bird over a peer's son', could not overcome his distaste for Westminster.[25] Another potential candidate was Robert Smillie, but he proved unwilling to transfer his campaign from Paisley where he had a reasonable chance of success.[26] Finally, Ferguson was again forced to call on West's services, despite worries that he would be seen as a carpetbagger.[27]

The appearance of the UILGB election manifesto for Scotland on 30 December at least helped clarify matters in the West of Scotland. It was a slate which Ferguson had done much to influence. Fifty-four Liberals were singled out, alongside Sullivan, Barnes and Burgess as 'approved' Labour candidates. [28]

Nationwide, the 1906 contest was an electoral flood-tide for the Liberals.[29] A Unionist majority of 74 was replaced by a Liberal majority of 241, with 30 Labour MPs and 83 Irish nationalists also returned. As Ferguson and Davitt conducted their usual post-election autopsy it was clear that there had also been missed opportunities. Barnes had been returned, but Burgess was defeated – a misfortune which Ferguson blamed squarely on T.P. O'Connor's pusillanimous conduct.[30] The direction of the Irish vote towards the Liberal in Paisley – in defiance of Ferguson's pleas for neutrality – had similarly robbed Smillie of the seat. Once targeted as a showcase of Irish political muscle, Midlothian had turned into another fiasco. Ferguson had been badly wrong-footed by West's sudden decision to quit the field, and by Dalmeny's equally sudden conversion to Campbell-Bannerman's Home Rule formula.[31] After months of denouncing Rosebery's son as a limb of Satan – 'with no educational value' – he realised, that with only a Unionist to face, he had become the only credible candidate.[32] He tried to make the Executive bow to the inevitable, but he had done his work too well. After some dithering, the Irish were instructed to oppose Dalmeny. When the young lord triumphed with a large majority, the Whiggish Liberals in the constituency were reported, 'rejoicing that the Irish vote should be done without'.[33]

It was not only in Midlothian that the unassailable Liberal position rapidly removed Ireland from the political equation. With the new Government consumed by a range of social reforms, the risk was that Home Rule would be completely omitted from the King's Speech.[34] This was averted, but the Irish policy which did emerge, with its promises of making economies in government and introducing means to associate the people with the conduct of Irish affairs, was at best 'sympathetic and somewhat vague'.[35] Yet Ferguson's faith survived the Liberals' reluctance to commit themselves immediately to major constitutional legislation. After all, there remained the prospect of the land tax which he described as, 'next to Home Rule . . . the chief work of my life'.[36] During the election, the country had been saturated with land values propaganda – the Scottish Liberal Association alone had circulated well over a million leaflets.[37] He remained adamant that the taxation of land values was, 'not a matter of politics but pure science', but after bills had been carried three times against an unfriendly government, there seemed much to hope for from an administration which was explicitly pledged to enact a land tax programme.[38]

He prepared the ground with a series of articles in the *Westminster Review* during January 1906.[39] The next month the battle began in earnest with another Municipal Committee deputation to London. [40] The immediate task was to find MPs willing to bring forward the Glasgow Bill as a private members bill. He was well acquainted with the problems involved – 700 members had the right to ballot and he needed 60 or 70 to enter the draw to have a fighting chance. On this occasion, he encountered unexpected difficulties. The new MPs, 'all needed educating on balloting techniques', with most sharing a complacent assumption that the government itself would initiate a suitable taxation measure. [41] With only fifty five MPs entering the ballot, the Bill failed to get a place. The situation was only retrieved by urging Mr Sutherland, MP for the Elgin Burghs, to use his slot to push the cause.

Yet these were piecemeal tactics. The real challenge was to persuade the government to take the issue out of the reformers' hands and bring forward its own legislation. At the sixth

Municipal Committee Conference in Manchester the previous November, it had been determined to petition the House of Commons praying for the passing of a bill for the separate assessment and rating of land values. On 26 February, Ferguson was in the vanguard of a 150–strong deputation which arrived to present the petition, signed by 115 authorities, to the new Prime Minister.[42] He still had high hopes of Campbell-Bannerman, whom he had recently lent upon to give the Glasgow agitation a favourable mention during a speech in the city.[43] On the day, however, the Premier was ailing and they were received by the Herbert Asquith, the new Chancellor of the Exchequer – a politician Ferguson had once described as an 'imbecile' over his handling of Irish political prisoners. The urbane Asquith praised their movement as one 'founded on the principles of common sense and equity', but refused to make a clear statement of the government's intentions, insisting that such a complex measure would take time to draft.[44] When he attempted to humour Ferguson by referring to his long years warring in the cause, the latter exploded: 'You have your years before you, and can afford to wait, but I have been half a century upon this job, and want to see results before I die'.[45]

He was indeed a dying man. He had set himself a punishing pace had during the general election, making a personal commitment to address two meetings every night of the campaign. On his way home from one of these events, he forgot his age for a moment and stepped hurriedly on a tramcar. He slipped and suffered what seemed to be a minor strain.[46] Typically, instead of resting he pushed on with his work in London, spending eight to ten hours a day for a period of two weeks lobbying on foot in the House of Commons.[47] By March 16, he was forced to enter a Glasgow nursing home in agony. He was deeply vexed at having to cancel meetings, especially his chairmanship of St Patrick's day, but from his bed he wrote to assure his comrades he would be back in harness within ten to twelve days.[48]

He came through an operation and seemed to be slowly

recovering, but his condition was to prove more than a simple injury.[49] As he lay in the nursing home, the demands of his public life would still not abate. He was besieged by well-wishers' telegrams and letters which queried if he would be able to keep his engagements. His family were forced to beg for peace, but they made one exception. Sutherland's Bill had passed its second reading on 23 March. Ferguson's delight on hearing of the latest parliamentary triumph of land values movement was described as 'almost childlike'.[50] Unfortunately, his pursuit of 'pawky Liberals' had also caught up with him. In the wake of election, the Roseberyite *Daily Record* had called for an end to his formal association with the Liberal party. At the beginning of April, he survived an attempt to oust him from the Glasgow Liberal Council only by the chairman's casting vote.[51]

It was not until Good Friday that he was strong enough to be removed to Lenzie. He remained in great pain, but his doctors were not unduly concerned. During Easter Week, he even seemed back to his old self, with some of his fire and vigour returning. On Sunday 22 April, he managed to get up and sit by the fire for a time. While resting in his chair he fainted and was immediately carried back to bed. His heart had proved unequal to the strain. He rallied a little, but his doctors saw that the situation was critical. They held a further consultation, but informed his family on Monday that there that all hope was gone. He grew weaker during the course of the day and at a quarter past nine in the evening, he slipped away.

It had been his wish to die at Benburb House. His wife, daughter and eldest son were by his side and he had remained conscious to the end – only a week after his seventieth birthday. After a life lived in public, his family could at last claim him for themselves. A huge official act of mourning was anticipated, with grandees from the Irish Party and a brace of municipal dignitaries poised to make the journey to Glasgow. Mary Ferguson and her children, however, had other ideas. On the afternoon of 26 April, the cortege left Benburb, impressing onlookers by its quiet simplicity. A private interment was held in the sequestered surroundings of Kirkintilloch's Old Aisle Cemetery. Only a handful of his closest friends on the Town Council were present, alongside a small deputation from Cameron, Ferguson and Co. Arthur Murphy, brother of Hugh, represented the local UILGB branches. [52] Under brilliant spring sunshine and a cloudless sky, John Ferguson was laid to rest beside the grave of his infant daughter, Elizabeth. He was buried, not in the raiment of the dead, but in his everyday frock coat – as if awaiting the call to action.

The news of his death dealt a grievous blow to Michael Davitt, himself recovering from an operation. [53] Their careers had been intertwined for over thirty years. He followed Ferguson to the grave within weeks.

For those left behind the immediate sensation was of 'a void, an utter vacuum'. [54] True to the traditions of the movement, Ferguson's friends formed a memorial committee, but even as they did so, his world seemed already to be vanishing. [55] Towards the end of his life he had been proud of his role as an Irish publisher, a contribution that the Gaelic activist, Stephen Gwynn fully acknowledged, commenting that he had, 'done more than any man to spread a knowledge of Anglo-Irish literature among the Irish throughout the world. [56] It soon transpired, however, that Cameron, Ferguson & Co. was burdened by almost a thousand unpaid customers' accounts, totalling over £10,000. This was only part of the problem: even when the firms assets were taken into account it was revealed that Ferguson's estate had debts of more than £20,000. [57] His nominated executors refused to become involved, and his widow and the family solicitor were left to sort out the mess. The main creditors were suppliers, but it was revealed that Ferguson had also been borrowing large cash sums from friends and business acquaintances – including his fellow councillors. In July, the Cameron, Ferguson & Co. was sold to R & T Washbourne of London, an old-established firm of Catholic publishers. [58] Benburb House was put on the market in October and was eventually disposed of at a knock-down price the next year. [59]

Ferguson's legacy in local politics seemed equally in peril. Within weeks of his death, Irish and Labour activists had fallen out over who would represent his Calton seat. As a result, the stronghold which he had made his own was lost at the by-election in May. It was to be the final blow for the Stalwart alliance. [60] The victory of 'Glasgow Bill' which had cheered Ferguson's last days was also to prove illusory. In December, the Select committee appointed to review it recommended that it be dropped for a more radical measure.[61] During 1907, a Valuation Bill, the Land Values (Scotland) Bill was introduced and passed its third reading, only to be rejected by the House of Lords. It was reintroduced the next year, but was so mutilated by the Lords, that the government abandoned it. There had always been a febrile quality to the ideas of Henry George – now they had run their course in a generation.

Above all, death had spared veterans like Ferguson the knowledge of Ireland's fate in the next decade. It had been his privilege – or misfortune – to realise the linkages and complexities in Irish politics, where others saw only absolutes. Beneath the florid rhetoric, he consistently rejected physical force and intimidation, separatism and partition. Instead, his credo was of Home Rule within the Empire through the cultivation of British opinion. In *Three Centuries* he had written of Irish bayonets reddening in a common struggle against European despots – a 'baptism of blood' which would forge a new imperial unity. When the baptism came, it was on the beaches of Gallipoli, and with it died Ferguson's dream of colonial self government.

Yet even if the Great War had eclipsed his cherished causes, it did not mean that Ferguson's career was one of failure. He was not an innovative thinker, but his great strength lay in synthesising a vast body of knowledge and applying it to real situations. As a theorist and an activist he had helped build successive popular movements in Ireland and Scotland, schooling his countrymen in political organisation and bringing them into contact with broader democratic forces. Unlike his parliamentary colleagues who were doomed to sterile opposition at Westminster, he found a further outlet for his talents in municipal government. His pursuit of the Single Tax may have proved chimerical, but for over a decade he employed his oratory, scholarship and sheer political acumen to achieve practical reforms which, if less exhilarating than George's utopia, still improved the lives and working conditions of many of his fellow citizens.

Ultimately, for the measure of the man, we must grasp not only his achievements, but what he represented. Part British radical, part Irish nationalist, he defended his social identity by drawing on a repertoire of roles. His obituarists struggled to encompass a career which was astonishing in its sweep: 'Celt of the Celts'; 'land reform pioneer'; 'great social reformer'; 'an Irishman first and always', 'soldier and servant of human liberty'; the 'seer'. The Ferguson who emerges from the reckoning of his contemporaries was a truly inspirational figure – a leader who possessed the stature and charisma to keep alive the self-belief of a migrant community through decades when it was shut out of Scottish mainstream.

His epitaph is best drawn from Emile de Laveleye, one of his 'highest authorities'. It was the vision which drove John Ferguson for almost half a century:

> There is in human affairs one order, which is the best. That order is not always the one which exists, but it is the order which should exist for the greater good of humanity. God knows it and wills it; man's duty is to discover and establish it.

Notes

1 *Glasgow Observer*, 28 Apr. 1906;TCD, Davitt, MSS 9331/217, J. Ferguson to M. Davitt, 30 Jan. 1906.

2 He refused to endorse the view expressed by Davitt in his Glasgow speech that forty or fifty Labour MPs should hold the balance of power at Westminster – the role traditionally played by the Irish party: *Glasgow Star*, 22 Oct. 1904.

3   *Glasgow Observer,* 30 Dec. 1905.

4   *Glasgow Star,* 10 Jun. 1905

5   TCD Davitt MSS 9330, K. Hardie to M. Davitt, 25 Dec. 1905; *Glasgow Star,* 3 Jun. 1905.

6   *Land Values,* May 1905. It was followed by a Scottish Convention in Edinburgh, attracting delegates from fifty-seven Scottish authorities: *Glasgow Herald,* 29 Apr. 1905.

7   *Land Values,* Jul. 1905; Ferguson, *Taxation,* pp. 6–7. An English measure had also passed its second reading in April, but was blocked by the Government from reaching the committee stage.

8   *Glasgow Observer,* 14 Jan. 1905. 'They were diddled', he commented. He had also taken up another land-related cause on the Town Council – the cheapening of the sale and transfer of land titles: *Glasgow News,* 9 Jun. 1905.

9   *Scottish Patriot,* Dec. 1905.

10 *Bailie,* 29 Mar. 1905.

11 *Land Values,* May 1906.

12 *Northern Star,* 19 Jul. 1906. The *Star* described him as, 'one of the most picturesque and interesting figures of his time'.

13 *Glasgow Observer,* 16 Dec. 1905.

14 *Glasgow Star,* 4 Nov. 1905. See also, NLS 11705/8, Minutes of the Western Committee, 15 Sept. 1905. Members agreed that the conduct of the government, trade disputes, the franchise, education and land reform should take precedence.

15 *Ibid.,* 18 Nov. 1905.

16 *Ibid.,* 2 Dec. 1905.

17 *Ibid.*

18 *Glasgow Observer,* 27 Jan. 1906. Some contests gave him particular relish. In Mid-Lanark, James Caldwell was

facing Scott Gibson, who had bizarrely taken the field as the Musician's Copyright Association candidate. *Glasgow Star*, 13 Jan. 1906. He also warmed to the fight in Glasgow Central where James Torrance was fighting the seat with the backing of the Young Scots.

19 TCD Davitt MSS 9330, K. Hardie to M. Davitt, 16 Dec. 1905.

20 Ibid. MSS 4770, K. Hardie to M. Davitt, 28 Dec. 1905. *Glasgow Herald*, 17 Jan. 1906.

21 *Glasgow Observer*, 23 Dec. 1905; *Glasgow Star*, 6 Jan. 1906.

22 TCD Davitt MSS 9485, K. Hardie to M. Davitt, 23 Dec. 1905.

23 Ibid. MSS 4775, J. Ferguson to M. Davitt 26 Dec. 1905; MSS 9330, J.F. Paterson to M. Davitt, 2 Dec. 1905. The seat in mind was originally Midlothian.

24 *Glasgow Observer*, 19 Nov. 1904.

25 TCD, Davitt MSS 9331, D. Donworth [John Dillon UIL Branch, Edinburgh] to M. Davitt, 29 Nov. 1905.

26 Ibid., MSS 9330 K. Hardie to M. Davitt, 16 Dec. 1905.

27 Ibid., MSS 9485, R. Smillie to Keir Hardie, 5 Dec. 1905.

28 *Ibid.*, 13 Jan. 1906.

29 *Glasgow Observer*, 20 Jan. 1906.

30 TCD Davitt MSS 9331, J. Ferguson to M. Davitt, 30 Jan. 1906.

31 *Glasgow Star*, 23, 30 Dec. 1906.

32 NLI, Redmond MSS 15246, J. F. Paterson [Midlothian Liberal Executive] to J. Redmond, 4, Jan. 1906.

33 Ibid., 31 Jan. 1906.

34 Lyons, *Dillon*, p. 284.

35 *Glasgow Star*, 3 Mar. 1906. He was also concerned about the continuing clericalist leanings of the Irish party as displayed on the education question. As he commented to Davitt: 'I

suppose we are getting away from the Bishops' control, but it is slow work': TCD, Davitt, MSS 9331/217, J. Ferguson to M. Davitt, 30 Jan. 1906.

36 *Glasgow Observer,* 24 Mar. 1906.

37 *Land Values,* Feb. 1906.

38 *Ibid.,* Mar. 1906.

39 Immediately reprinted as his *Taxation of Land Values* pamphlet.

40 *Glasgow Herald,* 20 Feb. 1906.

41 *Glasgow Observer,* 3 Mar. 1900.

42 *Land Values,* Mar. 1906. He reported that Dublin had also joined in the agitation with plans for a parallel petition.

43 *Glasgow Star,* 9 Dec. 1905.

44 *Land Values,* Mar. 1906.

45 *Glasgow Observer,* 3 Mar. 1906.

46 He had raised safety issues regarding the new Glasgow electric trams some years before: *Glasgow Herald,* 23 Aug. 1902.

47 *Glasgow Observer,* 16 Mar. 1906.

48 *Ibid.*

49 His cause of death was eventually given as sarcoma of the left testis (of three and a half months duration) and general and cardiac debility (of one month's duration). Sarcomata are tumours of the connective tissue and usually malignant.

50 *Glasgow Star,* 28 Apr. 1906.

51 *Daily Record* 4 Apr. 1906.The ostensible charge was supporting 'protectionist candidates'.

52 *Kirkintilloch Herald,* 2 May 1906; *Glasgow Star,* 28 Apr. 1906. His estrangement from the local Episcopalians had clearly

continued. The funeral was conducted by Rev. Mr Johnston of the Lenzie United Free Church.

53 F. Sheehy Skeffington, *Michael Davitt. Revolutionary, Agitator and Labour Leader* (London, 1967), p. 211. He had been operated on for a septic jaw, caused by a bungled tooth extraction. (My thanks to Andrew Newby for this reference).

54 *Glasgow Observer*, 28 Apr. 1906.

55 *Glasgow Star*, 7 Nov. 1906; *Glasgow Observer*, 2 Feb. 1907.

56 *Irish Packet*, 14 Nov. 1903; *Glasgow Observer*, 23 Mar. 1907.

57 SC48.200, Register of Inventories of the Sheriff Court of Glasgow; SC36.51 Register of Settlements of the Sheriff Court of Glasgow. There were 966 of these accounts, offering an indication of the scope of his business. He was owed £8147 15/1 by his Scottish customers and £2144 3/-6 by customers all over Ireland. He also had a few unpaid accounts in England, amounting to £541 4/1. See, *Evening Citizen*, 15 Aug. 1906.

58 *Glasgow Observer*, 11 Jul. 1906.

59 His will had been made in February 1894, naming Mary and Anna as his beneficiaries. For the fate of Benburb, see *Property Index 1906* (Glasgow, 1906). The villa originally went on sale at £1700, but the price was reduced by £700. Mary moved to a smaller house in Lenzie. She remained in touch with Irish political affairs and died in 1916, aged eighty-three. Ferguson's true heir, however, was his daughter Anna. She was a spirited, independent woman who fully embraced her father's causes. As 'A. B. Ochiltree Ferguson', she became a noted children's author with books such as *Saint Columba* (Dublin, 1920) and *sceúl ar dtíre* [Our Country's Story](Dublin, 1923). She was reputed locally in

Lenzie to be 'in league with the Irish' who found refuge at her house. She died in 1943.

60   When John Wilson, a Miner's Agent from Broxburn, was selected as the ILP challenger without reference to the UILGB, the branches were promptly advised to vote him down: *Glasgow Star,* 26 May 1906.

61   *Land Values,* Jun. 1913.

Bibliography

1. MANUSCRIPT SOURCES

NEW YORK

New York Public Library
Henry George Papers

DUBLIN

National Archives, Ireland
Chief Secretary's Office, Registered Papers
Fenian Papers
Irish National Land League and Irish National League papers
Marriage Licence Bonds, Down Connor and Dromore, 1721–1845

NATIONAL LIBRARY OF IRELAND

Butt MSS
J. F. X. O'Brien Papers
Redmond MSS

TRINITY COLLEGE DUBLIN

Davitt MSS
Dillon MSS
Galbraith Papers
Journal of the Irish Parliamentary Party

BELFAST

Public Records Office Northern Ireland
Documents Relating to the Land League
Glenavy Parish Register
Letterbook of the Home Government Association and Home Rule
League, 1873–8
Tithe Applotment Book, 1834, Parish of Glenavy

LIVERPOOL

University of Liverpool Library (Sidney Jones)
J.B Glasier Papers

LONDON

British Library
Campbell Bannerman Papers
Gladstone Papers

BIRMINGHAM

University of Birmingham
Joseph Chamberlain Papers

EDINBURGH

National Archives of Scotland
Lothian Papers
Ivory Papers
Police Reports, Glendale, 1882

National Library of Scotland

Cunninghame Graham Papers
General Council of the Scottish Liberal Association Minutes
Western Executive of the Scottish Liberal Association Minutes
Western Committee (Scottish Liberal Association) Minutes
Keir Hardie Correspondence

GLASGOW

Glasgow City Archives
Minutes of the Corporation of Glasgow
Minutes of the Town Council of Glasgow
Minutes of the Citizen's Union

Mitchell Library

General Election Ephemera, 1885
Independent Labour Party Archive, Francis Johnson
Correspondence (Mic.)

John Murdoch Ms. Autobiography

LENZIE

St Cyprian's Episcopal Church, Lenzie
Minute Book 1873–6

2. *PRIMARY PRINTED SOURCES*

Belfast and Ulster Directory 1856.
Corporation of Glasgow, Annual Report of Officials and Salaries as at 31 March 1906, (Glasgow, 1906).
Griffith's Valuation, 1864.
Henderson's New Belfast Directory, 1843–4.
Holland, Denis *The Landlord in Donegal. Pictures from the Wilds* (Belfast, nd.).
Cliffe Leslie, T. E., *On the Self Dependency of the Working Classes under the Law of Competition,* (Dublin 1851).
—*An Inquiry into the Progress and Conditions of Mechanics and Literary Institutions* (Dublin, 1852).
—*Military Systems of Europe Economically Considered* (London, 1856).
Matier's Belfast Directory, 1836.
Municipal Glasgow: Its Evolution and Enterprises (Glasgow, 1914).
Proceedings of the Home Rule conference held at the Rotunda, Dublin, on the 18th, 19th, 20th and 21st November 1873 (Dublin, 1874).
Seaver, Rev. Charles, *The Sunday School. A Nursery for the Church. A Lecture Delivered before the Belfast Sabbath School Union* (Belfast 1856).
—*The Ulster Revival. A paper read before the Evangelical Alliance, 22 September 1859,* (Belfast, 1859).
Report of the Commissioners of Enquiry into the Origin and Character of the Riots in Belfast in July and September 1857 (Dublin, 1858).
Report from the Select Committee on Municipal Regulation (Constabulary etc.) (Belfast) Bill, August, 1887.
Select Committee on the Land Values Taxation etc. (Scotland) Bill, 1906.

Scottish National Reform League: Great Reform Demonstration in Glasgow, Tuesday 16 October 1866 (Glasgow, 1866).

Special Commission Act 1888. Report of Proceedings before the Commissioners appointed by the Act. Reprinted from The Times (London, 1890).

Slater's Directory of Ireland, 1856.

Glasgow Trades Council Annual Report, 1892–3.

Twenty-Forth Annual Report on the Operations of the Sanitary Department of the City of Glasgow, 1893.

Watson, W., *Report on the Vital Social and Economic Statistics of Glasgow for 1868* (Glasgow 1869).

3. PERIODICALS

The Bailie

Belfast Newsletter

Bridgeton Advertiser and Single Tax Review,

Daily Record

Evening Citizen

Exile

Forward

Freeman's Journal

Glasgow Echo

Glasgow Free Press

Glasgow Herald

Glasgow Observer

Glasgow Sentinel

Glasgow Star

Highlander

Irish Catholic Banner

Irish News

Irish Packet

Irish World

Kirkintilloch Herald

Labour World

Land and Liberty

Land Values

Nation

Northern Star

North British Daily Mail

Scottish Leader

Single Tax

The Scotsman

Tuam Herald

United Irishman

Voice of the People

4. WORKS BY JOHN FERGUSON

The Land for the People. An Appeal to All who Work by Brain or Hand, (Glasgow [c.1881]).

Three Centuries of Irish History. From the Reign of Mary the Catholic to that of Victoria the Protestant. An Unbroken Record of Confiscation and Persecution, Mixed with Massacre, and Terminating in Extermination by Unjust and Ruinous Taxation, (Glasgow [c.1897]).

Glasgow : The City of Progress, (Glasgow 1900).

Address to the Citizens of the Twenty-Five Wards in General, and Particularly to the Electors of Calton Ward (Glasgow, 1902).

The Taxation of Land Values. A Retrospect and a Forecast (Glasgow, 1906).

5. MEMOIRS AND WRITINGS OF CONTEMPORARIES

Allen, Grant, *Individualism and Socialism* (Glasgow, 1889).

Bell, Sir James and Paton, James, *Glasgow. Its Municipal Organisation and Administration* (Glasgow, 1896).

Bradlaugh Bonner, Hypatica, *Charles Bradlaugh. His Life and Work* (London, 1895).

Cashman, D. B., *The Life of Michael Davitt, founder of the National Land League, to which is added the Secret History of the Land League* (London, 1882).

Clark, G. B., *The Highland Land Question* (London, 1883).

Colquhoun, James, *Reminiscences of Glasgow Town Council* (Glasgow, 1904).

Cronwright-Shreiner, S. C., *The Land of Free Speech: Record of a Campaign on Behalf of Peace in England and Scotland in 1900* (London, 1906).

Davis, Thomas, *Prose Writings, Essays on Ireland* (London, 1890).

Davitt, Michael, *The Fall of Feudalism in Ireland, or the Story of the Land League Revolution* (Shannon, 1970).

—*The Land League Proposal: a statement for honest and thoughtful men* (Glasgow and London, 1882).

—*Land nationalisation or national peasant proprietary, Michael Davitt's lectures in Scotland: the principles of radical reform in the land laws* (Glasgow and London, [1882]).

—*Leaves from a Prison Diary* (London, 1885).

O'Brien, W. and Ryan, D., *Devoy's Post Bag 1871–1928* (Dublin, 1948).

Denvir, John, *The Life Story of an Old Rebel* (Dublin, 1910).

—*The Irish in Britain from the Earliest Times to the Fall of Parnell* (London, 1892).

Duncan, J. D. (ed.), *The Life of Professor John Stuart Blackie* (Glasgow 1895).

Freer, Walter, *My Life and Memory* (Glasgow, 1929).

George, Henry, *Progress and Poverty an Inquiry into the cause of Industrial Depressions and of Increase of Want with Increase of Wealth: the Remedy* (London, 1883).

—*The Irish Land Question: What it Involves and how it can be Settled. An Appeal to the Land Leagues* (Glasgow, 1881).

Glasier, J. B., *On the Road to Liberty: Poetry and Ballad* (Manchester, 1920).

—*William Morris and the Earliest Days of the Socialist Movement* (London, 1921).

Haddow, W. M., *Socialism in Scotland. Its Rise and Progress* (Glasgow, nd.).

—*My Seventy Years* (Glasgow, 1943).

Healy, T. M., *Letters and Leaders of My Day* (London, 1928).

Hyndman, H. M., *The Record of an Adventurous Life* (London, 1911).

Innes Addison, W., *Roll of Graduates of the University of Glasgow, 1727–1897* (Glasgow, 1898).

Kettle (ed.), L. J. *The Material for Victory. Being the Memoirs of Andrew J. Kettle* (Dublin, 1958).

Lipton, Thomas, *Leaves from the Lipton Logs* (London, 1931).

Lloyd, Clifford, *Ireland Under the Land League: a Narrative of Personal Experiences* (London, 1892).

Lowe, D., *Souvenirs of Scottish Labour* (Glasgow, 1919).

Mavor, *My Windows on the Street of the World* (London, 1925).

McDonagh, M., *The Home Rule Movement* (Dublin, 1920).

Macdonald, J., *The Daily News Diary of the Parnell Commission* (London, nd.).

Mavor, James, *My Windows on the Street of the World*, vol. 1 (London, 1923).

Cross (ed.), I. B., *Frank Roney. Irish Rebel and California Labor Leader* (Berkley, 1931).

O'Brien, William, *Recollections* (London 1905).

O'Leary, J., *Recollections of Fenians and Fenianism*, (London, 1896).

O'Shea, K., *Charles Stuart Parnell* (London, 1914).

Sheehy-Skeffington, *Michael Davitt: Revolutionary Agitator and Labour Leader* (London, 1908).

Smillie, R., *My Life for Labour* (London, 1924).

Sullivan, A. M., *New Ireland* (Glasgow, 1877).

Webb, Beatrice, *My Apprenticeship* (London, 1926).

Mackenzie, N. and J. (eds.), *The Diary of Beatrice Webb* (London, 1982).

6. *Selected Secondary Works*

Bardon, J., *Belfast, An Illustrated History* (Belfast, 1982).

Barker, C. A., *Henry George* (New York, 1955).

Beckett, J. C. and Glasscock, R. E. (eds.), *Belfast, Origin and Growth of an Industrial City* (London, 1967).

Beckett, J. C. *et al.*, *Belfast: The Making of the City* (Belfast, 1983).

Belchem, J., 'The Irish middle class in Victorian Liverpool' in, R. Swift and S. Gilley (eds.), *The Irish in Victorian Britain: the Local Dimension* (Dublin, 2000).

Bell, R., *The Book of Ulster Surnames* (St Paul, Min., 1988).

Bew, P., *Land and the National Question in Ireland* (Dublin, 1980).

—*Conflict and Conciliation in Ireland: Parnellites and Radical Agrarians* (Oxford, 1987).

— *Parnell* (Dublin, 1991).

Bowman, T., *Peoples' Champion. The Life of Alexander Bowman, Pioneer of Labour Politics in Ireland.* (Belfast, 1997).

Boyce, D. G. and. O'Day, A., *The Revisionist Controversy in Irish History* (London, 1996).

Boyce, D. B. and O'Day, A., *Parnell in Perspective*, (London, 1991).

Brady, L. W., *T. P. O'Connor and the Liverpool Irish* (London, 1983).

Brown, M., *The Politics of Irish Literature: from Thomas Davis to W. B. Yeats* (Washington, 1972).

Brown, S. J., '"Echoes of Midlothian": Scottish Liberalism and the South African War, 1899–1902', *Scottish Historical Review,* vol. LXXI, (1992).

Brown, T. N., *Irish-American Nationalism 1870–1890* (Philadelphia and New York, 1966).

Callanan, F., *The Parnell Split 1890–1* (Cork, 1981).

—*T. M. Healy* (Cork, 1996).

Cameron, E. A. , *Land for the People? The British Government and the Scottish Highlands, c. 1880–1925* (E. Linton, 1996).

Clark, S., *The Social Origins of the Irish Land War* (Princeton, 1979).

Collison Black, R. D., *Economic Thought and the Irish Question, 1817–1870* (Cambridge, 1960).

Comerford, R. V., *The Fenians in Context* (Dublin, 1985).

D'Arcy, F., 'Charles Bradlaugh and the Irish Question: A Study in the Nature and Limits of British radicalism, 1853–91', in C. McCartney (ed.), *Studies in Irish History* (Dublin, 1979).

Day, A. and McWilliams, P. *Ordinance Survey Memoirs of Ireland. Parishes of Antrim, Volume VII, 1832–8,* (Belfast, 1993).

De Vere, T., *The Road to Excess* (London, 1946).

Devine, T., *The Great Highland Famine* (Edinburgh, 1988).

Devine, T. (ed.), *Irish Immigrants and Scottish Society in the Nineteenth and Twentieth Centuries* (Edinburgh 1990).

Douglas, R., *Land, People and Politics. A History of the Land Question in the United Kingdom* (London, 1976).

Dyer, M., *Men of Property and Intelligence. The Scottish Electoral System prior to 1884* (Aberdeen, 1996).

Ervine, St. J., *Parnell* (London, 1925).

Fielding, S., *Class and Ethnicity: Irish Catholics in England, 1880–1939,* (Buckingham, 1993.

Fraser, M., *John Bull's Other Homes. State Housing and British Policy in Ireland, 1883–1922* (Liverpool, 1996).

Fraser, W. H., 'From civic gospel to municipal socialism', in D. Fraser (ed.), *Cities, Class and Communications: Essays in Honour of*

Asa Briggs' (Hemel Hempstead, 1990).

— *Alexander Campbell and the Search for Socialism* (Manchester, 1996).

Fraser, W. H. and Maver, I. (eds.), *Glasgow 1830–1912* (Manchester, 1996).

Garvin, J. L., *Life of Joseph Chamberlain,* (London, 1933).

George, Henry Jr., *The Life of Henry George* (New York, 1949).

Gwynn, S. and Tuckwell, G. M., *Life of Rt. Hon. Sir Charles Dilke* (London, 1917).

Handley, J. E., *The Irish in Modern Scotland* (Cork, 1947).

Hanham, H. J., 'The problem of Highland discontent', *Transactions of the Royal Historical Society,* 5th Series (1969).

Himmelfarb, G., *Poverty and Compassion. The Moral Imagination of the Late Victorians* (New York, 1991).

Hoppen, K. T., *Elections, Politics and Society in Ireland, 1832–1885* (Oxford, 1984).

Holmes, P., *Henry Cooke* (Belfast, 1981).

Howell, D., *British Workers and the Independent Labour Party 1886–1906* (Manchester, 1984).

Hunter, J., 'The politics of highland land reform 1873–1895', *Scottish Historical Review,* vol. LIII, (1974).

— 'The Gaelic Connection: the Highlands, Ireland and nationalism, 1873–1922', *Scottish Historical Review,* vol. LIV (1975).

Hutchinson, J. and O'Day, A., 'The Gaelic revival in London, 1900–22: limits of ethnic identity', pp. 264–276, in Swift and Gilley (eds.), *Irish in Victorian Britain* (Dublin, 2000).

Jameson, J., *History of the Royal Belfast Academical Institute* (Belfast, 1959).

Jones, J. E., *A Social Geography of Belfast* (Oxford, 1960).

Joyce, P., *Democratic Subjects* (Cambridge, 1994).

Kellas, J., 'The Mid-Lanark By-election (1888) and the Scottish Labour Party', *Parliamentary Affairs,* (1964–5).

Kennedy, L. and Ollerenshaw, P., *An Economic History of Ulster 1820–1939* (Manchester, 1985).

Killen, J. (ed.), *The Famine Decade. Contemporary Accounts 1841–1851*

(Belfast, 1995).

Kinealy, L. and Parkhall, T. (eds.), *The Famine in Ulster,* (Belfast, 1997).

King, C., *Michael Davitt* (Dublin, 2000).

Koss, S., *The Pro-Boers. The Anatomy of an Anti-War Movement* (Chicago, 1973).

Lane, F., *Origins of Modern Irish Socialism 1881–1896* (Cork, 1997).

Lawrence, E. P., *Henry George in the British Isles* (Michigan, 1957).

Lyons, F. S. L., *The Irish Parliamentary Party 1890–1910* (London, 1951).

—*John Dillon: A Biography* (London, 1968).

—*Parnell* (London, 1977).

Martin, D. *The Story of Lenzie* (Strathkelvin, 1989).

I Maver, 'Local party politics and the temperance crusade 1890–1902', *Scottish Labour History Society Journal,* 27 (1992).

— *Glasgow* (Edinburgh, 2000).

McCaffrey, J. F., 'The Origins of Liberal Unionism in the West of Scotland', *Scottish Historical Review,* L (1971).

—*Scotland in the Nineteenth Century* (London, 1998).

Macdonald, C. M. M., *The Radical Thread* (E. Linton, 2000).

Macfarlane, J., *The Old Calton, Glasgow Green and the River Clyde* (Glasgow, 1921).

Macrae, D., *The Man versus the State,* (Harmondsworth, 1962).

MacRaild, D. M., *Irish Migrants in Modern Britain, 1750–1922* (London, 1999).

McFarland, E. W., '"A reality and yet impalpable": The Fenian panic in Mid-Victorian Scotland, in *Scottish Historical Review,* LXXVI, (1998).

— 'Marching from the Margins: Twelfth July Parades in Scotland 1820–1914,' in T. Fraser (ed.) *The Irish Parading Tradition, Following the Drum* (London 2000).

McMinn, J. R. B., *Against the Tide. A Calendar of the Papers of the Rev. J. B. Armour, Irish Presbyterian Minister and Home Ruler 1869–1914* (Belfast, 1985).

Moody, T. W., *Michael Davitt and the Irish Revolution* (Oxford, 1982).

— 'The IRB Supreme Council 1868–78', *Irish Historical Studies*, xix (1975).

— 'Michael Davitt and the British Labour Movement, 1882–1906', *Transactions of the Royal Historical Society*, cxiv, 1994.

— 'The new departure in Irish politics, 1878–9', in H. A. Cronne, T. W. Moody and D. B. Quinn (eds.), *Essays in British and Irish History in Honour of James Eadie Todd* (London, 1949).

Moody, T. W. and Beckett, J. C., *Queen's Belfast 1845–1949. The History of a University* (London, 1959).

Moran, G., *Father Patrick Lavelle. A Radical Priest in County Mayo* (Dublin, 1994).

Morgan, K. O., *Keir Hardie. Radical and Socialist* (London, 1975).

Nottingham, C. J., *The Pursuit of Serenity: Havelock Ellis and the New Politics* (Amsterdam, 1999).

O'Day, A., *The English Face of Irish Nationalism* (London, 1977).

— 'The Political Organisation of the Irish in Britain 1867–1890', in R. Swift and S. Gilley (eds.),*The Irish in Britain 1815–1939* (London, 1989).

O'Ferrall, F., *Daniel O'Connell* (Dublin, 1998).

Offer, A., *Property and Politics* (London, 1981).

Ord, J., *The Story of the Burgh of Calton* (Glasgow, nd.).

Reid, F., *Keir Hardie. The Making of a Socialist* (London, 1978).

Reisman, D., *Alfred Marshall. Progress and Politics* (New York, 1997).

Scott, A. R., *The Ulster Revival of 1859* (Ballymena, 1994).

Shannon, R., *Gladstone. Heroic Minister 1865–1898* (Harmondsworth, 1999).

Sheehy Skeffington, F., *Michael Davitt. Revolutionary, Agitator and Labour Leader* (London, 1967).

Smyth, J., 'The ILP in Glasgow, 1888–1906: the struggle for identity', in A. McKinley and R. J. Morris (eds.), *The ILP on Clydeside* (Manchester, 1991).

— *Labour in Glasgow 1896–1936* (E. Linton, 2000).

Steele, E. D., 'J. S. Mill and the Irish Question: the principles of political economy, 1848–65', *Historical Journal*, xii (1970).

Stewart, W., *J. Keir Hardie* (London, 1921).

Swift, R. and Gilley, S. (eds.), *The Irish in Britain, 1815–1939*, (London, 1989).

Thompson, L., *The Enthusiasts* (London, 1971).

Thornley, D. A., *Isaac Butt and Home Rule* (London, 1964).

Tribe, D., *President Charles Bradlaugh MP* (London, 1971).

Walker, G. and Officer, D., 'Scottish Unionism and the Ulster question', in C. M. M. Macdonald (ed.), *Unionist Scotland* (Edinburgh, 1998).

Warwick-Haller, S., *William O'Brien and the Irish Land War* (Dublin, 1990).

Watts, C. and Davies, L., *Cunninghame Graham: A Critical Biography* (Cambridge, 1979).

Whyte, J. H., *The Tenant League and Irish Politics in the Eighteen-fifties* (Dundalk, 1972).

Withers, C., 'Rural Protest in the Highlands of Scotland and Ireland, 1850–1930', in S. J. Connolly et al. (eds.), *Conflict, Identity and Economic Development* (Preston, 1995).

Wood, I. S., 'Irish Immigrants and Scottish Radicalism' in I. Macdougall, *Essays in Scottish Labour History* (Edinburgh, 1978).

Zimmerman, G., *Songs of the Irish Rebellion,* (Dublin, 1967).

Theses

Bell, D. D., 'The Reform League and its Origins to 1867' (University of Oxford D. Phil. Thesis, 1961).

Frame, J. R., 'America and the Scottish Left: the Impact of American Ideas on the Scottish Labour Movement from the American Civil War to World War One' (University of Aberdeen Ph.D. Thesis, 1998).

Hutchison, I. G. C. T., 'Politics and Society in Mid Victorian Glasgow 1846–86', (University of Edinburgh Ph.D. Thesis, 1975).

Kellas, J. G., 'The Liberal Party in Scotland, 1885–1895' (University of London PhD Thesis, 1961).

McCaffrey, J. F., 'Political Reactions in Glasgow Constituences in the General Elections of 1885 and 1886' (University of Glasgow Ph.D. Thesis, 1970).

McCann , P. J. O., 'The Protestant Home Rule Movement, 1885–95' (University College Dublin M.A. Thesis, 1972).

Morris, P. W., 'The Irish in Glasgow and the Labour Movement 1891–22'. (University of Oxford B.Phil. Thesis, 1989).

Smyth, J., 'Labour and Socialism in Glasgow 1880–1914: the Electoral Challenge Prior to Democracy', (University of Edinburgh Ph.D. Thesis, 1987).

Sweeney [Maver], I., 'The Municipal Administration of Glasgow, 1833–1912: Public Service and Scottish Civic Identity', (University of Strathclyde Ph.D. Thesis, 1990).

Index

PART I: JOHN FERGUSON

PART II: GENERAL